CONDENSED HISTORY
OF THE
143D REGIMENT
NEW YORK
VOLUNTEER INFANTRY

Reprinted with appreciation for the efforts of the
Sullivan County Historical Society
(sullivancountyhistory.org)
and the 143rd N.Y.Volunteer Infantry
(143rdnewyorkvolunteers.org)
to keep history alive

———————

ISBN 978-0-9626357-4-8
Condensed History of the 143d Regiment

First Published in 1909 by The 143d Regiment Association
at Newburgh Journal Printing House and Book Bindery
Newburgh, New York

Reprinted complete and unabridged
August 2012 by LoadNGo Press
Kiamesha Lake, New York
845-794-3772
myrongit@yahoo.com

Printed in the United States of America on acid-free paper

Back cover image of flag carried into battle by the
143rd Regiment courtesy of New York State Military Museum
& Research Center, Division of Military and Naval Affairs

DEDICATION

———

The reprint of this history of Sullivan County's Regiment
is a dedication to the Valor, Courage and Devotion to Duty
of the men who fought under her flag.

The historical significance of this work is invaluable to the
relatives of the members of the 143rd NYVI. It keeps alive
the memory of the sacrifice of each member of the unit.

GOD cradles in his arms each of them now and it is our
responsibility to see to the task that their endeavors
are never forgotten.

This publishing helps to honor that commitment.

Colonel Chuck Young Cmdg.
143rd NYVI Reenactor

June 22, 2011
Parksville, New York

GROUP OF OFFICERS OF THE 143D SOON AFTER THE CAPTURE OF ATLANTA.

1—Capt. Harrison Marvin.
2—Adjt. Rensselaer Hammond.
3—Lieut.-Col. Hezekiah Watkins.
4—Col. Horace Boughton.
5—Major John Higgins.
6—Q. M. Edward C. Howard.
7—Asst. Surgeon Wm. H. Stuart.
8—Lieut. Charles A. Smith.
9—Capt. William R. Bennett.
10—Surgeon David Mathews.
11—Lieut. Wallace Hill.
12—Lieut. Dewitt Apgar.
13—Capt. George H. Decker.
14—Lieut. Isaac Jelliff.
15—Lieut. Peter E. Palen.
16—Capt. Lewis W. Stanton.
17—Capt. Wm. T. George.
18—Capt. Edw. H. Pinney.
19—Lieut. Dwight Divine.
20—Capt. John F. Anderson.
21—Lieut. George Young.
22—Lieut. Richard M. J. Hardenbergh.
23—Capt. Benj. Reynolds.

A CONDENSED HISTORY

Of the

143d REGIMENT

New York Volunteer Infantry,

Of the

CIVIL WAR

1861-1865.

TOGETHER WITH A REGISTER OR ROSTER OF ALL THE MEMBERS
OF THE REGIMENT, AND THE WAR RECORD OF EACH MEMBER,
AS RECORDED IN THE ADJUTANT-GENERAL'S OFFICE,
AT ALBANY, N. Y.

═══════════

BY

A Committee of the 143d Regiment Association,

NAMED AS FOLLOWS:

William B. McMillen, of Co. A, Chairman,
Moses G. Young, of Co. A. Editor and Secretary,
Dwight Divine, of Co. F, Financial Secretary,

Isaac Jelleff, Co. B,
William F. Benedict, Co. E,
Thomas D. Collins, Co. H,
Peter E. Palen, Co. K,

McKendree N. Dodge, Co. C,
Jas, S. Beattie, Co. F,
Harrison H. Marvin, Co. I,
William Bennett, Co. A,

Joseph Cammer, Co. A.

Newburgh Journal Printing House and Book-Bindery,
1909.

CONTENTS.

DEDICATION.

This history is dedicated to the relatives of those of the 143d New York Volunteer Infantry, who answered final roll-call on Southern soil or since their return home, and to the survivors of the above and their friends.

We trust that it may prove of great interest as well as a source of pleasure to many. To secure all the data required much diligent research and labor, which have been cheerfully given.

The historical part narrates the immediate service of the regiment as a unit without mentioning acts of individuals, except in rare cases.

The committee takes pleasure in acknowledging the valuable assistance rendered by Comrade W. H. D. Blake, of the 56th N. Y. V. I., in the loan of valuable books of statistics; Senator John N. Cordts, of this State, and to all comrades who have contributed to whatever degree of success has been attained.

THE EDITOR.

CONDENSED HISTORY

OF

THE 143d REGIMENT

New York Volunteer Infantry.

CHAPTER I.

The Call for 300,000 Additional Troops in July, 1862—The Response in
Sullivan County—The War Committee—Colonel Ellis and the 124th
Regiment, N. Y. Volunteer Infantry—Enlistment Centers and Those in
Charge.

In July, 1862, after McClellan's failure to capture Richmond,
and the disastrous "Seven Days' Fight" in retreat to the James
River, the call from Washington for 300,000 additional troops resounded from ocean to ocean, and from the lakes to the gulf; and
the patriotic sons of Sullivan County were not deaf to the call.
Young men and married men stopped the team, dropped the hoe
or pen, closed the school book, and looking each other in the face,
said: "What does this mean?" And the response from the ma-
jority was, "It means me."

Early in July, Colonel Ellis was commissioned to enlist men in
Orange and Sullivan Counties to form the 124th Regiment, New
York Volunteer Infantry, and recruiting was progressing in several
places with the object of becoming a part of that organization.
Company A was completed under Captain Hezekiah Watkins, First
Lieutenant Wm. M. Ratcliff, and Second Lieutenant George Young,
and met at Monticello to proceed to Goshen as part of the 124th
Regiment. In the meantime, Judge Low, John C. Holley and others
were active in securing authority to enlist a regiment in Sullivan
County alone, and arrived at Monticello with such authority in time
to stop the departure of Company A. A War Committee, including Judge Henry R. Low, Hon. C. V. R. Ludington, John C. Holley,
and others, was appointed to push the enlistment and formation of
companies as rapidly as possible. Company A was already completed, with headquarters at Monticello, the men having been enlisted at Monticello, Liberty, Freemont, Parksville, Bethel and
Forestburgh.

Company B was enlisted by Captain Alfred J. Baldwin, First
Lieutenant Edwin C. Howard and Second Lieutenant Roberts C.

Benedict, at Bethel, Thompson, Fallsburgh, Forestburgh and. Stevensville.

Company C was enlisted by Captain James C. French, First Lieutenant Nathaniel C. Clark and Second Lieutenant Dwight. Divine, at Fallsburgh, Rockland, Grahamsville and Neversink.

Company D was enlisted by Captain John Higgins, First Lieutenant Caleb H. North and Second Lieutenant Edgar K. Apgar, at. Ithaca and Lansing in Tompkins County.

Company E was enlisted by Captain Ira Dorrance, First Lieutenant William R. Bennett and Second Lieutenant Peter L. Waterbury, at Wurtsborough, Bridgeville, Monticello and Phillipsport.

Company F was enlisted by Captain Edward H. Pinney, First Lieutenant John F. Anderson, and Second Lieutenant Marcus J. Fraser, Jr., at Fremont, Callicoon, Jeffersonville, Rockland and. Monticello.

Company G was enlisted by Captain Benjamin Reynolds, First Lieutenant Theron B. Luckey, and Second Lieutenant Alexander C. Kellam, at Freemont, Bloomingburgh, Neversink, Monticello, Cochecton and Tusten.

Company H was enlisted by Captain George H. Decker, First Lieutenant Jirah I. Young, and Second Lieutenant Rensselaer Hammond, at Liberty, Monticello and Rockland.

Company I was enlisted by Capt. Harrison Marvin, First Lieutenant William T. George, and Second Lieutenant William S. Moffat, at Dryden and Cochecton.

Company K was enlisted by Captain Anthony H. Bush, First Lieutenant Lewis N. Stanton, and Second Lieutenant Willett T. Embler, at Cochecton, Monticello, Tusten, Callicoon, Highland and' Thompson.

Companies D and I were secured largely from Tompkins County, by the active influence of the Hon. C. V. R. Ludington, in order to promptly complete the regiment and secure the desired regimental number and rank.

CHAPTER II.

Organization of the 143d Regiment, New York Volunteer Infantry—The Regimental Officers—The Regimental Life at Camp Holley—The Regiment Mustered into the United States Service.

The ten companies named in the foregoing chapter were brought together in camp on the northwestern shore of Pleasant Lake, since re-named Kiamesha, about two miles from Monticello. The camp was named "Camp Holley," in honor of John C. Holley, who had been appointed Colonel of the regiment August 14, 1862, but was not commissioned as such. The War Committee deemed it wise to secure, if possible, a man to command the regiment who had a military education, and one who had served at the front. Such an one was found in the person of Colonel David P. DeWitt, who had seen active service under General Banks and General Pope as Colonel of the 3d Maryland, which had been reduced by active service to 250 men. Colonel DeWitt was born at Hoboken, N. J., July 10th, 1817, and entered the West Point Military Academy in June, 1832. On his graduation in 1836, he was commissioned Second Lieutenant in the 2d U. S. Artillery. He resigned his commission in the army to accept a position as engineer in the survey and location of the Erie Railroad. Later he located the Ontario, Simcoe and Huron Railroad in Canada. In 1859, he entered the service of the United States Express Company. At the breaking out of the war he was commissioned Major of the Maryland Volunteers. In March, 1862, he was put in command of the 3d Maryland as its Colonel.

John C. Holley was appointed Lieut.-Colonel, but declined October 14th, 1862. Horace Boughton, who was a captain in the 13th N. Y. Infantry, was secured to take the office of Lieut-Colonel. He was born at Rust, N. Y., March 23d, 1833, and was educated at the Genesee Wesleyan Seminary and Genesee College. He studied law at Rochester, and enlisted in April, 1861, in the 13th N. Y. Volunteer Infantry, and was commissioned First Lieutenant. He came to the 143d Regiment in October, 1862, as Captain and was mustered in as Lieut.-Colonel.

Joseph B. Taft, who was commissioned Major, October 11th, 1862, was a young man of 23, who had been driven out of Texas because of his Union sentiments, having been given but a few hours in which to depart. He came to New York, where he became acquainted with Judge Low. He had a thorough military education, but where he obtained it we cannot learn, and proved to be a thorough disciplinarian and model soldier.

Barracks were erected for the accommodation of the regiment with board bunks, and a cook-house built down by the water large enough to accommodate one company at a time. The contract for supplying and preparing provisions was given to O'Neil and Royce, and the boys soon became dissatisfied with their rations. Very little butter was provided and that was rancid. One captain, Baldwin, I think, secured some that was good for his company. Other companies learned that some had good butter, and the next morning while companies C and D were being served, the cry, "butter, butter," was started. The butter not being forthcoming, the tables began to creak, tin plates sailed out of the windows, the roof boards began to dance to the music and presently floated off on the surface of the lake with the tin plates and other dishes. Very soon but a remnant of the cook-house remained and two men were seen racing across the pasture field as for their lives, evidently thinking it too late in the season to enjoy a bath for the amusement of the boys. The cook-house was soon repaired and thereafter the boys had no cause for complaint while at Camp Holley.

The first chapter in the life of a soldier was entered upon, such as squad and company drill, guard duty, etc. To be penned up by guards was not in accordance with the boys' ideas of freedom, and it was more difficult to keep them in at Camp Holley than it was to keep the enemy out later on.

On October 8th and 9th, 1862, Lieutenant Crowley, U. S. A., visited the camp and mustered the regiment into the United States service for three years, or during the war.

After muster Dr. J. D. Watkins presented each member of Company A with a crisp five-dollar bill, and John H. Divine, of Divine's Corners, did the same for the members of Company C. It is needless to say that the boys so favored appreciated and remembered the generous act of the donors.

CHAPTER III.

Flag Presentation by Patriotic Citizens—Hon. O. B. Wheeler's Speech— Reply by Colonel David P. DeWitt.

The next day after the regiment was mustered into the United States service, October 9th, 1862, an immense crowd of patriotic citizens of Sullivan County gathered at Camp Holley to present the regiment with a beautiful stand of colors, and to wish them "God speed," as they were about to leave for the field of action. The presentation speech was made by the Honorable O. B. Wheeler, and the reply by Colonel David P. DeWitt.

SPEECH OF HON. O. B. WHEELER.

"Colonel, Officers and Members of the Sullivan County Regiment:

"If I correctly understand the object of this immense gathering of the patriotic citizens of Sullivan County, it is to participate in the various patriotic exercises which are associated with the presentation of this beautiful stand of colors, and then bid your brave regiment—your regiment, which is composed of our sons, our brothers, and our neighbors—God speed in hastening to the seat of war, there to join the patriotic host, shoulder to shoulder, in putting down the wicked rebellion, and in restoring the Union as it was, and in maintaining the supremacy of the constitution throughout the whole length and breadth of this, our once prosperous and happy country.

"Ladies and gentlemen, your life-long devotion to, and your earnest, your intense, your undying love for, the best interests of your beloved country, and your munificent contributions for the support of the Union army, including this splendid stand of colors, and your immense rally on this occasion, may well be taken as a proof positive by this gallant regiment that you will continue to render to our beloved country—our country to which we all owe so much—all other material aid in your power, to put down the unholy rebellion, and preserve, and maintain, and perpetuate that precious, that sacred legacy, our glorious Union, which we, under God, have inherited from our sainted sires.

"Soldiers of the Sullivan County regiment, your purpose is a noble one! It is for the restoration of the Union—the Union as it was, and the constitution as it is—for the restoration of peace and tranquility. In your patriotic efforts to annihilate this stupendous rebellion, you have a great, an illustrious, an elevated charter—a sure guide. This charter, this sure guide, is nothing less than the constitution of the United States. The principles of this great charter are as broad as humanity— as eternal as truth. To it we owe everything. If we would have the veiled future a happy one to ourselves, and to those who may come after us, let us cling to it as the chief anchor of hope—cherish it as the epitome of earthly wisdom, justice and patriotism—bear it high up, that its light and glories may continue to shine forth pre-eminent among the nations of the world.

"If we cannot suppress the rebellion without sacrificing the fundamental principle of our political system, the work of suppression will cost very, very dear. In the memorable words of President Lincoln:—

"'I understand the ship to be made for the carrying and preservation of the cargo, and so long as the ship can be saved, with the cargo, it should never be abandoned. This Union should like-wise never be abandoned unless it fails, and the probability of its preservation shall cease to exist without throwing the passengers and cargo overboard. So long, then, as it is possible that the prosperity and the liberties of the people can be preserved in the Union, it shall be my purpose at all times to preserve it.'

"Here we have in the language of the President, the essence of loyalty. Fidelity to the constitution is loyalty to the United States! It was so proclaimed by Washington, and Madison, and Hamilton, and Morris, and Franklin; and to-day they speak to us in language which cannot be misunderstood, from that venerable charter.

"Sir, we do understand; and in response the very earth trembles with armed men. A million of brave patriots have rallied in support of the Union and the constitution, with not one conscript among them; and the patriotic cry still rolls up from the national capital, in trumpet tones: 'We come! We come! In the name of the Union and the Constitution, brother patriots, we come.' And may God grant the realization of the prayers of untold thousands, that the ushering in of December winds will find us at the close of a war, which will demonstrate to the people of this country that there is to be no more tampering with the Union and the Constitution of our fathers; and to the world that solid truth, 'We have a government.'

"And now, brave Regiment, in presenting to you this splendid stand of colors, allow me to say, that I am not delegated by the committee to present them in consideration of their intrinsic value; not because they contain a certain number of yards of the very finest bunting; but I am delegated by the committee to present them to you in consideration of their extrinsic value; because they are nothing less than the emblem of the greatness and power of this mighty nation, under the Constitution! And as such are the incentive to deeds of valor on the battlefield; and in your hands will prove a precursor of victory after victory, over armed rebels, and the restoration of the Union, the supremacy of the Constitution and the enforcement of the laws.

"Gallant Colonel, you have done your country valuable service on the battle field. You have proved yourself worthy to command this noble regiment. As its principal officer, may you, with them, win unfading laurels.

"Take this stand of colors, then, brave patriots. Soldiers of the Sullivan County Regiment, go forth to the war; unfurl this national ensign to the breeze; commit yourself into the keeping of the God of your fathers. And then,

" 'One glance where the banner floats gloriously, we pray;
    Let the sword flash on high; flinging the scabbard away;
    Roll on like the thunder bolt over the plain;
    Ye come back in glory, or come not again!' "

To which Colonel DeWitt replied as follows:

"To our friends of Sullivan County, donors of this splendid gift, and to you, sir, the eloquent medium through which it is presented, I, on the part of the 143d Regiment, tender our sincere thanks.

"Oratory not being my gift I regret exceedingly, for your sakes, yet with feelings of deep pride, that I accidently have been called upon, from my position as senior officer of the regiment, to receive this emblem of our glorious Union.

"This flag, dear to us all, scarce a year and a half since, waved in majestic beauty over every portion of the habitable globe, challenging admiration and respect. Now, in a certain portion of our own country it is trampled in the dust.

"We are here to-day before you, pledged to you, our government, and the world to assist in restoring the supremacy of our dear old flag, and with the blessing of Providence, we will succeed.

"This flag shall return. It may be old, faded, pierced with balls, and torn by shells; yet it shall return, were there only one poor wounded soldier left to bear it home.

"For the flattering allusion to myself I sincerely thank you, and feel that encouragement that every true soldier should, who receives praise for having endeavored to do his duty.

"I feel more than ordinary interest in this regiment, having been appointed a cadet at West Point, in 1832, from this, then my own Congressional District. I feel very near to you all, and pledge to carefully watch over those who are about to leave you, and link their fate with mine; and will endeavor to make their rough paths as smooth as possible, consistent with my duty to the government and them.

"I will state in conclusion, that I am under obligations to the War Committee for the offer for the appointment which I now hold, and as an assurance to them and you of my faithfulness in the discharge of my duty will say that I have been educated under this flag; I have fought under it; will fight under it again, and if God so wills it, will die beneath its folds."

HORACE BOUGHTON,
Colonel and Brvt. Brig. Genl. U. S. V.

CHAPTER IV.

"Good-Bye" to Camp Holley, and on to the Seat of War—The First March and Bivouac—Arrival and Sojourn in New York City—Trip to Washington, D. C.—In the Defences of Washington.

The preparatory stage of the soldier's life, such as running the guard, smashing cook-houses, scaling stone walls, and grumbling generally, had come to an end, and the regiment was about to enter upon the reality of a soldier's life. The Colonel had received orders to report with the Regiment at New York City, and the dawn of October 10th, 1862, found the camp in an uproar. What to take and what not to take was the question. Whatever the decision as to clothing was, nearly every man had a "pepper-box," or six-shooter, of some sort tucked away somewhere in his outfit. They were going to fight; why not be well armed? The nearest railroad station was at Middletown, some twenty-eight miles distant, and the boys were to have their first war experience in furnishing their own transportation to the cars. The bugle sounded the call, the long line formed, the new flag was flung to the breeze, and with bounding hearts full of anticipation they turned southward, leaving Camp Holley with its fun and frolic in the rear.

With easy swing, they soon reached the turnpike and halted on the flat just east of Monticello, where friends and relatives had gathered to say the parting word to brothers, sweethearts, sons, husbands and fathers. Little did any realize that out of the 1,007 in that line of stalwart young men, 187 would not return to the loved ones. But such was the fate of cruel war.

The partings over, the Colonel's voice rang out clear, "Attention! Right face, forward, route step, march," and away down the pike moved the pride of Sullivan County. This being the first march, frequent halts were made for rest. A luncheon was served at noon, and Wurtsboro was reached by early evening. Here the boys were given their first experience at "roughing it," as barns and out-sheds of every description had to be utilized to secure accommodations for them during the night. A large part of Company G, which had been enrolled at Bloomingburgh, crossed the mountain that evening to spend the night with loved ones.

Early the next morning those at Wurtsboro were up and off, facing Shawangunk Mountain. It was soon scaled and the Regiment halted in Bloomingburgh, where the friends of many were waiting to greet the boys and bid them "God speed" as they crossed the Shawangunk Kill and marched out of old Sullivan. They reached Middletown about noon, where a train of cars was in readiness for their transportation to New York City. Near Paterson, N. J., the train parted and the section with the engine was halted too suddenly, allowing the part broken loose to crash into the rear of that already stopped. The result was that some eight or nine were injured, causing the death of two or three. Two seized the occasion to desert.

New York was reached in the evening and the regiment were given quarters in barracks on City Hall Square, where the present post office stands. The square was surrounded with guards, nevertheless, many of the boys escaped, saw the town, saw so much of it that two days later when the Regiment moved on to Washington, D. C., they were left behind. A few of those left behind never found the Regiment and were enrolled as deserters. The Regiment left New York October 13th, going by boat to Perth Amboy, and thence by rail through Philadelphia and Baltimore to Washington, D. C., arriving about noon October 14th. They marched through the city, across the Long Bridge, and went into camp on Arlington Heights, being placed in the 4th Brigade, Abercrombie's Division, in the defences of Washington. Very soon thereafter they were moved to Camp DeWitt, Upton Hill, where thorough drilling, interspersed with picket and fatigue duties, was the order of each and every day. Snow and very cold weather were experienced while there, and the boys found shelter tents and army blankets quite a contrast to the homes and feather beds they had left in Sullivan.

The Regiment was at Camp DeWitt during November and December, 1862, when snow storms and very cold weather were experienced. On December 28th, rebel cavalry under Jeb Stuart were reported outside the lines, and some of the pickets had been driven in. Orders were given at about 10.30 p. m. directing that knapsacks be packed, haversacks filled, ammunition distributed, and all in readiness to form on the color line in fifteen minutes. At about midnight the brigade, composed of the 127th N. Y., the 144th N. Y. and the 143d N. Y., marched out on the Alexandria and Fairfax turnpike toward Fairfax Court House. When well out on the pike a halt was called and guns loaded. Annandale was reached about five o'clock on the 29th. A line of battle was formed, pickets posted and the men told to rest on their arms. It was a cold, frosty morning, and fires were soon started, about which the boys gathered. The cavalry pickets brought in six rebel cavalrymen, the only enemy in sight. About six p. m. orders were received to return to camp, which was reached about ten o'clock. This affair was known to the boys as "Bloody Annandale." Comrade Robert L. Tillotson, of Company A, was inspired to compose the following stanzas, which were frequently sung around the camp fires afterward:

FIGHT OF ANNANDALE.

(Air, "Annie of the Vale.")

"Oh, boys, ain't it jolly to march all night, my golly!
With nary a handy chance to get a shoot;
Some confounded fool swapped a horse for a mule,
And Gen'l Gurney sent us down to get the boot.

Chorus:

"March, march, march boys, march—
March till the night torches pale;
March with your knapsack,
Carrying all your hard-tack,
To brutal, to bloody Annandale.

"Oh, chilly were the breezes and bare were the treeses
And filthy were the ditches in the vale;
We liked to froze our faces a sleeping on such places,
And anathematize the dirty town of Annandale.
                                          Chorus.

"Now when the morning in the pale east was dawning,
We stripped the meadows bare of every rail;
The roosters were screaming and the streets fairly steaming,
In that dirty little town of Annandale.
                                          Chorus.

"Then boys, had we fit under David P. DeWitt,
We'd beaten all the rebels without fail;
But as we didn't fight, we surely have the right,
To blow that little town of Annandale.   Chorus.

"With Hughston in the front to bear the battle's brunt,
The Colonel who has never yet turned tail;
If we had only fought, we'd driven the rebels out
From that dirty little town of Annandale.

                                                 Chorus.

"Now boys, my song is ended, the least said the easiest
        mended,
And then I hope you'll never let my song get stale;
But boys, if you see Gurney, just remind him of our journey
From Upton Hill to 'Bloody Annandale.'

                                                 Chorus.

"Then boys here's to Gurney,
    In honor of our Journey,—
        Let us vote the Brigadier a handsome rail,
    May the devil make him stride it,
    Some cold night, and ride it,
        From Upton Hill to Bloody Annandale."   Chorus.

While at Upton Hill the Sullivan County farmers' sons were
transformed into an efficient organization to act as a fighting unit,
under the management of the regimental officers of skill and experience who had been secured to lead and instruct them.

In February, 1863, the Regiment was moved to Camp Chase,
near Cloud's Mills, Va., and placed in the 22d Army Corps. Here
they had heavy fatigue duty in erecting fortifications for the defences of Washington. Much of the time it stormed, and they had
to march long distances for both picket and fatigue duty. While
in camp here, wood was obtained along the Orange and Alexandria
Railroad. A detail from Company B was made to go with the train
of flat cars to load the wood. The engine was in the rear pushing
the train. When near the wood yard, the front car, on which the
men were riding, left the track, coming in contact with a mule, and
capsized, killing four men and mortally injuring two others.

As Spring had come, all were anticipating new developments,
and their anticipations were soon to be realities.

CHAPTER V.

Participation in Raising the Siege of Suffolk—Under General Keys at West Point, Va.—In the 4th Army Corps at White House—Return to Washington.

In April, 1863, the Regiment was marched to Alexandria, Va., where a transport was in waiting, which they boarded, pressing her deck down to near the water's edge. When all were on board the lines were cast off and they found themselves descending the Potomac. All went well until they were near Fortress Monroe, where the swells of the ocean tossed the transport as if a mere plaything. It seemed to the boys that they would be engulfed every time the vessel took the trough of the sea. They were cautioned not to move about, as by doing so they would cause the vessel to founder. In the evening they entered the harbor at Fortress Monroe, and in due time were landed at Suffolk, Va., and were placed in the 3d, Houston's, Brigade, Gurney's Division, Department of Va. They helped to raise the siege of Suffolk, taking part in the battle of Nansemond, April 15, 1863; Providence Church Road, May 3d, and Everett's Bridge, May 4th. After the siege of Suffolk was raised they were placed in the 1st Brigade, Gordon's Division, under General Keys, and were transported to West Point, Va., at the confluence of the Pamunky and Mattapony Rivers. While there, in May, they were required to build fortifications in the burning sun, and many were prostrated by the fatigue and heat. The water was scarce and impure, causing much sickness. In the short sojourn there nearly one-half of the men were on the sick list. About June 1 they were ordered to Yorktown, Va., and transferred to the Fourth Army Corps. The next move was to march up the Peninsula to White House, Va., which they reached June 27th. Richmond seemed to be their objective point, as they were almost in sight of the church spires of the Confederate Capital. On July 7th, orders were issued to be ready to march at daybreak the next morning. The railroad had been torn up some miles toward Richmond and most of the rails loaded on transports, and a part of the Regiment worked all night to complete the shipment.

The morning dawned with rain, and instead of "On to Rich-mond," as they supposed it might be, they were to retrace their steps down the Peninsula in the slippery Virginia mud. It rained all day, and early evening found them about twenty-three miles toward Yorktown, wet and about fagged out. They were halted in a piece of woods, all thinking they were to encamp for the night. Fires were started in spite of the rain, and coffee (the soldier's panacea for drenched backs and aching limbs) was being prepared, when, alas, that bugle call, "Fall in, fall in," brought dismay to all hearts. A road from Richmond joined the road they were on some five or six miles ahead, and it was feared they would be headed off there by the Confederates; hence they must struggle on through the mud and darkness as best they could. Very soon the boys be-gan to drop out unable to endure the fatigue longer, and sought the protection of some neighboring tree or a fence corner. At about 11 o'clock p. m. the Division, or about one-fifth of it, reached the junction, and the men dropped where halted, in the mud and rain, to be refreshed for the next day's march.

The next morning the army of stragglers reported in squads, and by nine a. m. the march was resumed, and Williamsburgh and Yorktown reached by nightfall. A transport was in waiting and in due time the Regiment was again landed at Washington, D. C.

CHAPTER VI.

In the 11th Army Corps, Army of the Potomac—With General Joseph Hooker to Bridgeport, Alabama—Head-on Collision—Opening the "Cracker
Route" and Midnight Fight—Camp in Lookout Valley.

The cause for the hasty retreat from White House and con-
centration at Washington, noted in the last chapter, was that General Lee was in Pennsylvania with his army threatening Washington, Baltimore, and Philadelphia. The Regiment boarded the
cars for Frederick City, Md., in order to join Meade's Army of the
Potomac, to head off and defeat the Confederate Army. They
reached Frederick, July 12th, and were placed in the 1st Brigade, 3d
Division, 11th Army Corps. They joined the Corps near Funkstown, and with it followed Lee's army into Virginia, crossing the
Potomac near Berlin, Md. After escorting General Lee and his
army back to their entrenchments in the vicinity of Richmond, the
Regiment went into camp near Warrenton Junction, where they
remained until September.

The great battle of Chickamauga, Ga., was fought, in which
General Rosecrans was defeated and besieged in Chattanooga,
Tenn. General Joseph Hooker was ordered to take the 11th and
12th Army Corps and proceed west to the relief of the besieged
army. The transfer by rail from Virginia to Bridgeport, Ala., on
the Tennessee River, was made in eight days, the troops passing
through Maryland, Pennsylvania, Ohio, and Indiana to Indianapolis; then south to and through Kentucky and Tennessee to Bridgeport, Ala. The 143d Regiment was packed in freight and cattle cars,
some of the men riding on the roofs of the cars because of their
crowded condition, the writer being one of such. The trip was one
of varied experience for the boys. At Xenia, Ohio, the patriotic
citizens came with wagons loaded with food and luxuries, such as
milk, biscuits, cookies, fruit, etc., to which the boys were to help
themselves, and no charges.

When within a few miles of Bridgeport the train carrying the
143d, while rounding a curve in a deep cut, met another train,
and a head-on collision was the outcome. The compact was such

that one locomotive was partly mounted on the other, and the two-front cars of the train were telescoped about half their length. A number of soldiers were hurt, but fortunately none were killed. The train was abandoned and the journey completed in true soldier fashion with no more collisions. A pontoon bridge was thrown across the Tennessee River, and the advance made up the south side of the river. At one stage of the advance, the Regiment marched into a large cave and bivouacked for the night. It was learned that a locomotive had been run off on a branch road up to a mine in the mountains, and the 143d was sent to capture and bring it out for use. The capture was not difficult, but an important part of the engine had been removed and hidden so as to make it useless. With characteristic Yankee ingenuity they set to work to find the missing piece and succeeded, returning highly elated with their success.

The 11th Corps reached Lookout Valley October 29th, 1863, and went into camp under Lookout Mountain, from whose summit bristled the Confederate cannon. The Confederates could look down on it and note every movement and the location of every camp. General Geary's Division was encamped about two miles in the rear of the 3d Division (of which the 143d was a part), at Wauhatchie. About 12 o'clock, midnight, heavy cannonading was heard in the direction of Geary's camp. The Regiment was called out and in double-quick time marched toward the firing. They ran right up against the Confederate line, and for a few minutes there was a lively time in the skirmish driving the rebels back across the creek. Geary had been sorely pressed by 10,000 picked men to make the capture of his Division by a surprise in moonlight. The timely arrival of the 3d Division saved the day.

Connection was made with Rosecrans' army the next day; pontoon bridges laid and part rations secured for the starving men and animals. The Regiment went into camp in this Lookout Valley, remaining about one month, or until the battle of Missionary Ridge. Their experience here was unique. They learned not only to live on half rations, but to take patiently the amusement of the Confederate artillerists on Lookout Mountain, who practiced, with small charges of powder, dropping shells and pieces of railroad iron in and about the camp. . Diarrhea was prevalent, the hospitals were full, and deaths were frequent.

HEZEKIAH WATKINS, C. E., A. M., LL. D.,
Lieut.-Colonel and Bvt. Col. U. S. V.

CHAPTER VII.

Temporary Transfer to the 14th Corps—Battle of Missionary Ridge—Death of Lieut.-Colonel Joseph B. Taft—Forced March to Knoxville, Tenn.— Bridging the Tennessee River at Night—Great Suffering from Cold— The Return to Camp in Lookout Valley—Winter Quarters at Bridgeport Ala.—The 20th Army Corps Formed.

On November 24th, 1863, the 3d Division, 11th Corps, was marched to and through Chattanooga and went into camp with the 14th Corps in front of Missionary Ridge. The next day, about 2 p. m. the Regiment was placed in the line of battle and advanced, capturing the first line of works before the Confederates realized that a battle was on. They could look down on the movement, and supposed the Yanks were having a grand review. The Regiment was then relieved and sent to the left to assist General Sherman in turning the Confederate right. On reaching the position assigned, they charged up the eastern end of Missionary Ridge, helping in the final charge that raised the siege of Chattanooga. For this charge, Lieut.-Col. Taft was detailed to command the 73d Pennsylvania, and fell, leading them in the charge. The next day the regiment pressed on with General Sherman's army after the retreating foe to Ringgold, and assisted in dislodging them from that stronghold. The pursuit was then abandoned.

The death of Lieut.-Colonel Taft was a great loss to the 143d, as he was a thorough disciplinarian and a model soldier, and had done much to bring the regiment to its high standard of efficiency.

While returning to Chattanooga, General Sherman received orders to proceed with his army, of which the 143d was then a part, to the relief of Burnside at Knoxville, 120 miles up the Tennessee River from Chattanooga.

The command had made a detour toward Knoxville on the return movement and was at the time at Hiawasse River, within eighty-four miles, but had provisions for but three days, and Knoxville must be reached in that time. Seven days before the regiment had left camp with two days' provisions in haversacks, without knapsacks, stripped for the fight, with but a single blanket or overcoat per man, and it was bitter cold. Ice froze about one inch thick every night. Twelve thousand of their fellow-soldiers were imprisoned and starving, and the regiment was off for their relief at daybreak the next morning. Camping places were selected where rail fences were plenty, and piles were kept burning all night, around which the boys slept as best they could, by alternately roasting one side and freezing the other. The fourth day the columns reached Marysville, within fifteen miles of Knoxville, when news was rceived that the siege was raised, and the command was given a couple of days' rest before the return.

During the night of December 4, near London, Tenn., the regiment was detailed to bridge the Little Tennessee, a swift-running stream some 300 yards wide. The bridge was made with over fifty captured wagons, by running stringers from wagon to wagon, on which were placed boards or planks. In the deepest part benches had to be constructed, and the boys were of necessity in the ice-cold water, and on coming out their clothes would freeze before they could reach the fires.

The return to Chattanooga was by easy marches, but over rough roads in a more mountainous country. One day a severe storm set in toward night and the regiment went into camp as darkness approached, supposing they were bivouacked for the night. Rails were secured and sheds made with rubber blankets for roofing. Under these, fires were started and coffee was nearly boiling when the bugle sounded "fall in," "fall in." The scene and language cannot be described. The Division had been halted because of the rain and impending darkness some three miles short of the camp ground assigned, and a request forwarded to headquarters to have the halt approved; but instead of approval, a peremptory order to move forward to the place assigned. Out into the blackness, pouring rain, and mud the regiment plunged. Men stumbled into the gutter, into each other, and said some things besides what they had been taught in Sunday School. About midnight they were turned into a field where corn had grown, and halted in mud and water ankle deep to rest and sleep preparatory for the next day's march. A few fires were started, and most of the boys took their rest standing around them till day appeared. The wind turned to the northwest, cold, and froze the ground as well as the wet clothes. The following quotation is from the pen of Major-General Carl Schurz:

HARD WORK AND SCANTY RETURNS.

"On December 5, not many miles from Knoxville, we were informed that Longstreet had not waited for the arrival of our forces of relief, but effected his retreat toward Virginia. Thus our expedition had accomplished its purpose. It was a victory achieved by the soldiers' legs. We were allowed a day's rest, and then started on our way back, the same hundred and twenty miles and a little more, to our old camp in Lookout Valley. We could march more leisurely, but the return seemed harder than the advance had been. There was not the same spirit in it. Our regular food-supplies were entirely exhausted. We had to 'lived upon the country.' We impressed what live stock we could, which was by no means always sufficient. The surrounding population, Union people, were friendly, but poor. Roasted wheat and corn had to serve for coffee; molasses, found on the farms, for sugar. But, far worse than this, the clothing of the men was in tatters, the shoes worn and full of holes. Perhaps one-fourth of the men had none at all. They protected their feet by winding rags around them.

"Their miseries were increased by occurrences like this: One day our march was unusually difficult. We passed through a hilly country. The roads were in many places like dry, washed-out beds of mountain torrents, full of boulders, large and small. The artillery-horses could not possibly pull their pieces and caissons over these obstacles. They had to be unhitched, and infantry detachments were called upon to help the artillerymen lift their guns and appurtenances over the rocks. This operation had to be repeated several times during the day. Thus the marching column was stopped, time and again, without affording the soldiers any real rest. On the contrary, such irregular stoppages for an uncertain length of time are apt to annoy and fatigue the marching men all the more. At last, toward dusk of the evening, I found on our route a large meadow-ground, through which a clear stream of water flowed. There was plenty of wood for fires near by. The spot seemed to be made for camping. My orders as to how far I was to march were not quite definite. I was to receive further instructions on the way. My troops, having been on their feet from early morning and having marched under the difficulties described, were tired beyond measure. They just dragged themselves painfully along. I resolved to rest them on this favored spot, if permitted, and despatched a staff-officer to corps-headquarters, two or three miles ahead, to obtain that permission. Meanwhile, waiting for an answer I did not doubt would be favorable, I assigned camping-places to the different brigades.

"After the lapse of about an hour, when a large part of my command had come in and were beginning to build fires and to prepare such food as they had, my officer returned from corps-headquarters with the positive order that I must—without loss of time—continue my march and proceed about three miles farther, where a camping-place would be assigned to me. There was now nothing to be done but to obey instantly. My division bugler sounded the signal. There arose something like a sullen groan from the bivouac, but the men emptied upon the ground the water which was just beginning to boil in their kettles, and promptly fell into line.

"We had hardly been on the way half an hour when a fearful thunder-storm broke upon us. The rain came down in sheets like a cloudburst, driving right into our faces. In a few minutes we were all drenched to the skin. I wore a stout cavalry overcoat with a cape, well lined with flannel, over my uniform. In an incredibly short time I felt the cold water trickle down my body. My riding-boots were soon full to overflowing. One may imagine the sorry plight of the poor fellows in rags. They had to suffer, too, not only from the water coming down from above, but also from water coming from below. We were again passing through a hilly district. The road ran along the bottom of a deep valley with high ridges on both sides. From these the rain-water rushed down in streams, transforming the road into a swelling torrent, the water reaching up to the knees of the men and higher. Meanwhile the thunder was rolling, the lightning flashing, and the poor sufferers stumbling over unseen boulders under the water and venting choler in wild imprecations.

"At last, after having struggled on in this way for about two hours, we emerged from the wooded hills into a more open country; at least, I judged so, as the absolute darkness seemed to be a little relieved. The storm had ceased."

In due time the old camp at Lookout Valley was reached, and then the boys could sleep without expecting a shell to drop among them from the crest of Lookout Mountain.

In the service in and about Chattanooga, the 143d was in Bushback's Brigade, of which General Sherman says: "The brigade of Colonel Bushback, belonging to the Eleventh Corps, which was the first to come out of Chattanooga to my flank, which fought at the Tunnel Hill, in connection with General Ewing's Division, displayed a courage almost amounting to rashness. Following the enemy almost to the tunnel gorge, it lost many valuable lives, prominent among them Lieutenant-Colonel Taft, spoken of as a most gallant soldier."

The regiment remained in camp in Lookout Valley until near the close of January, 1864, when it was ordered to Bridgeport, Ala., to guard the railroad.

Assistant Surgeon Herman Craft, writing from Lookout Valley, Jan. 12, 1864, says:

"Camp of the 143d Regiment, N. Y. S. V.,
"Lookout Valley, Tenn., January 12, 1864.

"Our regiment is in an alarmingly unhealthy condition. Day after day the destroying Angel continues to visit our already thinned ranks, and one after another of our bravest and once most robust boys, are numbered among the dead. Chronic diarrhœa is the prevailing disease. We have had since we came into this Department, upwards of seventy deaths from this direful malady, and probably before this articles reaches your paper, there may be added to this number ten or fifteen more of our bravest and best boys, who are now tottering on the verge of the grave. The boys are very much depressed in spirits, which makes them less able to resist the onward course of the diarrhœa. We report in the morning, at Surgeon's call, eighty unfit for duty, but there are actually some one hundred and seventy-six suffering in the regiment from the same disease, but some so slightly that they continue to duty until they get alarmed about themselves and are obliged to report. We have besides this number, 184 in the different military hospitals, making in the aggregate the enormous sick report of three hundred and sixty. The aggregate strength of the regiment, that is counting those present and absent, is 680. So you see at a glance that over half the regiment is suffering from sickness.

"The friends of the regiment will undoubtedly be glad to learn that Colonel Boughton, who always has been indefatigable in his efforts to promote the welfare of the regiment, is making every effort to have relief brought about, and they may rest assured that nothing on his part will be left undone to alleviate the suffering of the afflicted. From the encouragement the Colonel is meeting with, I should not be surprised if the regiment was either sent home, furloughed for a short time, or sent north to garrison some place. The causes of the sickness and mortality in our regiment will, I do not doubt, be attributed by many to the unhealthiness of this climate, but such an opinion would be, in a measure, erroneous. The climate of Tennessee is as healthy as any in the United States, but while making this statement I do not deny that the locality in which the army is encamped is made artificially unhealthy. The hundreds of dead and putrifying horses and mules that lie unburied, and strew the ground for miles around, and offal from cattle killed for the army, combine to render the locality peculiarly adapted to diarrhœa, dysentery and malarious fevers. But this is by no means the primary cause of our unhealthy condition. You are aware, I doubt not, that our regiment was enrolled in a high, salubrious district—indeed as salubrious as any section in the whole North, where malarias are almost entirely unknown. When we were organized and sent to the field, we were sent to Washington, where the climate is termed villainous by the resident physicians. From Washington we were sent to Suffolk in the southern part of Virginia, a still worse climate. From Suffolk we were order to West Point, Va., at the confluence of the Pamunky and Mattapony Rivers. Here the first seeds of disease and death were sown. The climate of this place is fully as unhealthy as the climate along the coast of the Mediterranean Sea—where the malaria floats as a halo o'er its victims. Indeed this place is so notoriously malarious, that the rebel journals predicted that sickness would soon thin our ranks, sand-flies fatten on our carcasses, and we would be compelled to abandon the place. Their predictions were too true, for before we had been there three weeks over half our regiment was prostrated by fever, dysentery and diarrhœa. From this place we were ordered back to York-town, and from Yorktown to the Peninsula. The unhealthiness of this latter place is too familiar with every reader in your section to need description by me. Suffice it to say, that in these unhealthy localities were sown the seeds of disease, which are now ripening into sickness and death, and threatening to annihilate the regiment.

"HERMAN CRAFT,
"Ass't Surgeon, 143d Regt., N. Y. V.'"

At Bridgeport, Ala., winter quarters were erected on high ground and the health of the regiment improved rapidly for the next four months. During this period of rest the 11th and 12th Corps were consolidated into the 20th Corps, under General Joseph Hooker, and the regiment was in the Third Brigade, First Division, with the red star as division badge. The division was commanded by General A. S. Williams, familiarly known as "Pop Williams."

CHAPTER VIII.

The Atlanta Campaign Begins—The Regiment at the Front at Rocky Faced
Ridge and at Rasaca, Ga.—Oostanaula River Bridged by the Regiment
—Battle of Cassville, Ga.—The Regiment Charges the Works at Punk-
invine Creek—In Front of Kenesaw Mountain and Marietta—The Chat-
tahoochee River Reached—Battle of Peach Tree Creek and Capture of
Atlanta.

On May 5, 1864, the great Atlanta campaign was opened,
in which the 143d Regiment was an active participant, doing its
full share as a unit of the Army of the Cumberland, commanded by
Major-General George H. Thomas. This army was the largest
of the three co-operating under General Sherman, and occupied
the center in the campaign. The enemy was found on Rocky Faced
Ridge, a mountain so steep that boulders could be rolled down
on the assaulting party, and so strongly fortified as to be impregna-
ble to assault from the front. To force Johnston out of this stronghold, a strong detachment, including the 143d, was sent around to
the right through Snake Creek Gap, near Resaca, Ga. Strong intrenchments were found to protect the railroad and Resaca. The
regiment was in the front line of investment. Sherman says of this
engagement: "Hooker's corps had some heavy and handsome fighting that afternoon and night on the left, where the Dalton road
entered the intrenchments, capturing a four-gun intrenched battery, with its men and guns."

On the night of May 15th, Johnston got his army across the
bridges of the Oostanaula River, set them on fire, and the troops
entered Resaca at daylight. Immediate pursuit was ordered, and to
facilitate that movement, the 143d Regiment was ordered to con-
struct a bridge for infantry service, which they did by taking bents
of barns for piers. By morning the bridge was completed and the
20th Corps was crossing.

"On the March, below Resaca, Ga.,
"Monday, May 16, 1864.
"My Dear Judge:—We had a general engagement with
Johnston's army in front of Resaca yesterday. Last night the

enemy left, leaving behind many of his dead and wounded. We are in pursuit this morning, and I avail myself of the hasty opportunity afforded by a halt to send this by Apgar, who goes home on leave.

"The cars to-day run to this place, but the Rebs burned a bridge across the river which will delay them a few days.

"The regiment behaved as well as men could. I know nothing to any man's discredit. Not a man or officer that did not stand up to his duty. Only two regiments of our brigade were engaged—the 101st Ill. and our own.

"We were on the extreme left of our line, which the Rebels endeavored to turn and flank. The Pioneer Corps of our Brigade this morning buried in front of our regiment 85 Confederates, including a Chaplain and 1st Lieutenant. A Captain and nine men raised a white flag, and when the firing ceased came in and gave themselves up.

"Butterfield's Division, joining our left, lost severely. Faulkner's regiment 98 in killed and wounded out of about 340 muskets—Faulkner not hurt.

"Have no time to write more now. I send list of killed and wounded.

"Sincerely yours,
"H. Watkins."

On May 17th the enemy was found intrenched again, near Cassville. Their lines were closely invested when darkness closed operations for that day. During the night the enemy made good their escape across the Etowah River. The army had distanced the trains of supplies, and a rest of four or five days was taken for them to catch up.

Johnston had taken a position at Allatoona Pass, very strong for defense by nature, which had been skillfully fortified. To avoid attacking this and force him to the open, the next movement was to the right through a rough, wild country toward Dallas, the 20th Corps on the main road in the lead. The enemy was found guarding a bridge across Pumpkin Vine Creek, and driven some four miles to a cross-road, called New Hope, where they were found in force, behind breastworks. The regiment was in the front line of battle, driving the enemy through the forest, when suddenly they found themselves within a few rods of fortifications, well

manned, from which poured forth a terrific fire. The Regiment was
ordered to lie down and fire. Lieutenant Stanton, of Company K,
saw the enemy in the act of unmasking a battery in their front,
and shouted, "Boys, don't let them fire those guns," and the boys
made it so warm for the gunners that they were unable to make
use of that battery. The ammunition carried was soon exhausted,
and as darkness approached another regiment took the place of
the 143d, not more than fifty paces from the rebel works. Firing
was kept up during the night, and the battle renewed in the morning. But the works were too strong to be carried by assault.

The next day the regiment was sent back to Kingston, Ga.,
some thirty miles, to guard the ammunition train, as it had to be
replenished there. On their return they were moved to the left
to extend the investment toward the railroad and Ackworth, about
eight miles distant. Every mile gained had to be fought over during the day, and at night rifle trenches with head logs were erected.
The fire of musketry and cannon resounded day and night for five
days, when the roads connecting New Hope, Ackworth and Allatoona were secured, which resulted in the evacuation of the
stronghold at Allatoona and the works in Sherman's immediate
front.

"On the Road to Sandtown, six miles
southwest of Ackworth Station.

"Tuesday, June 7th, 1864.

"My Dear Judge:—I think I wrote you last from Kingston. We returned on the following Tuesday p. m., and found
the position of affairs unchanged—the two lines confronting
each other not two hundred yards apart. Our next move
was to the extreme left of our line again, with incessant
skirmishing with the enemy.

"The rebels moved their force to their right on Saturday
and Saturday night, and we made a corresponding change.
Sunday night we encamped near the junction of the Ackworth
and Marietta turnpikes, about five miles from Ackworth. All
our movements since we left Kingston and Cassville have been
to strike the railroad somewhere below Allatoona. This position was so strong by nature as to defy a direct attack. In
fact, all our movements since we started have been made with
a view to flank their position and not to attack them in their

positions. I do not believe that the battle for the possession at Atlanta will be fought on this side of the Chattahoochee River.

"The excitement of constant skirmishes and alarms is very exhausting. Captains Reynolds and Bennett, and Lieutenants Hill and Pinney have gone to Chattanooga sick, and Captains Anderson and Pinney, and Lieutenant Palen are not well at all.

"Sincerely yours,
"Hezekiah Watkins."

Quotation from Sherman's Memoirs:

"Thus substantially in the month of May we had steadily driven our antagonist from the strong positions of Dalton, Resaca, Cassville, Allatoona, and Dallas; had advanced our lines in strong, compact order from Chattanooga to Big Shanty, nearly a hundred miles of as difficult country as was ever fought over by civilized armies; and thus stood prepared to go on, anxious to fight and confident of success, as soon as the railroad connections were complete to bring forward the necessary supplies."

During this time the 20th Corps had lost in killed and wounded, 3,568; sustaining the greatest loss of any corps in Sherman's army, and the 143d had its full share of honors and casualties.

At dawn on June 10th the advance was sounded and the Regiment was off, with the army, in search of the next line of fortifications occupied by the enemy. They were found on three prominent hills, known as Kenesaw, Pine Mountain, and Lost Mountain, the fortifications extending some ten miles. The skirmishers were driven in and fortifications erected facing theirs. From June 1st to the 15th it rained almost every day, making it very difficult to move artillery and trains, and unpleasant and trying for the men; yet, without murmur, they pushed and dug ahead. Roads had to be constructed to different parts of the army.

On the 15th of June an advance was made against Pine Mountain, and it was abandoned by the enemy. On the 16th Lost Mountain was secured in the same manner.

In pressing the enemy as he contracted his lines of defense around Kenesaw, the regiment was placed in support of a battery on quite an elevation, with half a mile of open plain in front, beyond which was a wooded ridge, fortified, to which the rebels had retreated. Shortly after being thus posted the enemy came out in force in plain view, to capture the battery and break our lines. The 143d could note every movement of the Confederates and the effect of the bursting shells over and among their ranks. It was the only instance in the history of the Regiment when they could see the battle as well as to participate therein. Two desperate attempts were made by the enemy to break the line where the Regiment was posted during that afternoon, but both were repulsed.

On July 2d the Confederate works were found abandoned, and another advance ordered. Thus Marietta was secured. The second day of advance disclosed the enemy very strongly intrenched at the Chattahoochee River, to cover crossings. A crossing was secured farther up the river, and the rebels were forced to abandon their position. Pontoons were laid, and the Regiment was with the army in pursuit of Johnston toward Atlanta.

On July 20th, after crossing Peach Tree Creek, while resting for noon, the 20th Corps was furiously attacked without notice by overwhelming numbers of the enemy in an effort to break through the Union lines. The Regiment was on a slight elevation in woods with dense undergrowth, and was charged upon three separate times, but held their position, the Confederates coming within a few yards of the line held by the 143d. The regimental loss was the heaviest they sustained in any action in which they participated. Adjutant Radcliff was killed while in the act of giving an order for the Colonel. Very little underbursh was left standing after the battle. Bullets had leveled it as with a scythe.

The writer was on the picket line in front of the Brigade, in dense underbrush. The first indication of impending battle was the discovery by the pickets of three lines of battle advancing through the brush in front of the pickets. The alarm was given and the line of battle formed. In the haste and confusion an order was sent to the regiments of the Brigade to fall back a short distance to another elevation, where the attack would be met. Col. Boughton and the Colonel of the 82d Ohio did not get the order and met the charge then and there, holding their position during the afternoon. By the line of battle being farther to the rear on either side exposed the two regiments to flank movements, which were attempted by the enemy, but promptly met and defeated. For some time Generals Hooker and Robinson thought the 143d N. Y. and the 82d Ohio captured. Thomas D. Collins, of Company H, 143d N. Y., was an orderly on General Robinson's Staff, and General Hooker asked him if he could find the 143d N. Y. Collins replied that he could. He was told to go, and through the brush and flying bullets he rode. He found the regiment and none too soon, for their ammunition was about exhausted. He reported back that Col. Boughton said that they were holding their line, but wanted reinforcements and ammunition. The ammunition was soon forwarded and the other lines advanced to conform with that held by the New York and Ohio regiments. Collins says that he went back with a box of ammunition on his horse.

The following resolutions were adopted:

"Peach Tree Creek,
"Camp of the 143d Regiment, N. Y. V.,
"Near Atlanta, Ga., July 27, 1864.

"The officers of the 143d Regiment, N. Y. Vols., in view of the death of Adjutant William M. Ratcliff, killed on the field, and First Lieut. Peter L. Waterbury, mortally wounded, in the battle of Peach-tree Ridge, before Atlanta, on the 20th inst., unanimously adopted the following resolutions:

"*Resolved,* That by the death of Adjutant Ratcliff and Lieutenant Waterbury, the Regiment sustains an irreparable loss, and the country is deprived of two of its most gallant and patriotic defenders.

"*Resolved,* That by their gentlemanly deportment and soldierly qualities, they had endeared themselves to the officers and men of the Regiment, so that we mourn their loss as brothers.

"*Resolved,* That we will more sacredly defend the cause of our beloved country, sanctified afresh by the blood of our two brothers-in-arms, and of the other brave men of the Regiment who have fallen upon the field of battle.

"*Resolved,* That we deeply sympathize with the friends of our comrades in battle, so hastily and so cruelly taken from

us, and while we mourn their loss, we will strive to emulate
their virtues.

"*Resolved,* That a copy of these resolutions be forwarded
to each of the Sullivan County papers for publication."

"Hezekiah Watkins, Chairman.
John Higgins,
E. H. Pinney,
W. T. George, Committee."

During the night the enemy withdrew within their fortifications
surrounding Atlanta, Ga.

The 143d Regiment was in the front line in pressing up to
the rebels' works. On reaching the heights in front of their fortifications, the Regiment occupied an exposed position to the shells
from the cannon of one of the forts. Orders were given to throw
up breastworks, but few picks or shovels were at hand. About one
pick was secured for each company, and by short relays it was
made to do the work of many, and the loosened earth was piled
up with tin plates in willing hands. One cannon had the range
of Company A, and James L. Brown, a member of the company,
spotted that gun and watched to see when it fired. On seeing the
puff of smoke from it, he would shout "duck," and down went the
heads into the hole dug, before the shell could reach them. In this
way they soon had ample protection, and the siege of Atlanta had
begun. The Regiment held this position secured in line, and did
not participate in the other battles fought in the siege. The Regiment was one of the first to scale the works and enter Atlanta on
September 2d, 1864. They remained in the city until it was
evacuated by Sherman in November. During this time the Regiment was detailed to accompany a wagon train for forage well out
into the country toward Madison. They had quite an exciting experience warding off a dash of Confederate cavalry to capture the
train, and returned with wagons loaded with corn.

"Camp 143d Regt., N. Y. S. V.,
"Near Atlanta, Ga., July 24, 1864.

"Friend Baldwin:—Yours of the 17th inst. is at hand.
Its perusal has afforded me much pleasure, and as I have a
few moments leisure to-day, I will improve them by writing.

You will perceive by the heading that we have kept moving toward.the place which was said to be our point of destination, when we started, viz: Atlanta.

"We have got the enemy in his last line of works, outside of the city, and are so close some of the church steeples can be plainly seen from our works. Our present position, however, was not obtained without a struggle. Sherman succeeded in getting his army this side of the Chattahoochee River without much fighting, and probably if he had had his own way, not much fighting would have occurred yet; for he would rather flank the enemy out of his position, than to move the troops on him in front, but it seems Jeff. Davis became dissatisfied with Johnston's way of fighting, and put Hood in command, who thought he could force us back and save Atlanta. This happened after we were across the river, or since Monday, as the last of our forces crossed then. Accordingly on Wednesday afternoon, a very fierce assault was made on our forces, nearly the whole length of the line; but mainly in the center, where the enemy were heavily massed. Our corps (which held the center) had hardly time to get in position before his forces were on us, and having a large space to fill, we could have only a single line of battle. But bravely did our men do their duty. The enemy made desperate and repeated attempts to break our line, but without success; and finally fell back, leaving his dead, and large numbers of his wounded on the field. This battle was fought nearly two miles farther back than where we now are. Our Brigade joined the 3d Brigade of the 2d Division on the right, and our Regiment was on the left of the Brigade. The 2d Division had formed on a side hill, descending toward the enemy, and when we were forming to continue the line, the Rebs opened fire on us. Owing to the shape of the ground, our position was very much exposed, and in about twenty minutes we lost in our Regiment six killed and thirty-eight wounded. The Adjutant was shot dead, and Lieutenant Waterbury severely wounded. There is very little hope of his recovery. This fire broke the 3d Brigade, and it fell back some distance; but our Regiment, by falling back about two rods, became sheltered by the crest of the hill, and there held its ground, only losing two more wounded, making in all forty-six. Some of those wounded have since died.

"While I write, sharp-shooters' balls, and shells from the enemy's guns, come whistling over, but we have got works thrown up, that neither musket balls or the largest shells can effect; so we feel perfectly safe. At the same time, we have some twenty and some thirty-two pound guns that are throwing shot and shell in the centre of the city. How long the enemy will be able to hold his present position it is hard to tell; but it is the general opinion he will soon 'dig out.' The health of the Regiment is very good at present. Sergts. Brown and Cantrell joined their company a few days since. They are both quite well. The boys all join in sending their best regards to you.

"R. M. J. HARDENBERG."

JOSEPH B. TAFT,
Lieut.-Colonel and Bvt. Col. N. Y. V.

CHAPTER IX.

Atlanta to Savannah, "Sherman's March to the Sea"—In the Enemy's Country and Living on His Sweet Potatoes and Bacon—Investment and Capture of Savannah—The Joy of Receiving the Mail.

During September, October, and part of November, while the Regiment was doing provost duty and recuperating in Atlanta, Sherman was preparing for the next great movement. What that movement would be none knew; but all felt assured that when undertaken it would be the right one, if planned and executed by their skillful and beloved leader.

The army had been reorganized; that under Major-General Thomas going to the rear to look after Hood, who had started northward to interfere with the supply route, and thus cause Sherman to give up Atlanta. But the Confederates did not realize that Sherman was all ready to give up Atlanta, in a very different manner from that which they anticipated. Four corps were retained near Atlanta and constituted Sherman's reorganized army, one of which was the 20th Corps, to which our Regiment belonged. On November 12th these four corps were ordered to concentrate on Atlanta, with limited wagons, cannon and rations; all not able for active campaigning being sent to the rear. Each soldier was provided with a rubber blanket, woolen blanket or overcoat, three-days rations, and forty rounds of ammunition, "light marching order." The following order was all that was known of the movement about to be executed:

"Headquarters, Military Division of the Mississippi,
"In the field, Kingston, Ga., Nov. 8, 1864.

"The General Commanding deems it proper at this time to inform the officers and men of the Fourteenth, Fifteenth, Seventeenth, and Twentieth Corps that he has organized them into an army for a special purpose, well known to the War Department and to General Grant. It is sufficient for you to know that it involves a departure from our present base, and a long and difficult march to a new one. All the chances of war have been considered and provided for, as far as human sagacity can. All he asks of you is to maintain that discipline, patience, and courage which have characterized you in the past; and he hopes through you to strike a blow at our enemy that will have a material effect in producing what we all so much desire, his complete overthrow.

"By order of

"MAJOR-GENERAL W. T. SHERMAN.

"L. M. DAYTON,

"Aide-de-Camp."

On the morning of November 15th, the Regiment, as a unit of the 20th Corps, "Pop" Williams commanding, marched out of Atlanta towards the east, which to them meant ultimately Richmond, and as the band struck up "John Brown," they sang it with a will, and as General Sherman rode by they shouted, "Uncle Billy, I guess Grant is waiting for us at Richmond." The general sentiment was that we were marching for Richmond. Following the Regiment was one army wagon drawn by six mules and one ambulance drawn by a span of horses. Ten days' rations were to be kept on hand, and to this end foragers were to be detailed every day to keep them replenished. These would start with the advance and branch off on either side, five or six miles if need be, visiting every house in search of corn, molasses, meal, bacon, and sweet potatoes, and when found, load what was needed into some vehicle and get this to the main road in time for the regimental wagon. Sherman says: "Often I would pass these foraging parties at the road-side, waiting for their wagons to come up, and was amused at their strange collections—mules, horses, even cattle, packed with old saddles and loaded with hams, bacon, bags of corn-meal, and poultry of every character and description."

This foraging was attended with great danger and hard work, yet there seemed to be a charm about it that attracted the boys, or many of them, and they freely volunteered for the detail. The wagon trains were ordered to keep closed up, and if one fell out to load up it had to fall in at the rear, and it was desirable to load in the provisions and still maintain the place in line. This required skill and dexterity, but the boys were equal to the occasion in most cases. The fences through the fields were opened back some distance, the wagon or wagons taken out and rushed ahead and loaded ready to retake their places in line when the train was passing.

The Regiment passed through Decatur and Madison, helping to destroy the railroad thus far. The track was upset by the troops being stationed along one side for a long distance, and by a united effort rolling the ties and rails over while spiked together. Then the ties were pried from the rails, piled, and fired, and the rails placed across these piles, and when red hot in the middle, removed to a telegraph pole or tree and wound around it, the men at the ends going in opposite directions. After reaching Madison the troops turned southward toward Milledgeville, one hundred miles distant, which was reached in seven days. After resting for a day, the march was resumed, crossing the Oconee and marching to the east again toward Sandersville, which was reached on the 26th. Here some resistance was shown, but it was soon overcome. From Sandersville the course was more to the south-east toward Millen, which was entered on December 3d.

Up to this time provisions had been plenty, but from Millen toward Savannah the country was more sandy and barren and the provisions stored in the wagons had to be drawn upon in part. The roads were good in the main and the fifteen miles per day seemed only a stimulant to the appetites, that they might the better enjoy the variety of goods things secured by the foragers, nick-named "bummers."

On the 9th of December, the Regiment encamped in front of the fortifications around Savannah. In front of these works was a swamp, and creek which had been dammed and the swamp flooded to the depth of five or six feet. While a portion of the army was capturing Fort McAllister and preparations were being made to carry their works, rations were very scarce. Rice was piled up in abundance near by, but in the hull, and the boys could not get rid of the hulls at first. Finally a negro showed them how, with the aid of a log with a hole cut into it, a sharpened stick, and the wind, they could eliminate the hulls, and thereafter they had plenty to eat. to eat.

Arrangements were made for the Regiment to take the works in their front by the use of bundles of rice straw, bound with telegraph wire. Every other man was to carry the guns of two, and the men without guns to carry a bundle of straw and wade until the water was too deep, then to make a filling of straw to cross the deeper part. But the works were evacuated the night before the charge was to have been made. On December 21st, the Regiment, with the army, crossed the fortifications and entered Savannah.

For nearly six weeks the boys had been cut off from communication with friends and home and surrounded by hostile foes. Who could depict their joy as they saw the transports approaching, loaded with provisions, which not alone were welcome, but with that which was even more precious to the boys. Hark! Loud cheering at the landing, and it is caught up by camp after camp. Two words, caught by the listening ear, "The mail," was enough to set that whole army wild; and when distributed, what a scene for an artist. The reading of the letters and papers from home, and comfortable quarters in Savannah was a most delightful Christmas ending of the great "March to the Sea."

Extract from a Sullivan County paper:

"Our 143d Regiment is with General Sherman, in his great movement from Atlanta to the sea coast. In the history of this war, this expedition will be considered one of the most remarkable. The whole nation stands breathless with excitement, awaiting the result. The North believes that it will be successful, because it is led by one of the greatest military commanders of our country. Nevertheless, a failure would be so disastrous that no one will feel relief until our army is fairly 'out of the woods.'

"Our own citizens are watching Sherman's movements with painful solicitude, because every one of them has some friend or neighbor whose life or liberty depends on the success of Sherman. If he fails, mourning and woe will visit hundreds of our families. The rich and the poor will be alike affected, except that the poor—Heaven shield and succor them!—in addition to the sorrow which will pierce their hearts at the loss or captivity of friends, will be thrown for support, in these times of want and suffering, upon the cold charities of the public.

"We copy in another column an article from the New York News—a paper not apt to speak hopefully of Northern success unless there is substantial ground for so doing. The editor expresses the opinion very decidedly that Sherman will succeed. So may it be!"

CHAPTER X.

"On to Richmond," or Campaign of the Carolinas—Flooded Swamps, Mud and Quicksand—Battle of Robertsville, S. C.—Battle of Averysboro, N. C.—Battle of Bentonville, N. C.—Goldsboro Occupied and Rest.

Sherman's army occupied Savannah and vicinity during January, 1865, preparatory to the "on to Richmond," the next wild chase through the Carolinas, the Regiment being encamped on the outskirts of the city. The campaign opened February 1st. The rainy season had commenced, causing swollen streams, mud, and mire. The roads on the lowlands near the streams, and there were many of these streams to be crossed, had to be corduroyed before the artillery and trains could be advanced. Many of the lowlands were flooded from knee-deep to waist-deep, through which the boys had to wade. The first brush with the enemy, for the Regiment, was in front of Robertsville, as skirmishers, driving the Johnnies through the town. On February 5th they encamped at Beaufort's Bridge.

The next objective point was Midway, on the railroad connecting Charleston and Augusta. General Sherman relates the following regarding the capture of the railroad, as told by General Howard:

"He (General Howard) was with the Seventeenth Corps, marching straight for Midway, and when about five miles distant he began to deploy the leading division so as to be ready for battle. Sitting on his horse by the road-side, while the deployment was being made, he saw a man coming down the road, riding as hard as he could, and as he approached he recognized him as one of his own 'foragers,' mounted on a white horse, with a rope bridle, and a blanket for a saddle. As he came near he called out, 'Hurry up General, we have got the railroad.' So while we, the generals, were proceeding deliberately to prepare for a serious battle, a parcel of our foragers, in search of plunder, had got ahead and actually captured the South Carolina Railroad, a line of vital importance to the Rebel Government."

The Regiment assisted in destroying some thirty miles of the railroad, to within about fifty miles of Augusta. The army had become very proficient in destroying railroads, following the general plan of piling and burning the ties, and heating the iron rails in the middle and then winding them around trees or telegraph poles.

The next objective point was Columbia, S. C., distant about seventy-five miles. The Regiment crossed the Saluda River and the Broad, west of Columbia, near Alston, not passing through Columbia. They crossed the Catawby River at Rocky Mount on February 23d. The march was then directed toward Cheraw, on the Great Pedee River. The Regiment, with the left wing of the army, crossed at Sneedsboro, some ten miles above Cheraw. The whole army was across the river, a large, deep, navigable stream, by March 6th, and the advance on Fayetteville ordered, which was reached on March 11th. March 12th was the Sabbath, and General Sherman states as follows what of great moment happened, not alone to the 143d, but to all in the army:

> "Shortly after noon we heard in the distance the shrill whistle of a steamboat, which came nearer and nearer, and soon a shout, long and continuous, was raised down by the river, which spread farther and farther, and we all felt that it meant a messenger from home. The effect was electric, and no one can realize the feeling unless, like us, he has been for months cut off from all communication with friends, and compelled to listen to the croakings and prognostications of open enemies. But in a very few minutes there came up through the town, to the arsenal on the plateau behind, a group of officers, among whom was a large, florid, seafaring man, named Ainsworth, bearing a small mail-bag from General Terry at Wilmington, having left at 2 p. m. the day before."

General Sherman had sent two scouts to work their way to the river and float down to Wilmington some days before, and this was the result. No news, except from rebel sources, had reached the army after leaving Savannah.

By the 15th of March the whole army was across the Cape Fear River, and at once began its march for Goldsboro, N. C. Near Averysboro, Hardee was found in force and the Regiment had its full share in sweeping the enemy out of the way and capturing nearly a whole brigade and a battery of three guns. The battle lasted all day, from early morning, the enemy making a stubborn resistance.

From Averysboro the march was more easterly toward Goldsboro. Johnston had collected some forty thousand in an army to oppose Sherman's progress, and much opposition was made as they moved on to Goldsboro. On March 19th the enemy was found in force intrenched near Bentonsville, N. C. The 143d formed line of battle and moved forward to a position from which a portion of the Fourteenth Corps had been driven. They were then drawn out and double-quicked to the left some half mile to guard against a flank attack, but soon returned on the double-quick to their former position. Soon after reaching the line of battle the Confederates came on in force, charging to within one hundred feet of our line. As our brigade was on the extreme left, their object was to break through and thus execute a flank movement on the rest of the corps. The boys had made good use of a rail fence, making it into breastworks behind which they could lie flat and have slight protection. Evidently the Johnnies did not like the reception the boys gave them, and retreated. They soon renewed the attack with results as before. After the second charge a movement of something tossed up in the air in the brush in front of Company A was noticed, and the Lieutenant cautioned the boys to be ready, as there was something going on in front. In a moment a hat was tossed up, and the Lieutenant called out: "Ho, Johnny, what do you want?" and back came the reply, "We want to come in." The Lieutenant shouted, "Come on," and some twenty came running in over our rails. A guard was detailed to escort them to headquarters, when two asked to be allowed to remain and be given the use of muskets. The request was granted. Presently on came the reorganized forces of the enemy for another attempt to break through our lines. The two recruits in gray fired as rapidly as any of us, and at each discharge would say, "—— you, take that; draft me will you." One or two more attempts were made to break through, when darkness closed the dreadful work for that day. Then our recruits in gray said: "We are ready to be sent to headquarters now."

Lieut.-Colonel Watkins was in command of the Regiment at this battle and performed a heroic act. During one of the charges the regiment to the right of the 143d broke and started to the rear across the open field. He saw the movement, ran in front of them, and shouted: "Halt! Who is in command?" Some one named their Lieut.-Colonel, and Watkins said: "I outrank him. About face and hold your line." He displayed a sword in one hand and a revolver in the other, and the regiment marched back into line and held it. In about two days the works in our front were deserted, and we marched to Goldsboro, going into camp on March 25th, 1865.

The Division Commander complimented the 143d for their staying qualities in this engagement.

General Sherman says of this campaign, of which the 143d took its full share:

"Thus was concluded one of the longest and most important marches ever made by an organized army in a civilized country. The distance from Savannah to Goldsboro is four hundred twenty-five miles, and the route traversed embraced five large navigable river, viz: the Edisto, Broad, Catawba, Pedee and Cape Fear, at either of which a comparatively small force, well handled, should have made the passage most difficult, if not impossible. The country generally was in a state of nature, with innumerable swamps, with simply mud roads, nearly every mile of which had to be corduroyed. In our route we had captured Columbia, Cheraw, and Fayetteville, important cities and depots of supplies; had compelled the evacuation of Charleston City and Harbor; had utterly broken up all the railroads of South Carolina, and had consumed a vast amount of food and forage essential to the enemy for the support of his own armies. We had in mid-winter accomplished the whole journey of four hundred twenty-five miles in fifty days averaging ten miles per day, and had reached Goldsboro with the army in superb order, and the trains almost as fresh as when we started from Atlanta."

We were dirty, ragged, and saucy, and needed to rest and fix up a little. All were in high spirits, not only because of what had been accomplished, but because of what was anticipated, as we would soon be "On to Richmond," and eventually to Washington.

WILLIAM M. RATCLIFF,
Adjutant.

CHAPTER XI.

Still "On to Richmond"—News of Lee's Surrender to Grant—Capture of Raleigh, N. C.—Johnston Surrenders to Sherman—March Through Richmond to Washington—The Grand Review—The Regiment Mustered Out—Sherman's Farewell to His Army.

The supplying of the army with needed clothing, supplies, ammunition, etc., took some twenty days, which gave the boys a much needed rest at Goldsboro; but they were facing homeward and were anxious and ready to press onward for what they hoped would be the last great struggle. During this interval the army was somewhat reorganized. The Twentieth Corps became a part of the "Army of Georgia," with General Joseph A. Mower in command of the Corps, and "Pop" Williams in command of the First Division again. The 143d Regiment was still in the Third Brigade.

On April 9th, haversacks were filled with ten days rations of coffee and sugar, five days rations of salt, and hardtack and pork for three days, with fifteen days rations in wagons, preparatory for another campaign, whither they knew not, but believed it to be "On to Richmond."

Early on the morning of April 10th, the Regiment, with the army, faced toward Raleigh, leaving Goldsboro in the rear. April 11th, p. m., they encamped in an open plain, where the camp-fires and movements of bodies of men could be seen for a long distance.

Early on the morning of April 12th, while preparing to move on, a commotion was seen at the corps headquarters. Presently an aid was seen to ride from regiment to regiment, delivering some message which was followed by prolonged cheering and the wildest scenes. Each regiment, as the messenger was seen approaching, rushed to headquarters to catch the news. Colonel Boughton was surrounded, the message delivered, and he announced, "General Lee has surrendered to Grant." How they shouted; not only shouted, but hugged each other and wept for joy. Presently they were off. No laggards that day. Hurrah, for Johnston. They reached the vicinity of Raleigh on the 13th. For the next few days many rumors were afloat regarding Johnston's surrender, but as the Regiment had nothing to do regarding the surrender, we omit comments thereon. The surrender was accomplished and that was enough for the boys.

On April 29th an order was read on dress parade that the Fourteenth, Fifteenth, Seventeenth and Twentieth Army Corps should proceed to Washington and be mustered out of the service.

Soon thereafter, with happy hearts and elastic step, the homeward march was begun. Richmond, distant 170 miles, was reached in nine days, crossing the James River and through the city on May 11th. The line of march was past Libby Prison and Castle Thunder, which were viewed by the boys with a far different interest to that of many who had viewed them in days gone by. The Regiment encamped some five miles out of the city. While in camp here a violent thunder storm was experiencd. The march was soon resumed toward Washington, passing over some of the noted battle-fields, as Spottsylvania Court House, Chancellorsville, and Bull Run. On May 19th the army encamped near Alexandria, Va., having marched some 1,200 miles or more since leaving Chattanooga. While encamped here preparations were being made for the final review, which was to take place in the streets of Washington.

May 23d was taken up with the Army of the Potomac passing in review. During that night and the following morning, Sherman's army crossed the Long Bridge and formed near the Capitol, and, at the signal, moved out along Pennsylvania Avenue toward the White House, in front of which was the reviewing stand. This rough and ready western army of Sherman's, with slouched hats, their easy swinging stride gained by their long marches, their pack mules or horses following every regiment, surmounted with the captured trained roosters, ready to crow as occasion offered, made a marked contrast to the appearance of those in review the day before, and elicited great applause.

"Who were these men being reviewed for the last time? They were the men who had escaped death by shot and shell! They were the men who had not succumbed to sickness; they were the men who had defied fatigue and hardships. They were the survivors of war's siftings." What an army that was, and the boys of Sullivan County were a part of that army.

Charles E. Benton, in his book entitled, "As Seen From the Ranks," refers to the review as follows:

"Column after column passed the reviewing stand, not with the quick and mincing steps of militia, but with that far-reaching, swinging stride which had carried its men around and through and over the Confederacy from the Mississippi to the Atlantic, and northward to Washington again.

"As the artillery rolled along Pennsylvania Avenue, its rumbling seemed the long-drawn echoes .of the innumerable conflicts of the years gone by. The cavalry, with horses' manes clipped to the crest, rode stirrup to stirrup with an alignment as perfect as that of infantry, and many a nicked and stained sabre was carried proudly to shoulder that day.

"Then followed the ambulances with the old bloodstained stretchers hanging on their sides, and the rumbling of their wheels seemed like a vast ghostly procession of the shrieks and groans of that great host of suffering ones, representatives of the nation's blood sacrifice, who had ridden in them, many of them to their last resting places."

General Sherman, in his "Memoirs," in reviewing his army while on the grand stand with the President and General Grant, says:

"It was, in my judgment, the most magnificent army in existence—sixty-five thousand men, in splendid physique, who had just completed a march of nearly two thousand miles in a hostile country, in good drill, and who realized that they were being closely scrutinized by thousands of their fellow-countrymen and by foreigners. Division after division passed, each commander of an army corps or division coming to the stand during the passage of his command. The steadiness and firmness of the tread, the careful dress on the guides, the uniform intervals between the companies, all eyes directly to the front, and the tattered and bullet-riven flags, festooned with flowers, all attracted universal notice. For six hours and a half that strong tread of the Army of the West resounded along Pennsylvania Avenue; not a soul of that vast crowd of spectators left his place; and, when the rear of the column had passed by, thousands still lingered to express their sense of confidence in the strength of a Government which could claim such an army."

After the review, the Regiment went into camp at Crystal Springs, north of Washington, while awaiting the completion of the muster-out rolls. The Twentieth Corps was disbanded and the Regiment was placed in a brigade of the Twenty-second Corps.

The Regiment was mustered out of the service in this camp near Washington on July 20th, 1865.

SHERMAN'S FAREWELL TO HIS ARMY.

"Headquarters Military Division of the Mississippi,
"In the Field, Washington, D. C., May 30, 1865.

"Special Field Orders No. 76.

"The General Commanding announces to the Armies of the Tennessee and Georgia that the time has come for us to part. Our work is done, and armed enemies no longer defy us. Some of you will go to your homes, and others will be retained in military service till further orders.

"And now that we are all about to separate, to mingle with the civil world, it becomes a pleasing duty to recall to mind the situation of national affairs when, but little more than a year ago, we were gathered about the cliffs of Lookout Mountain, and all the future was wrapped in doubt and uncertainty. Three armies had come together from distant fields, with separate histories, yet bound by one common cause—the union of our country, and the perpetuation of the Government of our inheritance. There is no need to recall to your memories Tunnel Hill, with Rocky-Face Mountain and Buzzard Roost Gap, and the ugly forts of Dalton behind.

"We were in earnest, and paused not for danger and difficulty, but dashed through Snake-Creek Gap and fell on Resaca; then on to Etowah, to Dallas, Kenesaw; and the heat of summer found us on the banks of the Chattahoochee, far from home, and dependent on a single road for supplies. Again we were not to be held back by any obstacle, and crossed over and fought four hard battles for the possession of the citadel of Atlanta. That was the crisis of our history. A doubt still clouded our future, but we solved the problem, destroyed Atlanta, struck boldly across the State of Georgia, severed all the main arteries of life to our enemy, and Christmas found us at Savannah.

"Waiting there only long enough to fill our wagons, we again began a march which, for peril, labor and results, will compare with any ever made by an organized army. The floods of the Savannah, the swamps of the Combahee and Edisto, the 'high hills' and rocks of the Santee, the flat quagmires of the Pedee and Cape Fear Rivers, were all passed in mid-winter, with its floods and rains, in the face of an accumulating enemy; and after the battles of Averysboro and Bentonsville we once more came out of the wilderness to meet our friends at Goldsboro. Even then we paused only long enough to get new clothing, to reload our wagons, and again pushed on to Raleigh and beyond, until we met our enemy suing for peace instead of war, and offering to submit to the injured laws of his and our country. As long as that enemy was defiant, nor mountains, nor rivers, nor swamps, nor hunger, nor cold, had checked us; but when he who had fought us hard and persistently offered submission, your general thought it wrong to pursue him farther, and negotiations followed which resulted, as you all know, in his surrender.

"How far the operations of this army contributed to the final overthrow of the Confederacy and the peace which now dawns upon us, must be judged by others, not by us; but that you have done all that men could do has been admitted by those in authority, and we have a right to join in the universal joy that fills our land because the war is over, and our Government stands vindicated before the world by the joint action of the volunteer armies and navy of the United States. * * *

"Your General now bids you farewell, with the full belief that, as in war you have been good soldiers, so in peace you will make good citizens; and if, unfortunately, new war should arise in our country 'Sherman's Army' will be the first to buckle on the old armor and come forth to defend and maintain the Government of our inheritance.

"By order of
"MAJOR-GENERAL W. T. SHERMAN.
"L. M. DAYTON,
"Assistant Adjutant General."

As soon as transportation could be secured, the Regiment boarded the cars, and looking back saw the great dome of the Capitol diminish and disappear in the distance. The theatre of war and desolation was left behind, and the Regiment was speeding forward to the cherished scenes of home, of which they had so long been deprived. They landed at the Battery, New York City; marched up Broadway to the Astor House, halted, faced toward the building, when their late General, "Fighting Joe Hooker," appeared on the steps and was saluted. He told them that he was not given to speech making, but that he could not let the Regiment disband without saying a word to them. After thanking them for the many times they had stood to their places, he said: "It could be said of them what could not be said of many regiments, he did not know as of any others—the Johnnies had never seen their backs; that if they had at Peech Tree Creek, God only knows what the result would have been."

The Regiment was then quartered in barracks at Hart's Island to await the coming of the paymaster, after which to be disbanded. An effort was made by the officers to hold the men after payment and return in a body to Sullivan; but as some were from Tompkins County, and all anxious to reach home as speedily as possible, the attempt failed, and the boys separated in groups as they were paid off. Thus ended the career of the 143d Regiment, New York Volunteer Infantry, as such.

CHAPTER XII.

Special Details—Company K Guarding the Woodchoppers.

In early January, 1863, while the 143d Regiment was encamped on Upton Hill, Va., Company K was detailed, under command of Lieut. L. N. Stanton, to guard a gang of wood choppers, and army teams, near Arlington Mills, Va. These men were chopping wood to supply the army camps. The timber was near the railroad. About seventy-five army teams were employed in hauling the wood to the railroad track. Four horses or six mules constituted a team.

The duty of Company K was to assist in loading wood in wagons in the woods and unload beside the railroad track; also to load on flat cars, to be taken to Alexandria, Va. At night wagons and teams were parked, and picket guard maintained. The company was quartered in the woods in shelter tents.

The company was divided in two parts. One half would load wood one day and do picket duty the next. About March 1, 1863, the wood at Arlington Mills was exhausted, and this entire working force was moved on up six miles, to Vienna, Va., where it continued the work until April 17, when the company was ordered to report to Alexandria and join the Regiment, where it was placed on transports, for Suffolk, Va. This ride of twelve miles from Vienna to Alexandria was made standing on open flat cars, in heavy rain.

During this entire period of detail, Company B, 144th Regiment, N. Y., Capt. William Plaskett, commanding, was working under this same order of detail with Company K, 143d N. Y. The two companies encamped near each other. While at Vienna, Company B, 144th, occupied the town. Company K, 143d, about a mile south on the Williams' plantation. The place had been abandoned by Williams, and Company K occupied the dwelling buildings for quarters, each mess occupying a separate room. They warmed and cooked with little sheet-iron stoves, pipes through the windows.

During the stay at Vienna, Moseby's Guerrillas kept lurking around, and keeping the men uneasy generally. Their main desire seemed to be the capture of mules and horses from this working force. In this they signally failed. On one occasion they ventured a real attack. The skirmish was spirited for awhile, but the repulse was prompt, and with slight injury to our men and camp. The attack was made during a heavy snow storm, and the men suffered in this respect.

All told, this detailed service of three months was not particularly hard. Company K, at the Williams house, passed the long winter evenings in song, and games, and dance, and in recounting recollections of home days. A few families of Williams' slaves remained in their little homes, but were having a hard time in keeping up a living. These black children were very amusing in dance. They often came in the rooms with the soldiers and entertained them with jig dancing. The bread ration there was a loaf per day for each man. This was more than most men ate. Surplus bread was given to little darkies in return for dancing. A specially amusing incident was when seven loaves of bread were offered to one little fellow if he would carry all the bread home to his mother at one trip, and not drop a loaf. He labored long and earnestly to get all the bread in his arms, but before the last loaf could be secured other loaves would drop away. Finally he was allowed to make two trips to take his bread.

DETAIL NO. 2.

During the Gettysburgh campaign, when most of the New York State Militia had been rushed to the defence of Washington, the bloody draft riots broke out in New York City. The draft was stopped, and a reign of terror prevailed for several days. The War Department ordered a detachment of three commissioned officers and six enlisted men from each New York Regiment to New York to assist in enforcing the draft and caring for the conscripts. The detail from the 143d Regiment consisted of:

Capt. Hezekiah Watkins, Lieut. Dwight Divine, Lieut. Willett T. Embler, Private Jonathan C. Loring, Co. B; Private William Criddle, Co. D; Corporal Jacob Sinsabaugh, Co. E; Corporal Paul P. Price, Co. G; Private Charles W. Travis, Co. H; Corporal Frank Jagger, Co. I.

The detachment left the Regiment while on the march, near Goose Creek, Va., taking cars for New York at Gainesville Station, July 24, 1863, reaching New York city, July 27, and were ordered to duty at the draft rendezvous on Riker's Island. This newly established Post was only a barren knob in the East River, without barracks, tents or organized commissary.

Several hundred officers and men, most of whom, like our own detachment, coming to this new camp direct from the field after a long and trying campaign, were without even blankets, shelter tents, or the ordinary scanty cooking utensils of the field, found it far from agreeable. All heartily wished themselves back with their regiments. By degrees the camp took on more orderly shape and became endurable.

The Post was later transferred to Hart's Island, where a model camp was established, and maintained until the close of the war, as a camp of instruction, and depot for recruits in transit to the army in the field, and also a large camp of rebel prisoners of war.

The machinery for enforcing the draft was rapidly put in order and a day was set for resuming the draft that the New York mobs had so summarily stopped. As the day approached anxiety increased, and civilians generally expected another carnival of blood and fire, but the War Department made such thorough preparation that failure was impossible. Every soldier in New York Harbor was under arms, ready to move at a moment's notice, with five days cooked rations and 100 rounds of cartridges. When dawn of the dreaded day arrived, New York City found that during the previous night some twenty thousand bronzed veterans of the army of the Potomac had quietly captured the city. Union Square and other parks in the center of the city were crowded with veteran troops fully prepared for serious work. The lawless mobs slunk to their hiding places and the draft proceeded without interruption. The local troops about the city had no occasion to move. The power of the government to raise troops by drafting was fully established for all time. Volunteers, conscripts and substitutes rapidly poured in and were hastened forward to the army in the field.

Guarding camp, drilling and conducting the new men to the army in the field kept the detachments busy. Of our detachment, Captain Watkins soon obtained leave to return to his Regiment. Lieutenant Divine's application to return to his Regiment was peremptorily refused by Post Commander General Jackson. Later an application to the War Department through Regimental Headquarters was granted and he returned to the Regiment, leaving balance of detachment at Hart's Island. Criddle was killed by a railroad accident. Loring and Price finally returned to the Regi-

ment. The other members never returned and were discharged
at close of the war.

THE PROVISIONAL COMPANY E,

Lieut. Dwight Divine, Commanding.

Early in October, 1864, General Hood tried to break Sherman's
cracker line and capture the depots of supplies between Chattanooga
and Atlanta. Chattanooga, at that time, was Sherman's base where
vast supplies were accumulated and its capture by Hood would have
spoiled all of Sherman's plans. The Post Commander, Col. Stanley,
at Chattanooga, feared that his post might be attacked before Sherman could reinforce, and a semi-panic condition prevailed. Orders
were issued for every officer and soldier within his command to report for duty. Lieutenant Dwight Divine, of the 143d Regiment,
arrived at Chattanooga on his way to the Regiment at this time, and
made immediate written application for order authorizing him to
form a Provisional Company of such recruits and veterans, belonging to the 143d, as could be found within the command. The order
was granted, and by midnight of October 14, he reported to the
ordnance officer with fifty-four recruits and four veterans. Before
daylight they had their arms and ammunition, and within a day
or two were attached to Col. Rhodes Provisional Battalion as
Company E. They were further armed with picks and shovels and
had pick and shovel drill in the morning on the fortifications, and
musket drill by way of dessert, both good and plenty, till Sherman's approach forced Hood off the railroad into Northern Alabama. Later they were sent out as railroad guards with headquarters at Adairsville, Ga., and finally march to Atlanta in time
to join in the "March to the Sea."

The Provisional Company E was then disbanded and the men
reported to the companies to which they were assigned.

MAJOR JOHN HIGGINS.

CHAPTER XIII.

How Comrade L——, of Company L, Milked the Cow—How Tommy Res-
cued the Wounded Man—Private William Berry, of Company D, Cap-
tures a Picket-Post of Corporal and Six Men—A Foot Race in Midst of
Battle—A Divy with Johnny Farmer—Another Pig Story—The Dispatch
that Closed the War.

The following amusing and interesting stories have been secured for the editor, but he does not vouch as to their historical
accuracy.

While the Regiment lay at Camp Chase, near Alexandria, a
farmer had a pasture field adjoining the camp, in which a milch
cow was grazing. Comrade L., of Company C, espied the cow,
liked her looks, and became interested in her to that extent that
he quietly scaled the fence, accompanied by a tin pail. Her fine
points attracted him more and more, and he approached nearer to
investigate. He liked the looks of her udder, and tried to manipu-
late it, but the cow positively objected, facing him with a look
which seemed to say no white trash can be so familiar. He pon-
dered, but presently he was observed to go to a bush, leave his pail
and return to his company street. Presently he returned, stepped
behind the bush, took off his soldier blouse and cap, and in a few
moments came out with face and hands black as coal. He took
his pail, approached the cow, and all was lovely now. While milking he realized that the Colonel was an observer, but continued
right on as if unobserved. When the milking was finished, he
donned his blouse and cap, returned by the way of some water,
washed, and proceeded directly to the Colonel's tent and said:
"Here is some milk for you, Colonel." At which the Colonel replied: "No, you earned it, but I would not advise you to do so
again."

The following was published in the New York Press of July
3, 1898:

REBS WOULDN'T KILL HIM.

To the Editor of the Press:

Sir:—Reading the account in your paper of the gallant deeds
of Lieut. Hobson and men of the Merrimac, brings fresh to my

memory a most brave and gallant deed I saw performed by a scout at the battle of Bentonville, in the Civil War. One of our men on the skirmish line was wounded severely in the head. The Johnnies drove our line back some distance and the soldier was left where he fell, we being unable to carry him off the field under such a galling fire of shot and shell. We were reinforced and checked the enemy's progress, but we were unable to drive them back to get possession of our man. He lay in the centre of the field, about thirty rods from our line. He was all the time trying to regain his feet, but could not.

About 4 p. m. a scout came riding at a swift gallop along our line, and as he passed us he called out: "Captain, why don't you advance your line and get possession of that wounded man?" The scout was gone about one hour, when he returned on foot. He crept along the line trying to have them make a bold dash and reach the man, but to no avail. The officer in charge was unwilling to make such a sacrifice, he said, for the purpose of regaining a man who could be of no use to us. The scout called for volunteers to go with him to recover our comrade, but none responded. "All right, boys," said the gallant fellow, "I will go alone." At this he left us, but soon returned on his horse, rode through a gap in the breastworks and dashed in the direction of the wounded soldier. We held our breath and reserved our fire. The enemy also ceased firing at the same time. He rode to the man, took off his hat, and sang out in a clear voice: "Soldiers of the Confederacy, I ask permission to remove this wounded soldier from the field!" They answered: "All right, Yank! Brave Yank! Give us your name Yank! You are too brave a soldier for we-uns to shoot." They gave him cheer after cheer while he was placing the wounded soldier across his saddle. When he was ready to start an officer of some importance asked him his name and rank, and he answered, "Certainly, sir; it will give me great pleasure. My name is Thomas D. Collins, my rank is sergeant, and I am one of General Sherman's scouts." "All right, sir," was the response, "now you may go. You are a brave man and an honor to your country." "Thank you for the compliment, sir," replied our hero, and he was off.

When he reached us we were scrambling over each other to shake his hand. Our boys cheered him and the "Rebs" cheered him. Presently they called out, "Collins, get out of the way; we are going to shoot and we don't want to shoot you, if we can help it." At this Collins leaped into his saddle and was soon lost to view in the timber.

Collins was from New York State and belonged to either the 43d or 143d Regiment, I have forgotten which.

Lincoln, Neb., June 27. D. E. GARDNER.

[Comrade Thomas D. Collins, of Company H, was the man; and say he knew nothing of the above publication till it was shown him in the papers, and says it happened in front of the skirmish line 3d Wisconsin, of the 2d Brigade, 1st Division, 20th Corps.— EDITOR.]

After the battle of Averysboro, N. C., March 16, 1865, was over, and the Regiment had stacked arms and broken ranks, Private William Berry, of Company D, took his gun from the stack and went out in front, passing through our skirmish line, to view the country and see what he could find. He ran upon a Confederate picket post of a corporal and six men that were cut off from their comrades and could not get away without coming out in sight of our line. Berry promptly ordered them to surrender, which they did, made them march around him at a safe distance, and drove them into our lines. On being questioned as to why they, seven men, surrendered to one man, the Confederate corporal said the Yank told them that if one of them advanced he would shoot. That they replied you can shoot only one of us; and his reply was, if I shoot, the boys will come with a rush, and if you shoot me they will kill every one of you. That after the parley they gave in.

During the fighting at Culp's Farm, Ga., June 21, 1864, the skirmish line of the 143d was forced back for lack of ammunition. They were given a new supply by the men in the Regiment and advanced, retaking the ground lost. The Confederate skirmishers fell back in turn as ours advanced, except one man, who was screened. He waited until our line was close to him, then took deliberate aim at Private ———— of Company I, fired, and missed. He dropped his gun and ran for his comrades. The Company I man had a fine chance to retaliate in kind with a loaded gun and plain mark, but instead of shooting his fleeing foe, he dropped his own gun and gave chase. The excitement of the race stopped all firing, one side shouting, "Go it Yank!" and the other, "Go it Johnny!" The Company I man won out and brought in his would-be slayer a prisoner of war.

About February 1, 1863, just before leaving camp DeWitt, having been in the enemy's country some four months without any very active duty, except picket duty, some of the boys became impressed with a great desire to forage on the enemy for a change of diet, although they had plenty to eat, such as their great Uncle Sam furnished. Accordingly, one bright night, about ten selected men quietly met and were off on a foraging expedition on their own orders, at about 10 o'clock. About three miles out, westerly, they approached a snug looking farm house, and in a pen near by found two hogs of about 200 pounds each. "Here we are, fresh pork, hurrah for a pig." On consultation, it was resolved to take one, and that they were quite liberal to divide equally with farmer Johnny. On attempting to get one out, the hogs (as is usual), set up an unearthly squealing, and several faces appeared at the windows of the house, but no objection was made. A hog was soon liberated and with one of the boys clinging to its tail tried to escape by encircling the house. The other boys, stationed at the corners, would fire their revolvers at the pig as it passed. Any one in the house, judging from the racket outside, would have thought a third Bull Run was being fought. They finally succeeded in killing the porker. As they had no means of scalding it, they tried to skin it, but found that the skin would not peel off, and when they had separated the skin and carcass, they could not tell for the life of them which had the most pork on. However, they quartered what was left and after securing a few heads of cabbage from a nearby cellar, returned to camp.

Early the next morning Johnny farmer is off on an expedition, and calls on Colonel Gurney, commanding the Brigade. Presently orders are issued for details of a corporal and file of men to be made to search each company for fresh pork. In Company A the corporal and one of the men in the foraging party were on the detail. Strange as it may seem, no fresh pork could be found. The 143d's reputation for soldierly bearing and honesty was not injured.

ANOTHER PIG STORY.

While the 143d Regiment was at Upton Hill, Va., in December, 1862, the boys discovered that a farmer near the camp had a fine hog, and for safety had made a pen for it right under his bed-room window, feeling that thus it was secure. One morning, after it had snowed, as he looked out of his window, he saw the pen, but no pig. The pen was all bloody instead. He tracked the foragers through the snow to the camp of the 127th N. Y. V., which lay just across the road from the 143d. The farmer felt sure that he was on the track of his man and went to the Colonel of the 127th, who was in command of the brigade at the time, with his complaint. The Colonel would not believe that the men of his regiment had stolen the hog, and went out to see the tracks for himself. When he saw them, he said: "There are only two men in the Brigade who can make those big tracks; one is Col. Curtis, of the 142d N. Y. V., and he is not stealing hogs, and the other is that big man in the 143d N. Y. V." An officer and detail of men were sent through the 144th and 143d to discover fresh pork, and though the odor of fresh meat cooking was strong, not a bit of the farmer's hog was found.

THE DISPATCH THAT CLOSED THE WAR.

Sherman's and Johnston's armies were facing each other near Raleigh, N. C., ready for immediate action, while negotiations were progressing for the surrender of Johnston's army. The terms agreed upon were rejected at Washington and orders issued to renew hostilities at once, unless Johnston accepted the terms required. An advance was to be made in the morning, and news was received at Sherman's headquarters in Raleigh that the terms were accepted by Johnston, only about one hour before the 20th Corps would advance for combat. A scout must cover the sixteen miles and deliver a message to stop the movement. One scout, Sergeant Thomas D. Collins, was from the 143d and he was selected to carry the dispatch, stating that Johnston had surrendered, and to march back to the vicinity of Raleigh. He was told in starting to reach the 20th Corps headquarters, if possible, before hostilities began. He covered the 16 miles in one hour and twenty minutes actual time, as he was timed. This dispatch, which a member of the Regiment had the honor to carry, brought great joy, not only to the boys of the 143d, but to every member of the army. Bugles were sounding and the regiments forming line as Tommy rode up to General Joseph A. Mower's headquarters. The Adjt. General tore open the dispatch, read it, called to the Corps bugler to sound the recall, which was done. When it was known why the recall was made the greatest rejoicing imaginable was experienced. By the cheering and hand shaking, an outsider would have thought friends and relatives were meeting after long separation.

LIEUTENANT S.'S CRACKERS.

On that march to "Bloody Annandale," Lieut. S. provided for emergencies by shouldering a large double-decker haversack, well filled with fresh crackers. His Orderly Sergeant had just returned from the hospital, and to secure his company, the boys proposed to carry his gun, accoutrements, etc., that he should not over-do himself.

When part way out the Lieutenant discovered the Sergeant marching light, and as his crackers were pulling rather heavily on his shoulder, he said: "Here, Sergt., take this," handing him the haversack of crackers. The big hearted boys behind the Sergeant thought it too bad for the convalescent Sergeant to carry such a load of nice fresh crackers, and devised how they might relieve him again. Presently the buckle of the haversack loosened, the haversack opened, and with the kindest intentions, the boys distributed the crackers, many sharing in the burden.

When the Lieutenant came for his haversack he was very much surprised to find it empty, and said some things we don't care to repeat. The boys were so willing to bear the extra burden, that none of the crackers were returned.

THE WAR FLAG AND A REMNANT OF THE 143D AT RE-UNION AT ELLENVILLE, N. Y., 1908.

1—Wm. F. Benedict.
2—Edward Cantrell.
3—Jas. H. Hodge.
4—David H. Keeler.
5—Moses Schoonmaker.
6—Wm. A. Briggs

7—Thomas Bates.
8—Frederick W. Burns.
9—John Vantran.
10—Abram Hunt.
11—Lewis S. Wheeler.
12—Moses Young

13—Aaron Dudley.
15—Thomas Corgill.
16—Joseph Cammer.
17—Elias G. DePew.
18—Samuel Lord.

19—Andrew S. Wilson.
20—Hiram Hector.
21—Wm. McMillen.
25—Isaac Jelliff.
26—James C. Leslie.
28—Wm. W. Bennett

29—M. P. Bennett.
30—John Darbee.
34—Chas. W. Travis.
35—Nelson T. Reynolds.
36—Dwight Divine.
40—Elijah Schoonmaker

ROSTER

ONE HUNDRED FORTY-THIRD REGIMENT,

New York Volunteer Infantry.

COLONEL DAVID P. DE WITT.

(Original.)

REGIMENTAL OFFICERS.

COLONELS.

David P. Dewitt, to April 29, 1863; resigned.

Horace Boughton, to July 20, 1865; mustered out with Regt. (Bvt. Brig. Gen. U. S. V.)

LIEUTENANT COLONELS.

John C. Holley, from Aug. 14, 1862, to Oct. 14, 1862; not mustered.

Horace Boughton, to May 9, 1863; promoted.

Joseph B. Taft, to Nov. 25, 1863; killed in action. (Bvt. Col. N. Y. V.)

Hezekiah Watkins, to July 20, 1865; mustered out with Regt. (Bvt. Col. U. S. V.)

MAJORS.

Joseph B. Taft, to Nov. 9, 1863; promoted.

Hezekiah Watkins, to Jan. 8, 1864; promoted.

John Higgins, to May 16, 1865; resigned. (Bvt. Lieut. Col. N. Y. V.)

Edward H. Pinney, from May 16, 1865; not mustered.

ADJUTANTS.

Edgar K. Apgar, to Feb. 1, 1863; dismissed.

William M. Ratcliffe, to July 20, 1864; killed in action. (Bvt. Maj. N. Y. V.)

Rensselaer Hammond, to July 20, 1865; mustered out with Regt.

Wallace Hill; not mustered.

QUARTERMASTERS.

Wallace W. Wheeler, to Mar. 26, 1864; dismissed.

Edwin C. Howard, to Aug. 10, 1865; mustered out at St. Louis, Mo.

SURGEONS.

Henry M. Edsall, to Feb. 28, 1863; resigned.
Orran A. Carroll, to Oct. 8, 1863; resigned. (Bvt. Lieut. Col. N. Y. V.)
David Mathews, to July 20, 1865; mustered out with Regt.

ASSISTANT SURGEONS.

David Mathews, to Feb. 4, 1864; promoted.
William H. Stewart, to July 20, 1865; mustered out with Regt.
Herman Craft, to April 11, 1864; resigned.

CHAPLAINS.

Jeremiah Searle, to Mar. 2, 1863; resigned.
Erastus Seymour; not mustered.
Isaac R. Gebbard, to Aug. 29, 1863; resigned.

MUSICIANS—DRUM AND FIFE CORPS.

August Rambour, principal musician, Co. A.
Chas. J. McPherson, Co. A.
Benjamin F. Allyn, Co. B.
James Low, Co. C.
Moses B. Cole, Co. E.
David W. Maston, Co. E.
Alfred Wormuth, Co. F.
Charles S. McWilliams, Co. G.
William H. French, Co. H.
Enos C. McKellips, Co. H.
Charles Terwilliger, Co. I.
William H. Hill, Co. K.

REGIMENTAL STAFF.

RECORD OF FIELD AND STAFF OFFICERS—ORIGINAL.

DEWITT, DAVID P.—Age, 45 years. Enrolled at Washington, D. C., to serve three years, and mustered in as colonel, October 8, 1862; discharged for disability, April 29, 1863. Commissioned colonel, September 25, 1862, with rank from same date, original.

HOLLY, JOHN C.—Appointed colonel, August 14, 1862; subsequently lieutenant-colonel, but declined, October 14, 1862. Not commissioned colonel; commissioned, not mustered, lieutenant-colonel, October 11, 1862, with rank from same date, original.

KIRKE, H. M.—Borne on muster-in roll of field and staff as lieutenant-colonel, with remark, "No authority to muster"; no further record. Not commissioned.

BOUGHTON, HORACE.—Captain, Thirteenth Infantry; mustered in as lieutenant-colonel, this regiment, October 20, 1862; as colonel, April 30, 1863; mustered out with regiment, July 20, 1865, at Washington, D. C. Commissioned lieutenant-colonel, October 20, 1862, with rank from same date, vice J. C. Holly, not mustered; colonel, May 9, 1863, with rank from April 29, 1863, vice D. P. Dewitt, resigned.

TAFT, JOSEPH B.—Age, 23 years. Enrolled, October 11, 1862, at New York City, to serve three years; mustered in as major, October 14, 1862; as lieutenant-colonel, November 18, 1863; killed in action, November 25, 1863, at Mission Ridge, Tenn. Commissioned major, October 11, 1862, with rank from same date, original; lieutenant-colonel, November 9, 1863, with rank from April 29, 1863, vice H. Boughton, promoted.

APGAR, EDGAR K.—Age, 19 years. Enrolled, September 2, 1862, at Monticello, to serve three years; mustered in as first lieutenant, Co. D, October 8, 1862; appointed adjutant, same date; dismissed, February 10, 1863. Not commissioned first lieutenant; commissioned adjutant, November 21, 1862, with rank from October 8, 1862, original; first lieutenant, not mustered, June 11, 1863, with rank from February 10, 1863, vice E. K. Apgar, dismissed.

EDSALL, HENRY M.—Age, 30 years. Enrolled at Albany, to serve three years, and mustered in as surgeon, August 23, 1862; discharged, February 28, 1863. Commissioned surgeon, November 21, 1862, with rank from August 22, 1862, original.

CARROLL, ORRIN A.—Assistant surgeon, Fifty-sixth Infantry; mustered in as surgeon, this regiment, May 10, 1863; discharged for disability, October 8, 1863. Commissioned surgeon, April 16, 1863, with rank from March 14, 1863, vice H. M. Edsall, resigned.

MATHEWS, DAVID.—Age, 32 years. Enrolled at Monticello, to serve three years, and mustered in as assistant surgeon, September 24, 1862; as surgeon, October 8, 1863; mustered out with regiment, July 20, 1865, at Washington, D. C. Commissioned assistant surgeon, November 21, 1862, with rank from September 24, 1862, original; surgeon, February 6, 1864, with rank from October 8, 1863, vice O. A. Carroll, resigned.

CRAFT, HERMAN.—Age, 27 years. Enrolled at New York city, to serve three years, and mustered in as assistant surgeon, October 6, 1862; discharged for disability, April 11, 1864. Commissioned assistant surgeon Nov. 21, 1862, with rank from October 6, 1862, original.

STEWART, WILLIAM H.—Age, 24 years. Enrolled, April 27, 1864, at Kingston, to serve three years; mustered in as assistant surgeon, June 1, 1864; mustered out with regiment, July 20, 1865, at Washington,. D. C., as Stuart; prior service as assistant surgeon, Twenty-seventh Infantry. Commissioned assistant surgeon, May 10, 1864, with rank from April 27, 1864, vice D. Matthews, promoted.

MOWRIS, J. A.—Assistant surgeon; reported absent on muster-in roll of field and staff; no further record. Not commissioned.

WHEELER, WALLACE W.—Age, 28 years. Enrolled, August 20, 1862, at Monticello, to serve three years; mustered in as first lieutenant and quartermaster, August 21, 1862; dismissed, April 20, 1864. Commissioned first lieutenant and quartermaster, November 21, 1862, with rank from August 21, 1862, original.

SEARLE, JEREMIAH.—Age, 26 years. Enrolled at Washington, D. C., to serve three years, and mustered in as chaplain, December 12, 1862; discharged, March 2, 1863. Commissioned chaplain, December 12, 1862, with rank from same date, original.

GEBBARD, ISAAC.—Age, 29 years. Enrolled at Suffolk, Va., to serve three years, and mustered in as chaplain, May 1, 1863; discharged for disability, August 29, 1863. Not commissioned chaplain.

SEYMOUR, ERASTUS.—Commissioned, not mustered, chaplain, February 9, 1864, with rank from January 12, 1864, vice I. Gebbard, resigned.

COMPANY A

Captains.

Hezekiah Watkins, original, promoted to Major.
William T. George, from Nov. 25, 1863, to muster out of Regt.

First Lieutenants.

William M. Ratcliff, original, promoted to Adjutant.
George Young, from Mar. 5, 1863; wounded in action.
Joseph Pierce, from Nov. 11, 1864, to muster out of Regt.

Second Lieutenants.

George Young, original, promoted to First Lieutenant.
DeWitt C. Apgar, from April 17, 1863; promoted to First Lieutenant, Co. D.
George C. Pinney, from May 1, 1864; promoted to First Lieutenant, Co. H.
David A. Wasim, from May 6, 1865, to muster out of Regt.
Samuel Lord, from July 24, 1865; not mustered.

Record of Members of Company A—Original.

Abberly, Thomas.—Age, 26 years. Enlisted, August 13, 1862, at Monticello, to serve three years; mustered in as private, Co. A, October 8, 1862; died January 13, 1863, in camp, at Upton's Hill, Va.

Akins, Amos P.—Age, 19 years. Enlisted, August 12, 1862, at Rockland, to serve three years; mustered in as private, Co. A, October 8, 1862; promoted corporal, prior to April, 1863; sergeant, no date; killed in action, July 20, 1864, at Peach Tree Ridge, Ga.

Akins, George H.—Age, 29 years. Enlisted, August 12, 1862, at Rockland, to serve three years; mustered in as private, Co. A, October 8, 1862; promoted corporal, September 1, 1863; mustered out with company, July 20, 1865, at Washington, D. C.

ALLAN, ARCHIBALD C.—Age, 18 years. Enlisted, August 9, 1862, at Monticello, to serve three years; mustered in as private, Co. A, October 8, 1862; mustered out with company, July 20, 1865, at Washington, D. C.

ALLAN, JOHN M.—Age, 21 years. Enlisted, August 11, 1862, at Monticello, to serve three years; mustered in as sergeant, Co. A, October 8, 1862; returned to ranks, prior to October, 1864; discharged, May 19, 1865, at hospital No. 15, Nashville, Tenn.

ALLAN, WILLIAM C.—Age, 22 years. Enlisted at Goshen, to serve one year, and mustered in as private, Co. A, September 8, 1864; mustered out with detachment, January 10, 1865, near Washington, D. C.

ALLEN, SEYMOUR R.—Age, 27 years. Enlisted, August 11, 1862, at Monticello, to serve three years; mustered in as private, Co. A, October 8, 1862; promoted corporal, prior to April, 1863; returned to ranks, no date; mustered out, August 19, 1865, at Elmira, N. Y.

ASHTON, WILLIAM H.—Age, 22 years. Enlisted, August 13, 1862, at Fremont, to serve three years; mustered in as private, Co. A, October 8, 1862; promoted corporal, no date; mustered out with company, July 20, 1865, at Washington, D. C.

BAILEY, CHARLES A.—Age, 29 years. Enlisted, August 12, 1862, at Forestburg, to serve three years; mustered in as private, Co. A, October 8, 1862; mustered out with company, July 20, 1865, at Washington, D. C.

BAKER, DAVID B.—Age, 19 years. Enlisted at Callicoon, to serve three years, and mustered in as private, Co. A, February 16, 1864; mustered out with company, July 20, 1865, at Washington, D. C.

BATES, THOMAS.—Age, 19 years. Enlisted, August 9, 1862, at Monticello, to serve three years; mustered in as private, Co. A, October 8, 1862; wounded in action, July 20, 1864, at Peach Tree Creek, Ga.; promoted corporal, May 18, 1865; mustered out with company, July 20, 1865, at Washington, D. C.

BEEBE, JOSEPH J.—Age, 18 years. Enlisted, August 12, 1862, at Liberty, to serve three years; mustered in as private, Co. A, October 8, 1862; wounded in action, July 20, 1864, at Peach Tree

Creek, Ga.; died of his wounds, October 5, 1864, at Hospital No. 1, Chattanooga, Tenn.

BEEBE, ROSWELL T.—Age, 24 years. Enlisted, August 13, 1862, at Monticello, to serve three years; mustered in as corporal, Co. A, October 8, 1862; transferred to Co. B, Eighteenth Regiment, Veteran Reserve Corps, March 8, 1865; mustered out with detachment, July 19, 1865, at Washington, D. C.

BENNETT, WILLIAM W.—Age, 28 years. Enlisted, August 13, 1862, at Rockland, to serve three years; mustered in as private, Co. A, October 8, 1862; transferred to Co. C, Eighteenth Regiment, Veteran Reserve Corps, September 3, 1863; mustered out with detachment, July 19, 1865, at Washington, D. C.

BLACK, JOHN.—Age, 42 years. Enlisted at New York city to serve one year, and mustered in as private, Co. A, October 7, 1864; captured, February 21, 1865; paroled, April 21, 1865; promoted sergeant, no date; discharged, July 1, 1865, at New York City.

BROWN, ALBERT.—Age, 38 years. Enlisted at Sanford, to serve one year, and mustered in as private, Co. A, February 15, 1865; mustered out with company, July 20, 1865, at Washington, D. C.

BROWN, JAMES L.—Age, 22 years. Enlisted, August 11, 1862, at Bethel, to serve three years; mustered in as private, Co. A, October 8, 1862; mustered out with company, July 20, 1865, at Washington, D. C.

BUCKLEY, PHILO.—Age, 21 years. Enlisted, August 12, 1862, at Bethel, to serve three years; mustered in as corporal, Co. A, October 8, 1862; promoted sergeant, April 17, 1863; wounded in action, July 20, 1864, at Peach Tree Creek, Ga.; promoted first sergeant, September 1, 1864; mustered out, May 19, 1865, as sergeant, at Louisville, Ky.

BURNS, FREDERICK W.—Age, 23 years. Enlisted, August 9, 1862, at Monticello, to serve three years; mustered in as sergeant, Co. A, October 8, 1862; wounded in action, July 20, 1864, at Peach Tree Creek, Ga.; discharged, May 22, 1865, at hospital, Chattanooga, Tenn.

CAMMER, JOSEPH.—Age, 23 years. Enlisted, August 14, 1862, at Rockland, to serve three years; mustered in as private, Co. A,

October 8, 1862; mustered out with company, July 20, 1865, at Washington, D. C.

CANTRELL, EDWARD R.—Age, 22 years. Enlisted, August 9, 1862, at Monticello, to serve three years; mustered in as private, Co. A, October 8, 1862; wounded in action, July 20, 1864, at Peach Tree Creek, Ga.; discharged for disability, June 26, 1865.

CANTRELL, JOHN.—Age, 21 years. Enlisted, August 12, 1862, at Monticello, to serve three years; mustered in as private, Co. A, October 8, 1862; mustered out with company, July 20, 1865, at Washington, D. C.

CANTRELL, THOMAS.—Age, 20 years. Enlisted, August 9, 1862, at Monticello, to serve three years; mustered in as private, Co. A, October 8, 1862; mustered out with company, July 20, 1865, at Washington, D. C.

CARPENTER, JOHN W.—Age, 25 years. Enlisted, August 6, 1862, at Monticello, to serve three years; mustered in as private, Co. A, October 8, 1862; died, July 17, 1863, at hospital, Portsmouth, Va.

CASTERLINE, EDWARD.—Age, 26 years. Enlisted, August 11, 1862, at Bethel, to serve three years; mustered in as private, Co. A, October 8, 1862; mustered out with company, July 20, 1865, at Washington, D. C.

COLEMAN, HENRY R.—Age, 22 years. Enlisted, August 9, 1862, at Monticello, to serve three years; mustered in as private, Co. A, October 8, 1862; absent, in hospital, at Murfreesboro, Tenn.; since June 15, 1864, and at muster-out of company.

CONNER, THOMAS O.—Age, 36 years. Enlisted, August 21, 1862, at Liberty, to serve three years; mustered in as private, Co. A, October 8, 1862; mustered out with company, July 20, 1865, at Washington, D. C.

CORBY, OREN T.—Age, 32 years. Enlisted, August 11, 1862, at Bethel, to serve three years; mustered in as private, Co. A, October 8, 1862; mustered out with company, July 20, 1865, at Washington, D. C.; also borne as Owen T.

CORGILL, THOMAS.—Age, 31 years. Enlisted, August 7, 1862, at Bethel, to serve three years; mustered in as private, Co. A, October 8, 1862; mustered out with company, July 20, 1865, at Washington, D. C., as Corgul.

Cox, ABRAHAM.—Age, 24 years. Enlisted, August 13, 1862, at Fremont, to serve three years; mustered in as private, Co. A, October 8, 1862; mustered out with company, July 20, 1865, at Washington, D. C.

DARLING, DAVID.—Age, 21 years. Enlisted, August 14, 1862, at Forestburg, to serve three years; mustered in as private, Co. A, October 8, 1862; wounded in action, May 25, 1864, at Dallas, Ga.; absent, in hospital, since at Louisville, Ky., and at muster out of company.

DECKER, JR., WILLIAM N.—Age, 27 years. Enlisted at Sanford, to serve one year, and mustered in as private, Co. A, February 15, 1865; mustered out with detchment, July 6, 1865, at Carver Hospital, Washington, D. C.

DICE, HENRY.—Age, 18 years. Enlisted at Goshen, to serve one year, and mustered in as private, Co. A, September 1, 1864; mustered out with detachment, June 10, 1865, near Washington, D. C.

DOBBS, MICHAEL.—Age, 34 years. Enlisted, August 11, 1862, at Bethel, to serve three years; mustered in as private, Co. A, October 8, 1862; died, July 19, 1863, at Chesapeake Hospital, Va.

DODGE, CYRUS.—Age, 21 years. Enlisted, August 8, 1862, at Liberty, to serve three years; mustered in as private, Co. A, October 8, 1862; died, February 2, 1864, at Murfreesboro, Tenn.

DRENNON, ROBERT.—Age, 21 years. Enlisted, August 15, 1862, at Liberty, to serve three years; mustered in as private, Co. A, October 8, 1862; discharged, June 19, 1865, at Albany, N. Y., while in hospital in Troy, N. Y.

ELDRIDGE, GEORGE D.—Age, 20 years. Enlisted, August 7, 1862, at Bethel, to serve three years, mustered in as private, Co. A, October 8, 1862; mustered out with company, July 20, 1865, at Washington, D. C.

EVERARD, ELEAZER.—Age, 22 years. Enlisted, August 11, 1862, at Bethel, to serve three years; mustered in as private, Co. A, October 8, 1862; discharged, March 15, 1865, at Nashville, Tenn.

EVERDEN, EDWIN J.—Age, 22 years. Enlisted, August 13, 1862, at Fremont, to serve three years; mustered in as private, Co. A, October 8, 1862; killed in action, July 20, 1864, at Peach Tree Creek, Ga.

FISHER, PETER A.—Age, 19 years. Enlisted, August 11, 1862, at Monticello, to serve three years; mustered in as private, Co. A, October 8, 1862; absent, on furlough, since June 30, 1865, and at muster-out of company.

FISHER, WILLIAM J.—Age, 20 years. Enlisted, August 11, 1862, at Monticello, to serve three years; mustered in as private, Co. A, October 8, 1862; absent, on furlough, since June 27, 1865, and at muster-out of company.

FOOT, EDWARD F.—Age, 21 years. Enlisted, August 11, 1862, at Forestburg, to serve three years; mustered in as private, Co. A, October 8, 1862; mustered out, July 18, 1865, at Elmira, N. Y.

GREGORY, STFPHEN J.—Age, 20 years. Enlisted, August 13, 1862, at Liberty, to serve three years; mustered in as private, Co. A, October 8, 1862; mustered out with company, July 20, 1865, at Washington, D. C., as Gregery.

GREGORY, STEPHEN P.—Age, 19 years. Enlisted, August 13, 1862, at Liberty, to serve three years; mustered in as private, Co. A, October 8, 1862; discharged for disability, March 4, 1863, at Judiciary Square Hospital, Washington, D. C.

HADDEN, JAMES H.—Age, 19 years. Enlisted at ·Goshen, to serve one year, and mustered in as private, Co. A, September 1, 1864; mustered out with detachment, June 10, 1865, near Washington, D. C.

HAIGHT, WALTER T.—Age, 18 years. Enlisted at New York City, to serve one year, and mustered in as private, Co. A, April 6, 1865; mustered out with company, July 20, 1865, at Washington, D. C.

HILL, WALLACE.—Age, 29 years. Enrolled, August 13, 1862, at Fremont, to serve three years; mustered in as first sergeant, Co. A, October 8, 1862; as first lieutenant, Co. I, May 1, 1864; mustered out with company, July 20, 1865, at Washington, D. C. Commissioned second lieutenant, not mustered, October 17, 1863, with rank from March 14, 1863, vice A. C. Kellam, resigned; first lieutenant, April 18, 1864, with rank from February 13, 1864, vice W. T. George, promoted; adjutant, not mustered, July 24, 1865, with rank from May 16, 1865, vice R. Hammond, promoted.

HODGE, JAMES H.—Age, 22 years. Enlisted, August 15, 1862, at Liberty, to serve three years; mustered in as private, Co. A, October 8, 1862; captured, no date; paroled, August 30, 1863; discharged, June 28, 1865, at Washington, D. C., while in hospital, Fairfax Seminary, Va.

HOLLIS, CHARLES S.—Age, 30 years. Enlisted, August 9, 1862, at Monticello, to serve three years; mustered in as private, Co. A, October 8, 1862; mustered out with company, July 20, 1865, at Washington, D. C.

HOUSTON, EDMOND.—Age, 25 years. Enlisted, August 11, 1862, at Monticello, to serve three years; mustered in as corporal, Co. A, October 8, 1862; returned to ranks prior to April, 1863; mustered out with company, July 20, 1865, at Washington, D. C.

HOXSIE, WILLIAM W.—Age, 28 years. Enlisted, August 11, 1862, at Liberty, to serve three years; mustered in as private, Co. A, October 8, 1862; mustered out with detachment, June 20, 1865, at Mower hospital, Philadelphia, Pa.

HOYT, LEWIS N.—Age, 20 years. Enlisted, August 14, 1862, at Bridgeville, to serve three years; mustered in as private, Co. A, October 8, 1862; transferred to Thirty-third Co., Second Battalion, Veteran Reserve Corps, September 26, 1863; mustered out, July 17, 1865, at Washington, D. C.

HUNT, ABRAM C.—Age, 21 years. Enlisted, August 6, 1862, at Bethel, to serve three years; mustered in as private, Co. A, October 8, 1862; transferred to Co. D, Seventeenth Regiment, Veteran Reserve Corps, January 10, 1865; discharged as corporal, July 20, 1865, at Indianapolis, Ind.

HUNT, JOHN.—Age, 21 years. Enlisted, August 6, 1862, at Bethel, to serve three years; mustered in as private, Co. A, October 8, 1862; mustered out with company, July 20, 1865, at Washington, D. C.

JOSCELYN, JOHN W.—Age, 23 years. Enlisted, August 11, 1862, at Liberty, to serve three years; mustered in as private, Co A, October 8, 1862; mustered out with company, July 20, 1865, at Washington, D. C.

KANISE, LEWIS J.—Age, 18 years. Enlisted at Callicoon, to serve three years, and mustered in as private, Co. A, February 16, 1864; wounded in action, July 20, 1864, at Peach Tree Creek, Ga.; absent, in hospital, at Jeffersonville, Ind., at muster-out of company; also borne as Kenise.

KEELER, BAILEY S.—Age, 23 years. Enlisted, August 12, 1862, at Monticello, to serve three years; mustered in as private, Co. A, October 8, 1862; mustered out with company, July 20, 1865, at Washington, D. C.

KEELER, DAVID H.—Age, 20 years. Enlisted at Goshen, to serve one year, and mustered in as private, Co. A, October 6, 1864; mustered out with company, July 20, 1865, at Washington, D. C.

KEENE, GILBERT.—Age, 21 years. Enlisted, August 15, 1862, at Rockland, to serve three years; mustered in as private, Co. A, October 8, 1862; mustered out with detachment, July 6, 1865, at Carver Hospital, Washington, D. C.; also borne as Kean.

KRUM, HERMAN M.—Age, 29 years. Enlisted, August 15, 1862, at Liberty, to serve three years; mustered in as private, Co. A, October 8, 1862; promoted corporal, April 17, 1863; returned to ranks, no date; promoted corporal prior to October, 1864; mustered out with company, July 20, 1865, at Washington, D. C.

LARAWAY, ABRAM.—Age, 38 years. Enlisted, August 13, 1862, at Jeffersonville, to serve three years; mustered in as private, Co. A, October 8, 1862; promoted quartermaster-sergeant, August 21, 1862; returned to ranks, January 16, 1864; mustered out with company, July 20, 1865, at Washington, D. C.

LARAWAY, HENRY.—Age, 23 years. Enlisted, August 14, 1862, at Beaverkill, to serve three years; mustered in as private, Co. A, October 8, 1862; mustered out with company, July 20, 1865, at Washington, D. C.

LARAWAY, MARTINUS.—Age, 34 years. Enlisted, August 16, 1862, at Callicoon, to serve three years; mustered in as wagoner, Co. A, October 8, 1862; mustered out with company, July 20, 1865, at Washington, D. C.

LARAWAY, WILSON.—Age, 33 years. Enlisted, August 14, 1862, at Beaverkill, to serve three years; mustered in as corporal,

Co. A, October 8, 1862; mustered out with company, July 20, 1865, at Washington, D. C.

LENT, NATHANIEL V.—Age, 30 years. Enlisted, August 11, 1862, at Monticello, to serve three years; mustered in as private, Co. A, October 8, 1862; wounded in action, July 20, 1864, at Peach Tree Creek, Ga.; discharged, June 17, 1865, at New York city.

LITTS, THOMAS H.—Age, 30 years. Enlisted, August 11, 1862, at Monticello, to serve three years; mustered in as private, Co. A, October 8, 1862; promoted sergeant prior to October, 1864; wounded in action, July 20, at Peach Tree Creek, Ga.; mustered out with company, July 20, 1865, at Washington, D. C.

LOHMANN, ADAM,—Age, 27 years. Enlisted, August 13, 1862, at Rockland, to serve three years; mustered in as private, Co. A, October 8, 1862; wounded in action, July 20, 1864, at Peach Tree Creek, Ga.: discharged, January 11, 1865, at hospital, Louisville, Ky.

LORD, JAMES.—Age, 28 years. Enlisted, August 14, 1862, at Liberty, to serve three years; mustered in as private, Co. A, October 8, 1862; mustered out with company, July 20, 1865, at Washington, D. C.

LORD, JOSEPH.—Age, 22 years. Enlisted, August 15, 1862, at Liberty, to serve three years; mustered in as private, Co. A, October 8, 1862; died, November 7, 1863, at hospital, near Alexandria, Va., as Joseph H.

LORD, SAMUEL.—Age, 25 years. Enrolled, August 14, 1862, at Parksville, to serve three years; mustered in as corporal, Co. A, October 8, 1862; promoted sergeant prior to April, 1863; first sergeant, no date; mustered out with company, July 20, 1865, at Washington, D. C. Commissioned, not mustered, second lieutenant, July 24, 1865, with rank from May 16, 1865, vice J. A. Eickenberg, promoted.

LOUNSBURY, JOHN M.—Age, 22 years. Enlisted, August 11, 1862, at Monticello, to serve three years; mustered in as private, Co. A, October 8, 1862; wounded in action, July 20, 1864, at Peach Tree Creek, Ga.; died of his wounds, November 12, 1864.

MAPLEDORAM, JAMES C.—Age, 34 years. Enlisted, August 9, 1862, at Monticello, to serve three years; mustered in as private, Co. A, October 8, 1862; died, December 30, 1863, at Lookout Valley, Tenn.

MASON, JAMES B.—Age, 18 years. Enlisted at Goshen, to serve one year, and mustered in as private, Co. A, September 9, 1864; discharged with detachment, June 10, 1865, near Washington, D. C.

McCORD, ANDREW J.—Age, 21 years. Enlisted, August 11, 1862, at Bethel, to serve three years; mustered in as private, Co. A, October 8, 1862; discharged for disability, January 13, 1864, at Murfreesboro, Tenn.

McMILLEN, WILLIAM.—Age, 20 years. Enlisted, August 9, 1862, at Monticello, to serve three years; mustered in as private, Co. A, October 8, 1862; absent, on furlough, since June 30, 1865, and at muster-out of company.

McPHERSON, CHARLES J.—Age, 34 years. Enlisted in Sixth Congressional District, to serve three years, and mustered in as private, Co. A, January 11, 1864; promoted principal musician, no date; mustered out with regiment, July 20, 1865, at Washington, D. C.

McWILLIAMS, JOHN.—Age, 21 years. Enlisted, August 12, 1862, at Monticello, to serve three years; mustered in as private, Co. A, October 8, 1862; died, July 21, 1864, at Peach Tree Ridge, Ga.

MEAD, WILLIAM H.—Age, 23 years. Enlisted, August 14, 1862, at Liberty, to serve three years; mustered in as private, Co. A, October 8, 1862; died, December 11, 1863, at Athens, Tenn.

MIDDAUGH, DENNIS S.—Age, 23 years. Enlisted, August 11, 1862, at Bethel, to serve three years; mustered in as private, Co. A, October 8, 1862; discharged, April 17, 1864, at Yorktown, Va.

MILLER, see Muller.

MILLER, SAMUEL J.—Age, 38 years. Enlisted, August 9, 1862, at Forestburg, to serve three years; mustered in as private, Co. A, October 8, 1862; mustered out with company, July 20, 1865, at Washington, D. C.

Morris, George J.—Age, 23 years. Enlisted, August 12, 1862, at Liberty, to serve three years; mustered in as private, Co. A, October 8, 1862; mustered out with company, July 20, 1865, at Washington, D. C.

Myers, Adelbert.—Age, 19 years. Enlisted at Goshen, to serve one year, and mustered in as private, Co. A, September 1, 1864; mustered out with detachment, June 10, 1865, near Washington, D. C.

Myers, Jr., Moses D.—Age, 21 years. Enlisted, August 11, 1862, at Bethel, to serve three years; mustered in as private, Co. A, October 8, 1862; mustered out with company, July 20, 1865, at Washington, D. C.

Myers, William D.—Age, 28 years. Enlisted, August 11, 1862, at Bethel, to serve three years; mustered in as private, Co. A, October 8, 1862; promoted sergeant, no date; mustered out with company, July 20, 1865, at Washington, D. C.

Myers, William H.—Age, 24 years. Enlisted, August 11, 1862, at Bethel, to serve three years; mustered in as corporal, Co. A, October 8, 1862; mustered out with company, July 20, 1865, at Washington, D. C.; also borne as Myres.

Newman, Thomas.—Age, 18 years. Enlisted at Callicoon, to serve three years, and mustered in as private, Co. A, February 16, 1862; mustered out with company, July 20, 1865, at Washington, D. C.

Ondet, C. G. A.—Age, 44 years. Enlisted, August 13, 1862, at Monticello, to serve three years; mustered in as private, Co. A, December 27, 1862; transferred to Veteran Reserve Corps, April 28, 1864.

Osborn, Peter V.—Age, 33 years. Enlisted, August 9, 1862, at Thompson, to serve three years; mustered in as corporal, Co. A, October 8, 1862; returned to ranks, no date; mustered out with company, July 20, 1865, at Washington, D. C.

Pierce, Joseph.—Age, 20 years. Enrolled at Atlanta, Ga., to serve three years, and mustered in as first lieutenant, Co. A, November 11, 1864; mustered out with company, July 20, 1865, at Washington, D. C. Commissioned first lieutenant, October 19,

1864, with rank from October 17, 1864, vice George Young, pro-moted.

PRICE, JAMES.—Age, 38 years. Enlisted at Goshen, to serve one year, and mustered in as private, Co. A, October 6, 1864; died, December 24, 1864, at Savannah, Ga.

PURVIS, GEORGE W.—Age, 18 years. Enlisted, August 13, 1862, at Rockland, to serve three years; mustered in as private, Co. A, October 8, 1862; wounded in action, July 20, 1864, at Peach Tree Creek, Ga.; mustered out with company, July 20, 1865, at Washington, D. C.

PURVIS, JOHN E.—Age, 25 years. Enlisted, August 12, 1862, at Rockland, to serve three years; mustered in as corporal, Co. A, October 8, 1862; died, June 18, 1863, at Nelson Hospital, York-town, Va.

QUACKENBUSH, FRANKLIN.—Age, 23 years. Enlisted, August 14, 1862, at Forestburg, to serve three years; mustered in as ser-geant, Co. A, October 8, 1862; returned to ranks prior to April 12, 1863; mustered out with company, July 20, 1865, at Washington, D. C.

RAMBOUR, AUGUST.—Age, 30 years. Enlisted, August 18, 1862, at Monticello, to serve three years; mustered in as private, Co. A, December 27, 1862; promoted principal musician, January 26, 1863; mustered out with regiment, July 20, 1865, at Washing-ton, D. C.

RATCLIFF, WILLIAM M.—Age, 29 years. Enrolled, August 26, 1862, at Monticello, to serve three years; mustered in as first lieu-tenant, Co. A, October 8, 1862; adjutant, March 1, 1863; killed in action, July 20, 1864, at Peach Tree Ridge, Ga. Commissioned first lieutenant, November 21, 1862, with rank from August 26, 1862, original; adjutant, February 23, 1863, with rank from Febru-ary 1, 1863, vice E. K. Apgar, dismissed.

RICHARDSON, LOUIS P.—Age, 35 years. Enlisted, August 21, 1862, at Liberty, to serve three years; mustered in as private, Co. A, October 8, 1862; mustered out with company, July 20, 1865, at Washington, D. C., as Richards.

RIDER, see Ryder.

ROBERTSON, LEVI.—Age, 25 years. Enlisted, August 14, 1862, at Monticello, to serve three years; mustered in as private, Co. A, October 8, 1862; mustered out with company, July 20, 1865, at Washington, D. C.

SHULY, DAVID J.—Age, 20 years. Enlisted at Goshen, to serve one year, and mustered in as private, Co. A, September 1, 1864; discharged with detachment, June 10, 1865, near Washington, D. C.

SHULY, TOBIES.—Age, 18 years. Enlisted at Goshen, to serve one year, and mustered in as private, Co. A, September 1, 1864; mustered out. with detachment, June 10, 1865, near Washington, D. C.

SMITH, ARTHUR W.—Age, 21 years. Enlisted, August 12, 1862, at Liberty, to serve three years; mustered in as private, Co. A, October 8, 1862; mustered out with company, July 20, 1865, at Washington, D. C.

SMITH, CHARLES A.—Age, 28 years. Enrolled, August 11, 1862, at Monticello, to serve three years; mustered in as sergeant, Co. A, October 8, 1862; promoted first sergeant, April 17, 1863; mustered in as first lieutenant, Co. E, August 29, 1864; mustered out with company, July 20, 1865, at Washington, D. C. Commissioned first lieutenant, August 12, 1864, with rank from July 24, 1864, vice P. L. Waterbury, died of wounds received in action.

SMITH, GEORGE.—Age, 40 years. Enlisted, August 7, 1862, at Monticello, to serve three years; mustered in as private, Co. A, October 8, 1862; mustered out, June 10, 1865, at McDougall Hospital, Fort Schuyler, New York Harbor.

SMITH, ORRION B.—Age, 42 years. Enlisted, August 11, 1862, at Monticello, to serve three years; mustered in as private, Co. A, October 8, 1862; transferred to Veteran Reserve Corps, September, 1863.

SMITH, WILLIAM.—Age, 38 years. Enlisted at Goshen, to serve one year, and mustered in as private, Co. A, September 8, 1864; mustered out with detachment, June 10, 1865, near Washington, D. C.

STRATTON, GEORGE W.—Age, 22 years. Enlisted, August 12, 1862, at Fallsburg, to serve three years; mustered in as private,

Co. A, October 8, 1862; mustered out with company, July 20, 1865, at Washington, D. C.

STURDEVANT, GEORGE.—Age, 22 years. Enlisted, August 6, 1862, at Jeffersonville, to serve three years; mustered in as private, Co. A, October 8, 1862; promoted commissary sergeant, October 9, 1862; present, October, 1864, but absent at muster-out of regiment.

TAGGETT, HENRY F.—Age, 24 years. Enlisted, August 13, 1862, at Rockland, to serve three years; mustered in as private, Co. A, October 8, 1862; mustered out with company, July 20, 1865, at Washington, D. C.

TERRY, SETH A.—Age, 18 years. Enlisted, August 11, 1862, at Monticello, to serve three years; mustered in as private, Co. A, October 8, 1862; absent, on furlough, since June 30, 1865, and at muster-out of company.

THOMPSON, JOHN.—Age, 20 years. Enlisted at Goshen, to serve one year, and mustered in as private, Co. A, October 1, 1864; mustered out with company, July 20, 1865, at Washington, D. C.

TILLOTSON, ROBERT L.—Age, 41 years. Enlisted, August 6, 1862, at Bethel, to serve three years; mustered in as private, Co. A, October 8, 1862; died, June 18, 1863, at Nelson Hospital, Yorktown, Va.; also borne as Tillertson.

TRAVIS, GEORGE W.—Age, 26 years. Enlisted, August 11, 1862, at Youngsville, to serve three years; mustered in as private, Co. A, October 8, 1862; absent, in hospital, since April 9, 1865, and at muster-out of company.

VAN ORDEN, PETER.—Age, 21 years. Enlisted, August 11, 1862, at Bethel, to serve three years; mustered in as private, Co. A, October 8, 1862; died of his wounds, July 22, 1864, at Peach Tree Ridge, Ga.

VAN SICLEN, THEODORE C.—Age, 19 years. Enlisted, August 13, 1862, at Monticello, to serve three years; mustered in as private, Co. A, October 8, 1862; killed in action, July 20, 1864, at Peach Tree Ridge, Ga.

WAGENER, FRANK.—Age, 23 years. Enlisted, August 11, 1862, at Bethel, to serve three years; mustered in as private, Co. A, Oc--

tober 8, 1862; discharged for disability, December 19, 1863, at Washington, D. C.; also borne as Wagner.

WALES, JOHN.—Age, 18 years. Enlisted, August 9, 1862, at Fallsburg, to serve three years; mustered in as private, Co. A, October 8, 1862; mustered out with company, July 20, 1865, at Washington, D. C.

WATKINS, HEZEKIAH.—Age, 25 years. Enrolled, August 2, 1862, at Monticello, to serve three years; mustered in as first lieutenant and adjutant, August 22, 1862; as captain, Co. A, October 8, 1862; as major, January 1, 1864; as lieutenant-colonel, January 9, 1864; wounded in action, March 16, 1865, at Averasboro, N. C.; mustered out with regiment, July 20, 1865, at Washington, D. C. Not commissioned first lieutenant and adjutant; commissioned captain, November 21, 1862, with rank from August 26, 1862, original; major, November 9, 1863, with rank from April 29, 1863, vice J. B. Taft, promoted; lieutenant-colonel, January 8, 1864, with rank from November 25, 1863, vice J. B. Taft, killed in action. Bvt. Colonel U. S. V.

WHISTON, DANIEL W.—Age, 29 years. Enlisted at Goshen, to serve one year, and mustered in as private, Co. A, September 24, 1864; mustered out, May 24, 1865, at McDougall Hospital, Fort Schuyler, New York Harbor.

WOOD, HEZEKIAH.—Age, 35 years. Enlisted at Tusten, to serve three years, and mustered in as private, Co. A, April 4, 1864; absent, on furlough, since July 3, 1865, and at muster-out of company.

WRIGHT, CHARLES.—Age, 23 years. Enlisted at Goshen, to serve one year, and mustered in as private, Co. A, September 28, 1864; mustered out, July 14, 1865, at David's Island, New York Harbor.

WRIGHT, GEORGE R.—Age, 21 years. Enlisted, August 14, 1862, at Forestburg, to serve three years; mustered in as private, Co. A, October 8, 1862; promoted corporal prior to October, 1864; sergeant, no date; mustered out with company, July 20, 1865, at Washington, D. C.

YORK, HERMAN.—Age, 27 years. Enlisted, August 11, 1862, at Fallsburg, to serve three years; mustered in as private, Co. A,

October 8, 1862; mustered out with company, July 20, 1865, at Washington, D. C., as Yorks.

YOUNG, GEORGE.—Age, 21 years. Enrolled at Parksville, to serve three years, and mustered in as second lieutenant, Co. A, August 26, 1862; as first lieutenant, March 5, 1863; wounded in action, July 20, 1864, at Peach Tree Creek, Ga.; discharged for disability caused from wounds, October 26, 1864. Commissioned second lieutenant, November 21, 1862, with rank from August 26, 1862, original; first lieutenant, October 17, 1863, with rank from March 5, 1863, vice W. R. Bennett, promoted; captain, not mustered, June 10, 1864, with rank from March 24, 1864, vice A. J. Baldwin, dismissed.

YOUNG, GILBERT J.—Age, 27 years. Enlisted, August 14, 1862, at Liberty, to serve three years; mustered in as private, Co. A, October 8, 1862; wounded in action, July 20, 1864, at Peach Tree Creek, Ga.; died of his wounds, August 5, 1864, at Kingston, Ga.

YOUNG, MOSES.—Age, 20 years. Enlisted, August 11, 1862, at Monticello, to serve three years; mustered in as private, Co. A, October 8, 1862; promoted corporal, no date; mustered out with company, July 20, 1865, at Washington, D. C.

KILLED IN ACTION.

Akins, Amos P., July 20, 1864, at Peach Tree Creek, Ga.
Everden, Edwin J., July 20, 1864, at Peach Tree Creek, Ga.
Van Siclen, Theodore C., July 20, 1864, at Peach Tree Creek, Ga.

WOUNDED IN ACTION.

Buckley, Philo, July 20, 1864, at Peach Tree Creek, Ga.
Burns, Frederick W., July 20, 1864, at Peach Tree Creek, Ga.
Cantrell, Edwin R., July 20, 1864, at Peach Tree Creek, Ga.
Darling, David, May 25, 1864, near Dallas, Ga.
Drennon, Robert, May 15, 1864, at Resaca, Ga.
Kanise, Lewis J., July 20, 1864, at Peach Treek Creek, Ga.
Lent, Nathaniel V., July 20, 1864, at Peach Tree Creek, Ga.
Litts, Thomas H., July 20, 1864, at Peach Tree Creek, Ga.

Lohman, Adam, July 20, 1864, at Peach Tree Creek, Ga.
Lounsbury, John M., July 20, 1864, at Peach Tree Creek, Ga.
Purvis, George W., July 20, 1864, at Peach Tree Creek, Ga.
Young, Gilbert I., July 20, 1864, at Peach Tree Creek, Ga.
Young, George, July 20, 1864, at Peach Tree Creek, Ga.
Watkins, Hezekiah, Mar. 16, 1865, at Averasboro, N. C.

DIED OF DISEASE AND WOUNDS.

Abberly, Thomas, Jan. 13, 1863, at Upton's Hill, Va.
Beebe, Joseph J., Oct. 5, 1864, at Chattanooga, Tenn.
Carpenter, John W., July 17, 1863, at Portsmouth, Va.
Dobbs, Michael, July 19, 1863, at Chesapeake Hospital, Va.
Lord, Joseph, Nov. 17, 1863, at Alexandria, Va.
Lounsbury, John M., Nov. 12, 1864, at Monticello, N. Y.
Mapledoram, James C., Dec. 30, 1863, at Lookout Valley, Tenn.
Mead, William H., Dec. 11, 1863, at Athens, Tenn.
Price, James, Dec. 24, 1864, at Savannah, Ga.
Purvis, John E., Jan. 18, 1863, at Yorktown, Va.
Tillotson, Robert L., Jan. 15, 1863, at Yorktown, Va.
Young, Gilbert I., Aug. 5, 1864, at Kingston, Ga.

CAPTURED.

Hodge, James H., no date; paroled Aug. 30, 1863.

DISCHARGED DURING SERVICE.

Allen, John M., May 19, 1865, for disability.
Burns, Frederick W., May 22, 1865, for disability.
Cantrell, Edward R., June 26, 1865, for disability.
Drennon, Robert, June 19, 1865, for disability.
Everard, Eleazer, Mar. 15, 1865, for disability.
Gregory, Stephen P., Mar. 4, 1863, for disability.
Hodge, James H., June 28, 1865, for disability.
Lohmann, Adam, Jan. 11, 1865, for disability.
McCord, Andrew J., Jan. 13, 1864, for disability.
Middaugh, Dennis S., April 17, 1864, for disability.
Smith, George, June 10, 1865, for disability.
Wagener, Frank, Dec. 19, 1863, for disability.
Whiston, Daniel W., May 24, 1865, for disability.

TRANSFERRED.

Beebe, Roswell T., Mar. 8, 1865, to Veteran Reserve Corps.
Hunt, Abram C., Jan. 10, 1865, to Veteran Reserve Corps.
Bennett, William W., Sept. 3, 1863, to Veteran Reserve Corps.
Hoyt, Lewis N., Sept. 26, 1863, to Veteran Reserve Corps.
Ondet, C. G. A., April 28, 1864, to Veteran Reserve Corps.
Smith, Orrin, Sept., 1863, to Veteran Reserve Corps.

COMPANY B

CAPTAINS.

Alfred J. Baldwin, original, dismissed.

George Young, from Mar. 24, 1864; disability prevented muster. (Bvt. Major N. Y. V.)

Rensselaer Hammond, from May 15, 1865, not mustered. (Bvt. Major N. Y. V.)

FIRST LIEUTENANTS.

Edward C. Howard, original, promoted to Quartermaster.

Isaac Jelliff, from Mar. 26, 1864, to muster out of Regt. (Bvt. Capt. N. Y. V.)

SECOND LIEUTENANTS.

Roberts C. Benedict, original, resigned.

Edward Carrington, from Oct. 27, 1862; killed in action. (Bvt. Capt. N. Y. V.)

William Smith, from July 24, 1864; not mustered.

RECORD OF MEMBERS OF COMPANY B—ORIGINAL.

ALLYN, BENJAMIN F.—Age, 24 years. Enlisted, August 20, 1862, at Thompson, to serve three years; mustered in as private, Co. B, October 8, 1862; appointed musician, prior to April, 1863; mustered out with company, July 20, 1865, at Alexandria, Va.

AVERY, WILLIAM L.—Age, 31 years. Enlisted, August 25, 1862, at Thompson, to serve three years; mustered in as private, Co. B, October 8, 1862; transferred to Co. D, Third Regiment, Veteran Reserve Corps, July 16, 1863; promoted corporal, July 8, 1865; mustered out with detachment, August 3, 1865, at Brattleboro, Vt.

BALDWIN, ALFRED J.—Age, 25 years. Enrolled, August 11, 1862, at Monticello, to serve three years; mustered in as captain, Co. B, August 30, 1862; dismissed, May 6, 1864. Commissioned captain, November 19, 1862, with rank from August 30, 1862, original.

BATES, BENJAMIN.—Age, 22 years.   Enlisted, August 20, 1862, at Forestburg, to serve three years; mustered in as private, Co. B, October 8, 1862; promoted corporal, prior to June 30, 1863; sergeant, June 19, 1865; absent, at home on furlough, July 6, 1865, and at muster-out of company.

BENEDICT, ROBERTS C.—Age — years.   Enrolled, August 30, 1862, at Monticello, to serve three years; mustered in as second lieutenant, Co. B, October 8, 1862; discharged, October, 1862. Commissioned second lieutenant, November 21, 1862, with rank from same date, original.   Resigned.

BLACK, JOHN.—Age, 32 years.   Enlisted, August 22, 1862, at Fallsburg, to serve three years; mustered in as private, Co. B, December 27, 1862; mustered out with company, July 20, 1865, near Alexandria, Va.

BLOOMINGBURGH, WILLIAM J.—Age, 20 years.   Enlisted, August 20, 1862, at Thompson, to serve three years; mustered in as private, Co. B, October 8, 1862; killed by accident, March 20, 1863, near Alexandria, Va.

BOLLMAN, CHRISTOPHER.—Age, 18 years.   Enlisted, August 19, 1862, at Thompson, to serve three years; mustered in as private, Co. B, October 8, 1862; promoted corporal, no date; mustered out with company, July 20, 1865, near Alexandria, Va.

BOLLMAN, CHRISTOPHER L.—Age, 45 years.   Enlisted, August 11, 1862, at Thompson, to serve three years; mustered in as private, Co. B, October 8, 1862; died of congestive fever, September 30, 1863, at Indianapolis, Ind.

BOWMAN, MAEGHER.—Age, 42 years.   Enlisted, August 22, 1862, at Thompson, to serve three years; mustered in as private, Co. B, October 8, 1862; discharged for disability, August 31, 1863; also borne as Malchoir Bowman.

BROADHEAD, URIAH M.—Age, 21 years.   Enlisted, August 13, 1862, at Monticello, to serve three years; mustered in as corporal, Co. B, December 27, 1862; returned to ranks, no date; promoted corporal, April 30, 1865; mustered out with company, July 20, 1865, near Alexandria, Va.

BROOME, ORVAL A.—Age, 18 years.   Enlisted, August 14, 1862, at Fallsburg, to serve three years; mustered in as private, Co. B, October 8, 1862; died of chronic diarrhea, April 2, 1864, at Hospital No. 3, Murfreesboro, Tenn.; also borne as Brown.

BROWN, LEANDER T.—Age, 25 years. Enlisted, August 14, 1862, at Bethel, to serve three years; mustered in as sergeant, Co. B, October 8, 1862; transferred to Signal Corps, August 12, 1863.

BROWN, MARCUS L.—Age, 18 years. Enlisted, August 20, 1862, at Fallsburg, to serve three years; mustered in as private, Co. B, October 8, 1862; died of typhoid fever, July 1, 1863, at Fort Monroe, Va.

BROWN, RENWICK.—Age, 25 years. Enlisted, August 20, 1862, at Bethel, to serve three years; mustered in as corporal, Co. B, October 8, 1862; promoted sergeant, May 20, 1863; mustered out with company, July 20, 1865, near Alexandria, Va.

BUTLER, PATRICK.—Age, 44 years. Enlisted, August 22, 1862, at Thompson, to serve three years; mustered in as private, Co. B, October 8, 1862; transferred to Co. D, Seventh Regiment, Veteran Reserve Corps, November 15, 1863; mustered out with detachment, July 14, 1865, at Washington, D. C.

CANTINE, NICHOLAS S.—Age, 23 years. Enlisted at New York city, to serve three years, and mustered in as private, Co. B, October 14, 1862; discharged for disability, June 30, 1864, at David's Island, New York Harbor.

CANTRELL, ROBERT.—Age, 23 years. Enlisted, August 15, 1862, at Thompson, to serve three years; mustered in as private, Co. B, October 8, 1862; promoted corporal prior to April, 1863; sergeant, no date; mustered out with company, July 20, 1865, at Alexandria, Va.

CARPENTER, BENJAMIN.—Age, 18 years. Enlisted, August 22, 1862, at Thompson, to serve three years; mustered in as private, Co. B, October 8, 1862; died of diarrhea, January 30, 1864, at City Hospital, Indianapolis, Ind.

CARPENTER, WILLIAM L.—Age, 18 years. Enlisted, August 19, 1862, at Thompson, to serve three years; mustered in as private, Co. B, October 8, 1862; killed by a sentinel, March 31, 1863, near Fort Worth, Va.

CARRINGTON, EDWARD.—Age, 24 years. Enrolled at Washington, to serve three years, and mustered in as second lieutenant, Co. B, October 27, 1862; killed in action, March 6, 1865, at Natural Bridge, Fla., while on detached service, Gen. Newton's staff. Commissioned second lieutenant, October 24, 1862, with rank from same date, vice R. C. Benedict, resigned.

CLARK, GARRETT T.—Age, 33 years.   Enlisted, August 20, 1862, at Bethel, to serve three years; mustered in as private, Co. B, October 8, 1862; discharged, May 28, 1865, at Hospital No. 1, Chattanooga, Tenn.

COGSWELL, RICHARD.—Age, 18 years.   Enlisted, August 18, 1862, at Thompson, to serve three years; mustered in as private, Co. B, October 8, 1862; died of typhoid pneumonia, March 7, 1864, at Eruptive Hospital, Louisville, Ky.

COMFORT, REEVE.—Age, 18 years.   Enlisted, August 16, 1862, at Bethel, to serve three years; mustered in as private, Co. B, October 8, 1862; transferred to One Hundred and Fifty-second Company, Second Battalion, Veteran Reserve Corps, April 22, 1864; mustered out, August 1, 1865, at Nashville, Tenn.

CONKLIN, EUGENE.—Age, 18 years.   Enlisted, August 14, 1862, at Fallsburg, to serve three years; mustered in as private, Co. B, October 8, 1862; mustered out with company, July 20, 1865, at Alexandria, Va.

CROMWELL, ALEXANDER.—Age, 19 years.   Enlisted, August 20, 1862, at Fallsburg, to serve three years; mustered in as private, Co. B, October 8, 1862; mustered out with company, July 20, 1865, at Alexandria, Va.

CROSBY, SCIPO L.—Age, 28 years.   Enlisted, August 20, 1862, at Bethel, to serve three years; mustered in as private, Co. B, October 8, 1862; wounded in action, May 15, 1864, at Resaca, Ga.; absent, in hospital, at Madison, Ind., since March, 1865, and at muster-out of company.

DEBENS, see Devens, Co. G.

DECKER, CHARLES H. T.—Age, 18 years.   Enlisted, August 13, 1862, at Forestburg, to serve three years; mustered in as private, Co. B, December 27, 1862; wounded in action, July 20, 1864, at Peach Tree Creek, Ga.; mustered out with company, July 20, 1865, near Alexandria, Va.; also borne as Charles H. D.

DEMOREST, JONATHAN O.—Age, 28 years. Enlisted, August 20, 1862, at Thompson, to serve three years; mustered in as private, Co. B, October 8, 1862; died from injuries received on the Orange and Alexandria Railroad, March 20, 1863, at hospital, Alexandria, Va.

DUN, SUMNER H.—Age, 22 years. Enlisted, August 12, 1862, at Forestburg, to serve three years; mustered in as private, Co. B, October 8. 1862; promoted corporal subsequent to October, 1864; mustered out with company, July 20, 1865, near Alexandria, Va, as Dunn.

DURLAND, JAMES T.—Age, 24 years. Enlisted, August 20, 1862, at Thompson, to serve three years; mustered in as private, Co. B, October 8, 1862; mustered out, June 30, 1865, at Carver Hospital, Washington, D. C.

DURLAND, STEPHEN D.—Age, 27 years. Enlisted, August 21, 1862, at Thompson, to serve three years; mustered in as private, Co. B, October 8, 1862; promoted corporal prior to April 11, 1863; returned to ranks, no date; died of disease, October 31, 1864, near Dallas, Ga.

EARNEST, ADAM.—Age, 23 years. Enlisted, August 14, 1862, at Lumberland, to serve three years; mustered in as private, Co. B, October 8, 1862; mustered out with company, July 20, 1865, at Alexandria, Va.

FERGUSON, JAMES.—Age, 19 years. Enlisted, August 22, 1862, at Bethel, to serve three years; mustered in as private, Co. B, October 8, 1862; mustered out, August 3, 1865, at St. Louis, Mo.

FISHER, IRA.—Age, 44 years. Enlisted, August 19, 1862, at Thompson, to serve three years; mustered in as private, Co. B, October 8, 1862; transferred to Veteran Reserve Corps, July 1, 1863.

FOOTE, SHUBAL.—Age, 44 years. Enlisted, August 22, 1862, at Forestburg, to serve three years; mustered in as private, Co. B, October 8, 1862; mustered out with company, July 20, 1865, at Alexandria, Va.

FRANCE, ISAAC C.—Age, 24 years. Enlisted, August 17, 1862, at Bethel, to serve three years; mustered in as private, Co. B, October 8, 1862; promoted corporal prior to October, 1864; mustered out with company, July 8, 1865, at Mount Pleasant Hospital, Washington, D. C.

FRASER, WILLIAM J.—Age, 24 years. Enlisted, August 14, 1862, at Bethel, to serve three years; mustered in as private, Co. B, December 27, 1862; promoted corporal and returned to ranks, no date; died of diphtheria, November 21, 1863, at Cumberland Hospital, Nashville, Tenn.

FREEMAN, DANIEL M.—Age, 28 years. Enlisted, August 13, 1862, at Woodbourne, to serve three years; mustered in as corporal, Co. B, October 8, 1862; discharged, January 28, 1863, at Upton's Hill, Va.

GEARY, DANIEL.—Age, 32 years. Enlisted, August 21, 1862, at Bethel, to serve three years; mustered in as private, Co. B, October 8, 1862; mustered out, July 3, 1865, at New York city; also borne as David.

HAINES, GEORGE N.—Age, 30 years. Enlisted at Kingston, to serve one year, and mustered in as private, Co. B, September 20, 1864; mustered out with detachment, June 10, 1865, at Washington, D. C.

HARDENBURGH, RICHARD M. J.—Age, 21 years. Enrolled, August 22, 1862, at Neversink, to serve three years; mustered in as sergeant, Co. B, October 8, 1862; promoted sergeant-major, April 18, 1863; mustered in as first lieutenant, Co. G, August 29, 1864; wounded in action and died of his wounds, March 16, 1865, at Averasboro, N. C. Commissioned first lieutenant, August 24, 1864, with rank from July 20, 1864, vice R. Hammond, promoted.

HENDRICKSON, JOHN M.—Age, 34 years. Enlisted, August 14, 1862, at Bethel, to serve three years; mustered in as private, Co. B, October 8, 1862; died, November 20, 1863, at Convalescent Camp, Bridgeport, Ala.

HOAR, JOHN.—Age, 32 years. Enlisted, August 18, 1862, at Thompson, to serve three years; mustered in as private, Co. B, October 8, 1862; died, February 14, 1864, at Bridgeport, Ala.

HOGANCAMP, JOHN W.—Age, 24 years. Enlisted, August 20, 1862, at Bethel, to serve three years; mustered in as private, Co. B,.

October 8, 1862; killed by accident, March 19, 1863, on the Orange and Alexandria Railroad.

HOWARD, EDWIN C.—Age, 24 years. Enrolled, August 11, 1862, at Monticello, to serve three years; mustered in as first lieutenant, Co. B, October 8, 1862; as quartermaster, March 26, 1864; mustered out, August 10, 1865, at St. Louis, Mo. Commissioned first lieutenant, November 19, 1862, with rank from August 30, 1862, original; first lieutenant and quartermaster, April 18, 1864, with rank from March 26, 1864, vice W. W. Wheeler, dismissed.

JACKSON, DAVID.—Age, 27 years. Enlisted, August 22, 1862, at Thompson, to serve three years; mustered in as private, Co. B, October 8, 1862; discharged, November 14, 1863.

JACKSON, JOHN H.—Age, 20 years. Enlisted, August 16, 1862, at Bethel, to serve three years; mustered in as corporal, Co. B, October 8, 1862; died, March 28, 1863, at Christ Church Hospital, Alexandria, Va., of injuries received on O. & A. Railroad.

JACOCKS, JOHN H.—Age, 28 years. Enlisted, August 16, 1862, at Bethel, to serve three years; mustered in as private, Co. B, October 8, 1862; promoted corporal prior to July, 1864; wounded in action, July 20, 1864, at Peach Tree Creek, Ga.; discharged for wounds, June 16, 1865, at Central Park Hospital, New York City; also borne as Jaycox.

JOYNER, JOSEPH.—Age, 18 years. Enlisted, at Goshen, to serve one year, and mustered in as private, Co. B, October 5, 1864; mustered out with company, July 20, 1865, near Alexandria, Va.

KENT, BURR S.—Age, 23 years. Enlisted, August 20, 1862, at Liberty, to serve three years; mustered in as private, Co. B, August 26, 1862; mustered out with company, July 20, 1865, near Alexandria, Va.

KENT, CHARLES.—Age, 43 years. Enlisted at Goshen, to serve one year, and mustered in as private, Co. B, October 5, 1864; died, February 11, 1865, at Savannah, Ga.

KENT, GEORGE A.—Age, 20 years. Enlisted, August 20, 1862, at Monticello, to serve three years; mustered in as private, Co. B, August 25, 1862; mustered out, June 10, 1865, at David's Island, New York Harbor.

KENT, JACOB.—Age, 18 years. Enlisted, August 20, 1862, at Liberty, to serve three years; mustered in as private, Co. B, October 8, 1862; mustered out with company, July 20, 1865, near Alexandria, Va.

KINNE, DANIEL I.—Age, 21 years. Enlisted, August 21, 1862, at Thompson, to serve three years; mustered in as private, Co. B, October 8, 1862; wounded in action, March 19, 1865, at Bentonville, N. C.; died of his wounds, March 20, 1865, near Bentonville, N. C.; also borne as Daniel Q. Kinnie.

KIRK, see Kyrk, Co. G.

KNOX, ADNA L.—Age, 23 years. Enlisted, August 16, 1862, at Rockland, to serve three years; mustered in as corporal, Co. B, October 8, 1862; discharged for disability, February 17, 1864.

KRUM, LUTHER S.—Age, 18 years. Enlisted, August 20, 1862, at Thompson, to serve three years; mustered in as private, Co. B, October 8, 1862; killed by accident on O. & A. Railroad, March 20, 1863, as Luther.

LAWSON, BENJAMIN.—Age, 37 years. Enlisted, August 16, 1862, at Bethel, to serve three years; mustered in as private, Co. B, October 8, 1862; died of chronic diarrhea, December 3, 1863, at hospital, Murfreesboro, Tenn.

LINSON, LYMAN S.—Age, 25 years. Enlisted, August 14, 1862, at Bethel, to serve three years; mustered in as sergeant, Co. B, October 8, 1862; discharged, March 4, 1863, for promotion to first lieutenant, Eighty-first Regiment, U. S. Colored Troops.

LORGAN, JAMES A.—Age, 39 years. Enlisted, August 11, 1862, at Bethel, to serve three years; mustered in as private, Co. B, October 8, 1862; discharged, December 12, 1863, at New York city.

LORING, JONATHAN C.—Age, 33 years. Enlisted, August 16, 1862, at Thompson, to serve three years; mustered in as private, Co. B, October 8, 1862; mustered out with company, July 20, 1865, near Alexandria, Va.

LYBOLT, HENRY C.—Age, 22 years. Enlisted, August 20, 1862, at Bethel, to serve three years; mustered in as private, Co. B, October 8, 1862; absent, sick in Joe Holt Hospital, Jeffersonville, Ind., since November 10, 1864, and at muster-out of company.

LYON, GEORGE.—Age, 23 years. Enlisted, August 22, 1862, at Bethel, to serve three years; mustered in as private, Co. B, December 27, 1862; killed by accident, on Orange and Alexandria Railroad, March 20, 1863, near Alexandria, Va.

McINTINE, JOHN L.—Age, 20 years. Enlisted at Goshen, to serve one year, and mustered in as private, Co. B, October 5, 1864; mustered out with company, July 20, 1865, at Alexandria, Va.

MORRIS. JAMES D.—Age, 43 years. Enlisted, August 20, 1862, at Forestburg, to serve three years; mustered in as private, Co. B, October 8, 1862; mustered out with company, July 20, 1865, at Alexandria, Va.

O'NEIL, TERRENCE.—Age, 28 years. Enlisted, August 21, 1862, at Monticello, to serve three years; mustered in as private, Co. B, December 27, 1862; died of chronic diarrhea, February 20, 1864, at Clay Hospital, Louisville, Ky.

PALMER, ASHER B.—Age, 42 years. Enlisted, August 11, 1862, at Thompson, to serve three years; mustered in as private, Co. B, October 8, 1862; absent, sick in field hospital, Bridgeport, Ala., since May 2, 1864, and at muster-out of company.

PALMER, RUFUS.—Age, 19 years. Enlisted at Neversink, to serve three years, and mustered in as private, Co. B, September 9, 1864; mustered out with detachment, June 10, 1865, at Washington, D. C.

PATTERSON, JOHN.—Age, 44 years. Enlisted, August 25, 1862, at Thompson, to serve three years; mustered in as private, Co. B, October 8, 1862; promoted corporal prior to April 11, 1863; transferred to Veteran Reserve Corps, July 1, 1863.

PERRY, SENECA W.—Age, 23 years. Enlisted, August 22, 1862, at Thompson, to serve three years; mustered in as private, Co. B, October 8, 1862; promoted quartermaster-sergeant, November 22, 1864; mustered out with regiment, July 20, 1865, at Washington, D. C.

PINTLER, JOHN C.—Age, 36 years. Enlisted, August 16, 1862, at Bethel, to serve three years; mustered in as corporal, Co. B, October 8, 1862; promoted sergeant, no date; died of chronic diarrhea, January 29, 1864, at Hospital No. 19, Nashville, Tenn.

PINTLER, WILLIAM.—Age, 23 years. Enlisted, August 16, 1862, at Bethel, to serve three years; mustered in as private, Co B, October 8, 1862; died of chronic diarrhea, January 7, 1864, at Lookout Valley, Tenn.

PREDMORE, ABRAM S.—Age, 43 years. Enlisted, August 14, 1862, at Bethel, to serve three years; mustered in as sergeant, Co. B, October 8, 1862; promoted first sergeant prior to April 11, 1863; died of typhoid fever, August 2, 1863, at Convalescent Camp, Va.

RALSTON, GEORGE.—Age, 20 years. Enlisted, August 13, 1862, at Thompson, to serve three years; mustered in as private, Co. B, August 26, 1862; mustered out with company, July 20, 1865, near Alexandria, Va.

RAY, EDWARD.—Age, 18 years. Enlisted, August 13, 1862, at Stevensville, to serve three years; mustered in as private, Co. B. October 8, 1862; killed by accident, March 19, 1863, on Orange and Alexandria Railroad.

ROBINSON, PHILIP S.—Age, 21 years. Enlisted, August 15, 1862, at Bridgeville, to serve three years; mustered in as private, Co. B, October 8, 1862; promoted corporal, September 1, 1864; mustered out with company, July 20, 1865, near Alexandria, Va.

ROSE, AUSTIN J.—Age, 34 years. Enlisted, August 21, 1862, at Monticello, to serve three years; mustered in as private, Co. B, October 8, 1862; discharged for disability, December 24, 1863, at Nashville, Tenn.

ROSE, GUSTUS.—Age, 27 years. Enlisted, August 22, 1862, at Forestburg, to serve three years; mustered in as private, Co. B, October 8, 1862; promoted corporal prior to July, 1864; wounded in action, July 20, 1864, at Peach Tree Creek, Ga.; died of his wounds, August 1, 1864, at hospital, Lookout Mountain, Tenn.

RUMSEY, CYRUS.—Age, 21 years. Enlisted, August 21, 1862, at Thompson, to serve three years; mustered in as private, Co. B, October 8, 1862; mustered out with company, July 20, 1865, near Alexandria, Va.

RUMSEY, JOHN J.—Age, 22 years. Enlisted, August 21, 1862, at Thompson, to serve three years; mustered in as wagoner, Co. B,

October 8, 1862; mustered out with company, July 20, 1865, near Alexandria, Va.

SECOR, LORENZO.—Age, 19 years. Enlisted, August 13, 1862, at Stevensville, to serve three years; mustered in as private, Co. B, October 8, 1862; promoted corporal, no date; mustered out with company, July 20, 1865, near Alexandria, Va.

SISSON, WILLIAM D.—Age, 38 years. Enlisted, August 15, 1862, at Thompson, to serve three years; mustered in as private, Co. B, October 8, 1862; promoted corporal prior to April 11, 1863; discharged, June 29, 1863, at Alexandria, Va.

SLATER, ALBERT H.—Age, 26 years. Enlisted, August 16, 1862, at Bethel, to serve three years; mustered in as private, Co. B, October 8, 1862; mustered out, July 15, 1865, at Lovell Hospital, Portsmouth Grove, R. I.

SMITH, JAMES.—Age, 18 years. Enlisted, August 18, 1862, at Thompson, to serve three years; mustered in as private, Co. B, October 8, 1862; mustered out with company, July 20, 1865, near Alexandria, Va.

SMITH, WILLIAM.—Age, 25 years. Enlisted, August 14, 1862, at Bethel, to serve three years; mustered in as private, Co. B, August 25, 1862; promoted sergeant prior to April, 1863; first sergeant, June 19, 1865; mustered out with company, July 20, 1865, at Alexandria, Va. Commissioned, not mustered, second lieutenant, July 24, 1865, with rank from May 16, 1865, vice W. Hill, promoted.

STANTON, CHARLES C.—Age, 18 years. Enlisted, August 11, 1862, at Bethel, to serve three years; mustered in as private, Co. B, October 8, 1862; mustered out, September 4, 1865, at Elmira, N. Y.; also borne as Charles E.

STANTON, JOHN S.—Age, 43 years. Enlisted, August 11, 1862, at Bethel, to serve three years; mustered in as private, Co. B, October 8, 1862; transferred to Forty-eighth Company, Second Battalion, Veteran Reserve Corps, November 15, 1863, thence to Co. K, Seventh Regiment, Veteran Reserve Corps, January 17, 1865; mustered out, July 3, 1865, at Washington, D. C.

STURGES, WILLIAM.—Age, 32 years. Enlisted at Monticello, to serve three years, and mustered in as private, Co. B, August 20, 1862; no further record.

SURINE, see Sarine, Co. E.

SUTTER, HENRY.—Age, 20 years. Enlisted, August 20, 1862, at Bethel, to serve three years; mustered in as private, Co. B, October 8, 1862; died of chronic diarrhea, November 25, 1863, at Lookout Valley, Tenn.

TRAVIS, ORRIN.—Age, 29 years. Enlisted at Kingston, to serve three years, and mustered in as private, Co. B, September 15, 1864; mustered out with detachment, June 10, 1865, at Washington, D. C.

TUCKER, WILLIAM.—Age, 23 years. Enlisted, August 14, 1862, at Thompson, to serve three years; mustered in as private, Co. B, October 8, 1862; discharged for disability, March 23, 1864, at Nashville, Tenn.

VANTRAN, JOHN.—Age, 19 years. Enlisted at Neversink, to serve one year, and mustered in as private, Co. B, September 9, 1864; mustered out with detachment, June 10, 1865, at Washington, D. C.

WADDELL, NEIL.—Age, 23 years. Enlisted, August 19, 1862, at Bethel, to serve three years; mustered in as private, Co. B, October 8, 1862; mustered out with company, July 20, 1865, at Alexandria, Va.

WAGER, DAVID H.—Age, 23 years. Enlisted, August 13, 1862, at Monticello, to serve three years, as private, Co. B, and deserted, December 16, 1862, at Washington Hospital.

WARRING, HIRAM B.—Age, 32 years. Enlisted, August 22, 1862, at Thompson, to serve three years; mustered in as private, Co. B, October 8, 1862; transferred to Veteran Reserve Corps, July 1, 1863.

WARRING, JOHN W.—Age, 27 years. Enlisted, August 20, 1862, at Thompson, to serve three years; mustered in as private, Co. B, October 8, 1862; died of diarrhea, December 15, 1863, at Lookout Valley, Tenn.

WASIM, DAVID A.—Age, 26 years. Enrolled, August 13, 1862, at Liberty, to serve three years; mustered in as corporal, Co. B, October 8, 1862; promoted sergeant prior to April, 1863; first sergeant, no date; mustered in as second lieutenant, Co. A, May 6, 1865; mustered out with company, July 20, 1865, at Washington, D. C. Commissioned second lieutenant, April 15, 1865, with rank from March 6, 1865, vice E. Carrington, killed in action; first lieutenant, not mustered, July 24, 1865, with rank from May 16, 1865, vice D. Divine, promoted.

WATSON, MARTIN.—Age, 26 years. Enlisted, August 14, 1862, at Forestburg, to serve three years; mustered in as private, Co. B, October 8, 1862; died of bronchitis, January 1, 1863, at Upton's Hill, Va.

WATTS, GEORGE B.—Age, 20 years. Enlisted, August 21, 1862, at Thompson, to serve three years; mustered in as private, Co. B, October 8, 1862; mustered out with company, July 20, 1865, near Alexandria, Va.

WATTS, JOHN C.—Age, 18 years. Enlisted, August 15, 1862, at Thompson, to serve three years; mustered in as private, Co. B, October 8, 1862; mustered out with company, July 20, 1865, near Alexandria, Va.

WEBER, JOHN.—Age, 18 years. Enlisted at Goshen, to serve one year, and mustered in as private, Co. B, October 6, 1864; absent, sick at Slough Hospital, Alexandria, Va., at muster-out of company.

WHEELER, LEWIS S.—Age, 28 years. Enlisted, August 15, 1862, at Thompson, to serve three years; mustered in as private, Co. B, October 8, 1862; promoted corporal prior to April 11, 1863; sergeant prior to October, 1864; mustered out with company, July 20, 1865, at Alexandria, Va.

WHITE, JOSEPH.—Age, 24 years. Enlisted, August 16, 1862, at Bethel, to serve three years; mustered in as private, Co. B, October 8, 1862; died of heart disease, November 10, 1864, at Bethel, N. Y.

WHITLEY, GEORGE W.—Age, 41 years. Enlisted, August 22, 1862, at Thompson, to serve three years; mustered in as private,

Co. B, October 8, 1862; died of chronic diarrhea, February 11, 1864, at Seminary Hospital, Covington, Ky.

WRIGHT, JOSEPH.—Age, 35 years. Enlisted, August 14, 1862, at Bethel, to serve three years; mustered in as private, Co. B, October 8, 1862; mustered out with company, July 20, 1865, near Alexandria, Va.

YEOMANS, BENJAMIN M.—Age, 21 years. Enlisted, August 14, 1862, at Forestburg, to serve three years; mustered in as private, Co. B, October 8, 1862; died of chronic diarrhea, October 9, 1863, at Alexandria, Va.

YEOMANS, WILLIAM H.—Age, 18 years. Enlisted, August 14, 1862, at Forestburg, to serve three years; mustered in as private, Co. B, October 8, 1862; accidentally wounded, October 17, 1864; mustered out with company, July 20, 1865, near Alexandria, Va.

YORKS, NICHOLAS.—Age, 40 years. Enlisted, August 18, 1862, at Thompson, to serve three years; mustered in as private, Co. B, October 8, 1862; died of injuries received by railroad accident, March 20, 1863, at Christ Church Hospital, Alexandria, Va.

KILLED IN ACTION.

Bloomingburgh, William J., Mar. 20, 1863, near Alexandria, Va., (accident).

Carpenter, Wm. L., Mar. 31, 1863, killed by sentinel near Fort Worth, Va.

Carrington, Edward, Mar. 6, 1865, at Natural Bridge, Fla.

Hogancamp, John W., Mar. 20, 1863, at Alexandria R. R. accident.

Krum, Luther S., Mar. 20, 1863, at Alexandria R. R. accident.

Lyon, George, Mar. 20, 1863, at Alexandria R. R. accident.

Ray, Edward, Mar. 20, 1863, at Alexandria R. R. accident.

Yorks, Nicholas, Mar. 20, 1863, at Alexandria R. R. accident.

WOUNDED IN ACTION.

Crosby, Scipo L., May 15, 1864, at Resaca, Ga.

Decker, Charles H. T., July 20, 1864, at Peach Tree Creek, Ga.

Hardenburgh, Richard M. J., Mar. 16, 1865, at Averysboro, N. C.

Jacocks, John H., July 20, 1864, at Peach Tree Creek, Ga.
Kinne, Daniel I., Mar. 19, 1865, at Bentonville, N. C.
Rose, Gustus, July 20, 1864, at Peach Tree Creek, Ga.

DIED OF DISEASE AND WOUNDS.

Bollman, Christopher L., Sept. 30, 1863, at Indianapolis, Ind.
Broome, Orval A., April 2, 1864, at Murfreesboro, Tenn.
Brown, Marcus L., July 1, 1863, at Fort Monroe, Va.
Cantine, Nicholas S., June 30, 1864, at David's Island, N. Y.
Carpenter, Benjamin, Jan. 30, 1864, at Indianapolis, Ind.
Cogswell, Richard, Mar. 7, 1864, at Louisville, Ky.
Demorest, Jonathan O., Mar. 20, 1863, at Alexandria, Va.
Durland, Stephen D., Oct. 31, 1864, near Dallas, Ga.
Fitzgerald, James, Dec. 13, 1863, near Athens, Tenn.
Fraser, William J., Nov. 21, 1863, at Nashville, Tenn.
Hardenburgh, Richard M. J., Mar. 16, 1865, at Averysboro,.
N. C.
Hendrickson, John M., Nov. 20, 1863, at Bridgeport, Ala.
Hoar, John, Feb. 14, 1864, at Bridgeport, Ala.
Jackson, John H., Mar. 28, 1863, at Alexandria, Va.
Kent, Charles, Feb. 11, 1865, at Savannah, Ga.
Kinne, Daniel I., Mar. 20, 1865, near Bentonville, N. C.
Lawson, Benjamin, Dec. 3, 1863, at Murfreesboro, Tenn.
O'Neil, Terence, Feb. 20, 1864, at Louisville, Ky.
Pintler, John C., Jan. 29, 1864, at Nashville, Tenn.
Pintler, William, Jan. 7, 1864, at Lookout Valley, Tenn.
Predmore, Abram S., Aug 2, 1863, at Convalescent Camp, Va..
Sutter, Henry, Nov. 25, 1863, at Lookout Valley, Tenn.
Warring, John W., Dec. 15, 1863, at Lookout Valley, Tenn.
Watson, Martin, Jan. 1, 1863, at Upton's Hill, Va.
White, Joseph, Nov. 10, 1864, at Bethel, N. Y.
Whitley, George W., Feb. 11, 1864, at Covington, Ky.
Yeomans, Benjamin M., Oct. 9, 1863, at Alexandria, Va.

DISCHARGED DURING SERVICE.

Baldwin, Alfred J., May 6, 1864, dismissed by General Order.
Benedict, Roberts C., October, 1862.
Bowman, Maegher, Aug. 31, 1863, for disability.

Clark, Garrett T., May 28, 1865, for disability.
Durland, James T., June 30, 1865, for disability.
Jackson, David, Nov. 14, 1863, for disability.
Kent, George A., June 10, 1865, for disability.
Knox, Adna L., Feb. 17, 1864, for disability.
Rose, Austin J., Dec. 24, 1863, for disability.
Sisson, William D., June 29, 1863, for disability.
Slater, Albert H., July 15, 1865, for disability.
Tucker, William, Mar. 23, 1864, for disability.

TRANSFERRED.

Avery, William L., July 16, 1863, to Veteran Reserve Corps.
Brown, Leander T., Aug. 12, 1863, to Signal Corps.
Butler, Patrick, Nov. 15, 1863, to Veteran Reserve Corps.
Comfort, Reeve, April 22, 1864, to Veteran Reserve Corps.
Fisher, Ira, July 1, 1863, to Veteran Reserve Corps.
Howard, Edwin C., Mar. 26, 1864, to Regimental Staff.
Linson, Lyman S., Mar. 4, 1863, to 81st Regt. U. S. C. T.
Lorgan, James A., Dec. 12, 1863, at New York City.
Patterson, John, Feb. 16, 1864, to Veteran Reserve Corps.
Perry, Seneca W., Nov. 22, 1864, to Regimental Staff.
Stanton, John S., Jan. 17, 1865, to Veteran Reserve Corps.
Warring, Hiram B., July 1, 1863, to Veteran Reserve Corps.

DESERTED.

Wager, David H., Dec. 16, 1862, at Washington Hospital.

COMPANY C.

CAPTAINS.

James C. French, original, resigned Mar. 6, 1863.

William R. Bennett, from Mar. 6, 1863, to muster-out of Regt.

FIRST LIEUTENANTS.

Nathaniel C. Clark, original, resigned Feb. 8, 1864.

John R. Groo, from April 19, 1864; resigned Mar. 20, 1865.

Henry H. Hemingway, from April 15, 1865, to muster-out of Regt.

SECOND LIEUTENANTS.

Dwight Divine, original, promoted to First Lieut., Co. F.

Jelliff, Isaac, from Mar. 30, 1863; promoted to First Lieut. Co. B.

Bruce, Elmore, July 24, 1865, not mustered.

RECORD OF MEMBERS OF COMPANY C—ORIGINAL.

ATWELL, GEORGE.—Age, 20 years. Enlisted, August 14, 1862, at Fallsburg, to serve three years; mustered in as private, Co. C, October 8, 1862; promoted corporal, prior to October, 1864; mustered out with detachment, June 24, 1865, at Mt. Pleasant Hospital, Washington, D. C.

BAHRLEY, ANTHONY.—Age, 42 years. Enlisted, August 15, 1862, at Neversink, to serve three years; mustered in as private, Co. C, October 8, 1862; died, October 7, 1863, at Fairfax Seminary Hospital, Va.; also borne as Barhly.

BARNHART, HERMAN A.—Age, 28 years. Enlisted, August 22, 1862, at Rockland, to serve three years; mustered in as private, Co. C, October 8, 1862; died, October 29, 1863, at field hospital, Bridgeport, Ala.

BARNHART, WILLIAM.—Age, 32 years.   Enlisted, August 16, 1862, at Rockland, to serve three years; mustered in as private, Co. C, October 8, 1862; absent, at hospital, Washington, D. C., at muster-out of company.

BENNETT, ASA A.—Age, 29 years.   Enlisted at Goshen, to serve one year, and mustered in as private, Co. C, September 17, 1864; mustered out with detachment, June 10, 1865, near Washington, D. C.

BENNETT, MILTON P.—Age, 20 years.   Enlisted at Goshen, to serve one year, and mustered in as private, Co. C, September 3, 1864; mustered out with detachment, June 10, 1865, near Washington, D. C.

BLACK, JAMES A.—Age, 22 years.   Enlisted, August 10, 1862, at Neversink, to serve three years; mustered in as private, Co. C, October 8, 1862: died, November 5, 1863, at hospital, Murfreesboro, Tenn.

BOWERS, ALFRED.—Age, 25 years.   Enlisted, August 12, 1862, at Fallsburg, to serve three years; mustered in as private, Co. C, October 8, 1862; mustered out with company, July 20, 1865, near Alexandria, Va.

BOWERS, HERMAN.—Age, 28 years.   Enlisted, August 14, 1862, at Fallsburg, to serve three years; mustered in as private, Co. C, October 8, 1862; deserted, April 30, 1863, at hospital, Philadelphia, Pa.

BOWERS, PALMER.—Age, 22 years.   Enlisted, August 15, 1862, at Fallsburg, to serve three years; mustered in as private, Co. C, October 8, 1862; discharged for disability, December 18, 1862, at hospital, Philadelphia, Pa.

BRIGGS, WILLIAM A.—Age, 19 years.   Enlisted, August 8, 1862, at Neversink, to serve three years; mustered in as private, Co. C, October 8, 1862; mustered out with company, July 20, 1865, near Alexandria, Va.

BROCK, ALANSON G.—Age, 41 years.   Enlisted at Goshen, to serve three years, and mustered in as private, Co. C, January 30, 1864; mustered out with company, July 20, 1865, at Washington, D. C.

BROWN, ALBERT.—Age, 26 years. Enlisted, August 15, 1862, at Fallsburg, to serve three years; mustered in as private, Co. C, October 8, 1862; mustered out with company, July 20, 1865, near Alexandria, Va.

BROWN, WILLIAM B.—Age, 26 years. Enlisted, August 22, 1862, at Rockland, to serve three years; mustered in as private, Co. C, October 8, 1862; mustered out with company, July 20, 1865, near Alexandria, Va.

CAUTHERS, HENRY A.—Age, 28 years. Enlisted, August 14, 1862, at Fallsburg, to serve three years; mustered in as private, Co. C, October 8, 1862; mustered out with company, July 20, 1865, near Alexandria, Va.; also borne as Cothers.

CHAPMAN, JONES.—Age, 33 years. Enlisted at Goshen, to serve one year, and mustered in as private, Co. C, September 3, 1864; mustered out with detachment, June 10, 1865, near Washington, D. C.

CLARK, NATHANIEL C.—Age, 27 years. Enrolled, August 6, 1862, at Neversink, to serve three years; mustered in as first lieutenant, Co. C, September 1, 1862; discharged for disability, February 8, 1864. Commissioned first lieutenant, November 21, 1862, with rank from September 1, 1862, original.

CODDINGTON, ABNER J.—Age, 28 years. Enlisted, August 12, 1862, at Fallsburg, to serve three years; mustered in as private, Co. C, October 8, 1862; promoted corporal prior to October, 1864; mustered out with company, July 20, 1865, near Alexandria, Va.

CODDINGTON, MONROE.—Age, 20 years. Enlisted at Goshen, to serve three years, and mustered in as private, Co. C, January 30, 1864; mustered out with company, July 20, 1865, near Alexandria, Va.

CONKLIN, BENJAMIN.—Age, 19 years. Enlisted, August 15, 1862, at Neversink, to serve three years; mustered in as private, Co. C, October 8, 1862; wounded, no date; mustered out with company, July 20, 1865, near Alexandria, Va.

CONKLIN, THEODORE.—Age, 22 years. Enlisted, August 10, 1862, at Neversink, to serve three years; mustered in as private, Co. C, October 8, 1862; discharged for disability, April 14, 1863.

Cox, Joseph E.—Age, 19 years. Enlisted, August 14, 1862, at Neversink, to serve three years; mustered in as private, Co. C, October 8, 1862; discharged for disability, December 26, 1863, at hospital, Louisville, Ky.

Cross, Cornelius.—Age, 24 years. Enlisted, August 20, 1862, at Fallsburg, to serve three years; mustered in as private, Co. C, October 8, 1862; mustered out with company, July 20, 1865, near Alexandria, Va.

Cross, George W.—Age, 18 years. Enlisted, August 14, 1862, at Fallsburg, to serve three years; mustered in as private, Co. C, October 8, 1862; wounded in action, May 25, 1864, at Dallas, Ga.; reported, died of his wounds.

Darbee, Cleavland.—Age, 21 years. Enlisted at Goshen, to serve one year, and mustered in as private, Co. C, September 3, 1862; mustered out with detachment, June 10, 1865, at Washington, D. C.

Darbee, John G.—Age, 25 years. Enlisted at Poughkeepsie, to serve one year, and mustered in as private, Co. C, September 13, 1864; mustered out with detachment, June 10, 1865, at Washington, D. C.; also borne as John A.

Darbee, John W.—Age, 21 years. Enlisted, August 18, 1862, at Rockland, to serve three years; mustered in as corporal, Co. C, October 8, 1862; promoted sergeant, October 12, 1864; mustered out with company, July 20, 1865, near Alexandria, Va.

Dekay, James C.—Age, 18 years. Enlisted, August 21, 1862, at Fallsburg, to serve three years; mustered in as corporal, Co. C, October 8, 1862; mustered out with company, July 20, 1865, near Alexandria, Va.

De Munn, Francis M.—Age, 22 years. Enlisted at Goshen, to serve one year, and mustered in as private, Co. C, September 10, 1864; mustered out with detachment, June 10, 1865, near Washington, D. C.; also borne as Dennin.

Deniston, John G.—Age, 44 years. Enlisted at Goshen, to serve one year, and mustered in as private, Co. C, October 6, 1864; mustered out with company, July 20, 1865, near Alexandria, Va.

DENNIS, WILLIAM C.—Age, 23 years. Enlisted, August 6, 1862, at Neversink, to serve three years; mustered in as private, Co. C, October 8, 1862; discharged for disability, February 23, 1864, at hospital, Nashville, Tenn.

DEWITT, JOHN.—Age, 35 years. Enlisted, August 6, 1862, at Fallsburg, to serve three years; mustered in as private, Co. C, October 8, 1862; deserted, July 14, 1863, on march near Funkstown, Md.

DIVINE, DWIGHT.—Age, 21 years. Enrolled, August 23, 1862, at Fallsburg, to serve three years; mustered in as second lieutenant, Co. C, September 1, 1862; as first lieutenant, Co. F, April 17, 1863; mustered out with company, July 20, 1865, at Washington, D. C. Commissioned second lieutenant, November 21, 1862, with rank from September 1, 1862, original; first lieutenant, October 17, 1863, with rank from March 30, 1863, vice J. F. Anderson, promoted; captain, not mustered, July 24, 1865, with rank from May 16, 1865, vice E. H. Pinney, promoted.

DODGE, McKENDREE N.—Age, 18 years. Enlisted, August 22, 1862, at Fallsburg, to serve three years; mustered in as corporal, Co. C, October 8, 1862; promoted sergeant, May 1, 1864; wounded in action, July 20, 1864, at Peach Tree Creek, Ga.; mustered out with company, July 20, 1865, near Alexandria, Va.

DOLAWAY, STEPHEN L.—Age, 30 years. Enlisted, August 14, 1862, at Fallsburg, to serve three years; mustered in as private, Co. C, October 8, 1862; mustered out with company, July 20, 1865, near Alexandria, Va.; also borne as Dolloway.

DONELSON, JOHN B.—Age, 21 years. Enlisted, August 14, 1862, at Neversink, to serve three years; mustered in as private, Co. C, October 8, 1862; died, February 5, 1864, at Field Hospital, Bridgeport, Ala.

EBERLIN, HENRY.—Age, 30 years. Enlisted, August 21, 1862, at Rockland, to serve three years; mustered in as private, Co. C, October 8, 1862; promoted corporal prior to April, 1863; sergeant, no date; mustered out with company, July 20, 1865, near Alexandria, Va.

ELMORE, BRUCE.—Age, 27 years. Enrolled, August 12, 1862, at Fallsburg, to serve three years; mustered in as sergeant, Co. C,

October 8, 1862; promoted first sergeant prior to October, 1864; mustered out with company, July 20, 1865, near Alexandria, Va. Commissioned, not mustered, second lieutenant, July 24, 1865, with rank from May 16, 1865, vice D. A. Wasim, promoted.

ELMORE, WILLARD.—Age, 24 years. Enlisted, August 14, 1862, at Fallsburg, to serve three years; mustered in as corporal, Co. C, October 8, 1862; returned to ranks prior to April, 1863; promoted corporal, no date; mustered out with company, July 20, 1865, near Alexandria, Va.

EVERITT, CHARLES H.—Age, 28 years. Enlisted, August 6, 1862, at Neversink, to serve three years; mustered in as private, Co. C, October 8, 1862; mustered out with detachment, August 19, 1865, at hospital, Fort Monroe, Va.

EVERITT, GEORGE H.—Age, 22 years. Enlisted, August 15, 1862, at Neversink, to serve three years; mustered in as private, Co. C, October 8, 1862; mustered out with detachment, August 19, 1865, at hospital, Fort Monroe, Va.

FERDON, ANTHONY H.—Age, 32 years. Enlisted, August 22, 1862, at Rockland, to serve three years; mustered in as private, Co. C, October 8, 1862; transferred to Co. F, March 1, 1863; mustered out with company, July 20, 1865, at Washington, D. C., as Furdon.

FINCH, ISAAC NEWTON.—Age, 18 years. Enlisted, August 18, 1862, at Fallsburg, to serve three years; mustered in as private, Co. C, October 8, 1862; discharged for disability, February 9, 1863, at hospital, Philadelphia, Pa.

FINCLE, WILLIAM.—Age, 18 years. Enlisted, August 14, 1862, at Fallsburg, to serve three years; mustered in as private, Co. C, October 8, 1862; mustered out with company, July 20, 1865, near Alexandria, Va.

FIRCH, see Furch.

FRENCH, JAMES C.—Age, — years. Enrolled, August 22, 1862, at Fallsburg, to serve three years; mustered in as captain, Co. C, October 8, 1862; discharged, March 6, 1863. Commissioned captain, November 21, 1862, with rank from September 1, 1862, original.

FURCH, GEORGE H.—Age, 18 years. Enlisted, August 18, 1862, at Fallsburg, to serve three years; mustered in as private, Co. C,

October 8, 1862; mustered out with company, July 20, 1865, near Alexandria, Va.; also borne as Firch.

GARDNER, AUSTIN.—Age, 21 years. Enlisted, August 14, 1862, at Fallsburg, to serve three years; mustered in as private, Co. C, October 8, 1862; mustered out with company, July 20, 1865, near Alexandria, Va.

GORTON, JAMES D.—Age, 38 years. Enlisted, August 15, 1862, at Neversink, to serve three years; mustered in as private, Co. C, October 8, 1862; wounded in action, May 25, 1864, near Dallas, Ga.; mustered out with company, July 20, 1865, near Alexandria, Va.

GORTON, JOHN T.—Age, 20 years. Enlisted, August 14, 1862, at Neversink, to serve three years; mustered in as private, Co. C, October 8, 1862; mustered out with company, July 20, 1865, near Alexandria, Va.

GORTON, NELSON.—Age, 28 years. Enlisted, August 15, 1862, at Fallsburg, to serve three years; mustered in as private, Co. C, October 8, 1862; discharged, May 13, 1865, at Fort Columbus, New York Harbor; also borne as Girton.

HENDRIXON, BLAKE.—Age, 32 years. Enlisted, August 14, 1862, at Fallsburg, to serve three years; mustered in as private, Co. C, October 8, 1862; died, June 30, 1863, at Yorktown, Va.

HENDRIXSON, WILLIAM.—Age, 32 years. Enlisted, August 14, 1862, at Fallsburg, to serve three years; mustered in as private, Co. C, October 8, 1862; wounded, September 22, 1863, at Catlett's Station, Va.; discharged for disability, February 13, 1864, at hospital, Alexandria, Va.

HILL, MATHEW.—Age, 20 years. Enlisted, August 15, 1862, at Neversink, to serve three years; mustered in as private, Co. C, October 8, 1862; died, December 2, 1864, at hospital, Covington, Ky.

HILL, WILLIAM.—Age, 25 years. Enlisted, August 15, 1862, at Neversink, to serve three years; mustered in as private, Co. C, October 8, 1862; promoted corporal prior to April, 1863; wounded in action, October 29, 1863, at Wauhatchie, Tenn.; discharged for disability, February 27, 1865, at hospital, New York.

HITT, FRANKLIN M.—Age, 18 years. Enlisted at Goshen, to serve one year, and mustered in as private, Co. C, September 3, 1864; mustered out, July 6, 1865, at McDougall Hospital, New York Harbor.

HITT, JAMES M.—Age, 43 years. Enlisted, August 22, 1862, at Rockland, to serve three years; mustered in as sergeant, Co. C, October 8, 1862; died, August 11, 1863, in hospital at Annapolis, Md.

HOOD, GEORGE W.—Age, 34 years. Enlisted at Goshen, to serve one year, and mustered in as private, Co. C, September 17, 1864; mustered out with detachment, June 10, 1865, near Washington, D. C.

HORNBECK, JOHN.—Age, 18 years. Enlisted, August 12, 1862, at Fallsburg, to serve three years; mustered in as private, Co. C, October 8, 1862; mustered out with company, July 20, 1865, near Alexandria, Va.

JONES, BENJAMIN.—Age, 38 years. Enlisted, September 1, 1862, at Fallsburg, to serve three years; mustered in as private, Co. C, October 8, 1862; transferred to Co. H, Tenth Regiment, Veteran Reserve Corps, July 10, 1864; discharged, July 13, 1865, at Washington, D. C.

JONES, JONATHAN.—Age, 19 years. Enlisted, August 12, 1862, at Fallsburg, to serve three years; mustered in as corporal, Co. C, October 8, 1862; promoted sergeant, no date; died, December 5, 1863, at hospital, Louisville, Ky.

LAWRENCE, GILBERT.—Age, 19 years. Enlisted, August 12, 1862, at Fallsburg, to serve three years; mustered in as private, Co. C, October 8, 1862; wounded in action, July 20, 1864, at Peach Tree Creek, Ga.; died of his wounds, July 26, 1864, at Field Hospital, Ga.

LAWRENCE, PETER E.—Age, 21 years. Enlisted, August 12, 1862, at Fallsburg, to serve three years; mustered in as private, Co. C, October 8, 1862; mustered out with company, July 20, 1865, near Alexandria, Va.

LEROY, PETER H.—Age, 30 years. Enlisted, August 12, 1862, at Fallsburg, to serve three years; mustered in as private, Co. C,

October 8, 1862; deserted, April 30, 1863, from hospital, Philadelphia, Pa.; also borne as Peter W.

LESLIE, JAMES C.—Age, 18 years. Enlisted, August 15, 1862, at Neversink, to serve three years; mustered in as private, Co. C, October 8, 1862; mustered out with company, July 20, 1865, near Alexandria, Va.; also borne as James E.

LEWIS, REUBEN A.—Age, 20 years. Enlisted, August 10, 1862, at Neversink, to serve three years; mustered in as private, Co. C, October 8, 1862; mustered out with company, July 20, 1865, near Alexandria, Va.

LEWIS, WILLIAM B.—Age, 27 years. Enlisted, August 10, 1862, at Neversink, to serve three years; mustered in as private, Co. C, October 8, 1862; mustered out with company, July 20, 1865, near Alexandria, Va.

LOCKWOOD, DANIEL C.—Age, 22 years. Enlisted, August 12, 1862, at Fallsburg, to serve three years; mustered in as private, Co. C, October 8, 1862; discharged for disability, April 27, 1863, at Fairfax Seminary Hospital, Va.

LOW, JAMES.—Age, 23 years. Enlisted, August 14, 1862, at Fallsburg, to serve three years; mustered in as private, Co. C, October 8, 1862; appointed musician prior to April 11, 1863; mustered out with company, July 20, 1865, near Alexandria, Va.

LOW, JONATHAN W.—Age, 44 years. Enlisted, August 19, 1862, at Fallsburg, to serve three years; mustered in as sergeant, Co. C, October 8, 1862; returned to ranks, December 14, 1862; discharged for disability, May 3, 1865, at McDougall Hospital, Fort Schuyler, New York Harbor.

MACKNEY, SAMUEL J.—Age, 32 years. Enlisted, August 11, 1862, at Fallsburg, to serve three years; mustered in as private, Co. C, October 8, 1862; drowned, June 1, 1864, at Madison, Ind.; also borne as McKeny.

MANETT, GEORGE V.—Age, 23 years. Enlisted, August 14, 1862, at Fallsburgh, to serve three years; mustered in as corporal, Co. C, October 8, 1862; promoted sergeant prior to October, 1864; mustered out with company, July 20, 1865, near Alexandria, Va.

MARRICLE, see Merical, Co. C.

MARTIN, GIDEON W.—Age, 23 years. Enlisted at Goshen, to serve one year, and mustered in as private, Co. C, September 3, 1864; mustered out with detachment, June 10, 1865, near Washington, D. C.

MATHEWS, LORENZO.—Age, 22 years. Enlisted at Goshen, to serve one year, and mustered in as private, Co. C, September 13, 1864; mustered out with detachment, June 10, 1865, near Washington, D. C.

MEDDEUCH, ABRAM.—Age, 28 years. Enlisted, August 14, 1862, at Fallsburg, to serve three years; never mustered in as private, Co. C, on account of injuries received after enlistment.

MEDLER, WILLIAM O.—Age, 18 years. Enlisted, Augsut 14, 1862, at Fallsburg, to serve three years; mustered in as private, Co. C, October 8, 1862; discharged for disability, April 23, 1863, at hospital, Washington, D. C.

MERICAL WILLIAM P.—Age, 21 years. Enlisted, August 15, 1862, at Fallsburg, to serve three years; mustered in as private, Co. C, October 8, 1862; mustered out with company, July 20, 1865, near Alexandria, Va., as Marricle.

MILLER, DAVID.—Age, 24 years. Enlisted, August 15, 1862, at Neversink, to serve three years; mustered in as private, Co. C, October 8, 1862; transferred to Co. B, Tenth Regiment, Veteran Reserve Corps, July 21, 1863; mustered out, July 13, 1865, at Washington, D. C.

MORGAN, ISAAC.—Age, 26 years. Enlisted, August 6, 1862, at Neversink, to serve three years; mustered in as private, Co. C, October 8, 1862; wounded in action, May 25, 1864, at Dallas, Ga.; mustered out with company, July 20, 1865, near Alexandria, Va.

NEWMAN, AUSTIN D.—Age, 20 years. Enlisted, August 22, 1862, at Fallsburg, to serve three years; mustered in as private, Co. C, October 8, 1862; transferred to Veteran Reserve Corps, May 15, 1864.

NEWMAN, WILLIAM H.—Age, 19 years. Enlisted, August 14, 1862, at Fallsburg, to serve three years; mustered in as private, Co. C, October 8, 1862; promoted corporal, no date; mustered out with company, July 20, 1865, near Alexandria, Va.

PALEN, PETER E.—Age, 19 years. Enrolled, August 12, 1862, at Fallsburg, to serve three years; mustered in as first sergeant, Co. C, October 8, 1862; mustered in as second lieutenant, Co. F, March 27, 1863; as first lieutenant, Co. K, May 1, 1864; mustered out with company, July 20, 1865, at Washington, D. C. Commissioned second lieutenant, October 17, 1863, with rank from March 26, 1863, vice F. Buckley, resigned; first lieutenant, April 18, 1864, with rank from February 13, 1864, vice W. T. George, promoted.

PALMER, JOHN J.—Age, 34 years. Enlisted, August 14, 1862, at Fallsburg, to serve three years; mustered in as private, Co. C, October 8, 1862; mustered out with company, July 20, 1865, near Alexandria, Va.

PATMORE, DAVID A.—Age, 32 years. Enlisted, August 12, 1862, at Fallsburg, to serve three years; mustered in as private, Co. C, October 8, 1862; mustered out, May 16, 1865, at Nashville, Tenn.

PERKLEY, ELIJAH P.—Age, 20 years. Enlisted, August 12, 1862, at Fallsburg, to serve three years; mustered in as private, Co. C, October 8, 1862; died, April 15, 1864, at hospital, Nashville, Tenn.; also borne as Perkey.

POWELL, RUSSELL.—Age, 25 years. Enlisted at Goshen, to serve one year, and mustered in as private, Co. C, September 3, 1864; mustered out with detachment, June 10, 1865, at Washington, D. C.

PURHAMUS, EMERY.—Age, 26 years. Enlisted, August 6, 1862, at Fallsburg, to serve three years; mustered in as private, Co. C, October 8, 1862; discharged for disability, January 19, 1863, at Central Park Hospital, New York city; also borne as Perhamous.

REYNOLDS, NELSON T.—Age, 19 years. Enlisted, August 22, 1862, at Fallsburg, to serve three years; mustered in as private, Co. C, October 8, 1862; discharged for disability, March 20, 1863, at hospital, Philadelphia, Pa.

ROOSA, FRANCIS M.—Age, 19 years. Enlisted, August 12, 1862, at Fallsburg, to serve three years; mustered in as private, Co. C, October 8, 1862; died, October 21, 1864, while on furlough, at Neversink, N. Y.; also borne as Francis J.

Rowe, Orin D.—Age, 22 years. Enlisted at Goshen, to serve one year, and mustered in as private, Co. C, September 3, 1864; mustered out with company, July 20, 1865, at Washington, D. C.

Rowe, Samuel A.—Age, 24 years. Enlisted, August 22, 1862, at Rockland, to serve three years; mustered in as private, Co. C, October 8, 1862; promoted corporal prior to October, 1864; mustered out, October 3, 1865, at Elmira, N. Y.

Rusa, John C.—Age, 45 years. Enlisted, August 15, 1862, at Neversink, to serve three years; mustered in as private, Co. C, October 8, 1862; died, October 8, 1863, at hospital, Fairfax Seminary, Va.; also borne as Roosa.

Schoonmaker, Moses.—Age, 30 years. Enlisted, August 14, 1862, at Fallsburg, to serve three years; mustered in as private, Co. C, October 8, 1862; transferred to One Hundred and Fifty-fifth Company, Second Battalion, Veteran Reserve Corps, March 15, 1865; mustered out, August 1, 1865, at Nashville, Tenn.

Scoonmaker, Moses H.—Age, 23 years. Enlisted, August 14, 1862, at Fallsburg, to serve three years; mustered in as private, Co. C, October 8, 1862; died, July 26, 1863, at hospital, Hampton, Va.

Shelley, Tobias C.—Age, 22 years. Enlisted, August 6, 1862, at Fallsburg, to serve three years; mustered in as corporal, Co. C, October 8, 1862; promoted sergeant prior to April 11, 1863; transferred to Veteran Reserve Corps, December 1, 1863.

Shultis, William H.—Age, 22 years. Enlisted, August 15, 1862, at Neversink, to serve three years; mustered in as private, Co. C, October 8, 1862; mustered out with company, July 20, 1865, near Alexandria, Va.; also borne as Shultze.

Simpson, Charles H.—Age, 19 years. Enlisted, August 14, 1862, at Fallsburg, to serve three years; mustered in as private, Co. C, October 8, 1862; wounded in action, October 29, 1863, at Lookout Valley, Tenn.; died of his wounds, November 26, 1863, at hospital, Nashville, Tenn.

Sprague, Dewitt C.—Age, 27 years. Enlisted, August 22, 1862, at Rockland, to serve three years; mustered in as private, Co. C, October 8, 1862; mustered out, June 17, 1865, at Lincoln Hospital, Washington, D. C.

STARE, SANFORD M.—Age, 19 years. Enlisted, August 14, 1862, at Fallsburg, to serve three years; mustered in as private, Co. C, October 8, 1862; discharged for disability, March 5, 1863, at Stanton Hospital, Washington, D. C.; also borne as Starr.

STEWART, JAMES W.—Age, 19 years. Enlisted, August 12, 1862, at Fallsburg, to serve three years; mustered in as private, Co. C, October 8, 1862; promoted corporal, no date; mustered out with company, July 20, 1865, near Alexandria, Va.

STRATTON, CYRUS J.—Age, 28 years. Enlisted at Kingston, to serve one year, and mustered in as private, Co. C. September 20, 1864; mustered out with detachment, June 10, 1865, near Washington, D. C.

SWARTHOUT, ALEXANDER E.—Age, 44 years. Enlisted at Goshen, to serve one year, and mustered in as private, Co. C, September 15, 1864; mustered out with detachment, June 10, 1865, near Washington, D. C.

TAYLOR, JAMES M.—Age, 35 years. Enlisted, August 15, 1862, at Neversink, to serve three years; mustered in as private, Co. C, October 8, 1862; died, January 31, 1864, at hospital, Nashville, Tenn.

TAYLOR, WILLIAM J.—Age, 20 years. Enlisted, August 15, 1862, at Neversink, to serve three years; mustered in as private, Co. C, October 8, 1862; discharged for disability, December 10, 1862, at College Hospital, Georgetown, D. C.

TERWILLIGER, BENJAMIN.—Age, 18 years. Enlisted at Goshen, to serve one year, and mustered in as private, Co. C, October 13, 1864; mustered out, July 1, 1865, at Carver Hospital, Washington, D. C.

TERWILLIGER, SEVERYN M.—Age, 43 years. Enlisted, August 15, 1862, at Fallsburg, to serve three years; mustered in as private, Co. C, October 8, 1862; died, November 6, 1863, at hospital, Washington, D. C.

TRIPP, PETER C.—Age, 32 years. Enlisted, August 22, 1862, at Rockland, to serve three years; mustered in as private, Co. C, October 8, 1862; mustered out with company, July 20, 1865, near Alexandria, Va.

TYRELL, WILLIAM.—Age, 18 years. Enlisted, August 19, 1862, at Fallsburg, to serve three years; mustered in as private, Co. C, October 8, 1862; mustered out, June 9, 1865, at hospital, Fort Monroe, Va.

UPHAM, GEORGE W.—Age, 33 years. Enlisted, August 12, 1862, at Fallsburg, to serve three years; mustered in as private, Co. C, October 8, 1862; mustered out with company, July 20, 1865, near Alexandria, Va.

VAN WAGONER, GEORGE W.—Age, 21 years. Enlisted, August 12, 1862, at Fallsburg, to serve three years; mustered in as private, Co. C, October 8, 1862; mustered out with company, July 20, 1865, near Alexandria, Va.

VREDENBURGH, HENRY H.—Age, 44 years. Enlisted, August 6, 1862, at Neversink, to serve three years; mustered in as private, Co. C, October 8, 1862; discharged for disability, August 18, 1863, at hospital, Hampton, Va.

VREDENBURGH, HENRY J.—Age, 24 years. Enlisted, September 1, 1862, at Fallsburg, to serve three years; mustered in as private, Co. C, October 8, 1862; discharged for disability, June 1, 1863, at hospital, Fairfax Seminary, Va.

VREDENBURGH, JACOB C.—Age, 22 years. Enlisted, September 1, 1862, at Fallsburg, to serve three years; mustered in as private, Co. C, October 8, 1862; mustered out with company, July 20, 1865, near Alexandria, Va.

WAMSLEY, JOHN.—Age, 21 years. Enlisted, August 22, 1862, at Rockland, to serve three years; mustered in as private, Co. C, October 8, 1862; transferred to Thirtieth Company, Second Battalion, Veteran Reserve Corps, September 26, 1863; mustered out, October 7, 1865, at Fort Monroe, Va.; also borne as Wansley.

WHITE, ABRAHAM.—Age, 38 years. Enlisted, August 22, 1862, at Rockland, to serve three years; mustered in as private, Co. C, October 8, 1862; died, July 20, 1863, near Boonsboro, Md.

WHITTAKER, HENRY.—Age, 36 years. Enlisted, August 18, 1862, at Fallsburg, to serve three years; mustered in as private, Co. C, October 8, 1862; mustered out, May 31, 1865, at McDougall Hospital, Fort Schuyler, New York Harbor.

WICKS, CHARLES.—Age, 26 years. Enlisted, August 12, 1862, at Fallsburg, to serve three years; mustered in as private, Co. C, October 8, 1862; promoted corporal, October 12, 1864; mustered out with company, July 20, 1865, near Alexandria, Va.

WILSON, ANDREW S.—Age, 27 years. Enlisted, August 14, 1862, at Fallsburg, to serve three years; mustered in as private, Co. C, October 8, 1862; discharged for disability, April 13, 1863, at Fairfax Seminary Hospital, Alexandria, Va.

WILSON, JAMES B.—Age, 21 years. Enlisted, August 22, 1862, at Rockland, to serve three years; mustered in as sergeant, Co. C, October 8, 1862; discharged for disability, October 11, 1864.

WOUNDED IN ACTION.

Conklin, Benjamin, no date.
Cross, George W., May 25, 1864, near Dallas, Ga.
Dodge, McKendree N., July 20, 1864, at Peach Tree Creek, Ga.
Gorton, James D., May 25, 1864, near Dallas, Ga.
Hendrixon, William, Sept. 22, 1863, at Catlett's Station, Va.
Hill, William, Oct. 29, 1863, at Wauhatchie, Tenn.
Lawrence, Gilbert, July 20, 1864, at Peach Tree Creek, Ga.
Morgan, Isaac, May 25, 1864, near Dallas, Ga.
Simpson, Charles H., Oct. 29, 1863, at Lookout Valley, Tenn.

DIED OF DISEASE AND WOUNDS.

Bahrley, Anthony, Oct. 7, 1863, at Fairfax Seminary, Va.
Barnhart, Herman, Oct. 29, 1863, at Bridgeport, Ala.
Black, James A., Nov. 5, 1863, at Murfreesboro, Tenn.
Donelson, John B., Feb. 5, 1864, at Bridgeport, Ala.
Hendrixon, Blake, June 30, 1863, at Yorktown, Va.
Hill, Mathew, Dec. 2, 1864, at Covington, Ky.
Hitt, James M., Aug. 11, 1863, at Annapolis, Md.
Jones, Jonathan, Dec. 5, 1863, at Louisville, Ky.
Lawrence, Gilbert, July 26, 1864, at Field Hospital, Ga.
Mackney, Samuel J., June 1, 1864, drowned at Madison, Ind.
Perkley, Elijah P., April 15, 1864, at Nashville, Tenn.
Roosa, Francis M., Oct. 21, 1864, at Neversink, N. Y.
Rusa, John C., Oct. 8, 1863, at Fairfax Seminary, Va.
Simpson, Charles H., Nov. 26, 1863, at Nashville, Tenn.

Taylor, James M., Jan. 31, 1864, at Nashville, Tenn.
Terwilliger, Severyn M., Nov. 6, 1863, at Washington, D. C.
White, Abraham, July 20, 1863, at Boonsboro, Md.

DISCHARGED DURING SERVICE.

Bowers, Palmer, Dec. 18, 1862, for disability.
Clark, Nathaniel C., Feb. 8, 1864, for disability.
Conklin, Theodore, April 14, 1863, for disability.
Cox, Joseph E., Dec. 26, 1863, for disability.
Cross, George W., reported, died of wounds.
Dennis, William C., Feb. 23, 1864, for disability.
Finch, Isaac Newton, Feb. 9, 1863, for disability.
French, James C., Mar. 6, 1863, for disability.
Gorton, Nelson, May 13, 1865, for disability.
Hendrixon, William, Feb. 13, 1864, for disability.
Hill, William, Feb. 27, 1865, for disability.
Hitt, Franklin M., July 6, 1865, for disability.
Lockwood, Daniel C., April 27, 1863, for disability.
Low, Jonathan W., May 3, 1865, for disability.
Medler William O., April 23, 1863, for disability.
Patmore, David A., May 16, 1865, for disability.
Purhamus, Emery, Jan. 19, 1863, for disability.
Reynolds, Nelson T., Mar. 20, 1863, for disability.
Sprague, Dewitt C., June 17, 1865, for disability.
Stare, Sanford M., Mar. 5, 1863, for disability.
Taylor, William J., Dec. 10, 1862, for disability.
Terwilliger, Benjamin, July 1, 1865, for disability.
Tyler, William, June 6, 1865, for disability.
Vreedenburgh, Henry H., Aug. 18, 1863, for disability.
Whittaker, Henry, May 31, 1865, for disability.
Wilson, Andrew, April 13, 1863, for disability.
Wilson ,James B., Oct. 11, 1864, for disability.

TRANSFERRED.

Ferdon, Anthony H., to Co. F, Mar. 1, 1863.
Jones, Benjamin, July 10, 1864, to Veteran Reserve Corps.
Miller, David, July 21, 1863, to Veteran Reserve Corps.
Newman, Austin D., May 15, 1864, to Veteran Reserve Corps.

Schoonmaker, Moses, Mar. 15, 1865, to Veteran Reserve Corps.
Shelley, Tobias C., Dec. 1, 1863, to Veteran Reserve Corps.
Wamsley, John, Sept. 26, 1863, to Veteran Reserve Corps.

Deserted.

Bowers, Herman, April 30, 1863, at Philadelphia, Pa.
Davitt, John, July 14, 1863, near Finkstown, Md.
Leroy, Peter H., April 30, 1863, at Philadelphia, Pa.

COMPANY D.

CAPTAINS.

John Higgins, original, promoted to Major, Jan. 9, 1864.
Lewis N. Stanton, from May 1, 1864, to muster-out of Regt..
(Bvt. Major N. Y. V.)

FIRST LIEUTENANTS.

C. Howell North, original, promoted to Captain Co. K.
William S. Moffat, from Jan. 1, 1864; resigned, Feb. 13, 1864..
DeWtit C. Apgar, from Feb. 14, 1864; promoted to Captain,
Co. E.
Albert B. Gordon, from April 26, 1865, to muster-out of Regt..

SECOND LIEUTENANTS.

John R. Groo, original, promoted to First Lieut. Co. C.
William A. Bennett, July 24, 1865; not mustered.

RECORD OF MEMBERS OF COMPANY D—ORIGINAL.

ALLEN, DAVID L.—Age, 26 years. Enlisted, August 19, 1862,.
at Ithaca, to serve three years; mustered in as private, Co. D, October 8, 1862; deserted, October 14, 1862, at New York city.

ANDERSON, JARED.—Age, 26 years. Enlisted, August 6, 1862..
at Ithaca, to serve three years; mustered in as sergeant, Co. D,.
October 8, 1862; promoted first sergeant, no date; discharged for
disability, December 25, 1862, at Ascension Hospital, Washington, D. C.

APGAR, DEWITT C.—Age, 23 years. Enrolled, September 5,.
1862, at Ithaca, to serve three years; mustered in as first sergeant,
Co. D, October 8, 1862; promoted sergeant-major, October 9,.
1862; mustered in as second lieutenant, Co. A, April 17, 1863; as.

first lieutenant, Co. D, February 14, 1864; as captain, Co. E,. April 1, 1865; mustered out with company, July 20, 1865, at Washington, D. C. Commissioned second lieutenant, October 17, 1863, with rank from March 5, 1863, vice G. Young, promoted; first lieutenant, April 18, 1864, with rank from February 13, 1864, vice W. S. Moffat, resigned; captain, April 15, 1865, with rank from February 10, 1865, vice J. F. Anderson, discharged.

BEMENT, ALBERT.—Age, 28 years. Enlisted, August 19, 1862, at Ithaca, to serve three years; mustered in as private, Co. D, October 8, 1862; promoted corporal, June 1, 1865; mustered out with company, July 20, 1865, at Washington, D. C.

BENNETT, WILLIAM A.—Age, 31 years. Enrolled, August 21, 1862, at Ithaca, to serve three years; mustered in as corporal, Co. D, October 8, 1862; promoted sergeant prior to April 11, 1863; first sergeant, no date; mustered out with company, July 20, 1865, at Washington, D. C. Commissioned, not mustered, second lieutenant, July 24, 1865, with rank from May 16, 1865, vice J. R. Gros, promoted.

BERRY, WILLIAM.—Age, 18 years. Enlisted, August 20, 1862, at Ithaca, to serve three years; mustered in as private, Co. D, October 8, 1862; discharged, July 6, 1865.

BICKEL, ADAM.—Age, 40 years. Enlisted, August 17, 1862, at Lansing, to serve three years; mustered in as private, Co. D, October 8, 1862; discharged for disability, December 22, 1862, at Columbia College Hospital, Washington, D. C.

BISHOP, JEREMIAH.—Age, 42 years. Enlisted, August 20, 1862, at Ithaca, to serve three years; mustered in as private, Co. D, October 8, 1862; discharged, February 16, 1863.

BREITENBUCHER, ADAM.—Age, 35 years. Enlisted, August 6, 1862, at Ithaca, to serve three years; mustered in as private, Co. D, October 8, 1862; mustered out with company, July 20, 1865, at Washington, D. C.

BUNNELL, LUTHER G.—Age, 26 years. Enlisted, August 16, 1862, at Lansing, to serve three years; mustered in as private, Co. D, October 8, 1862; promoted corporal prior to April 11, 1863; died of wounds received in action, June 26, 1864, at hospital, Chattanooga, Tenn.

BURTON, CHARLES.—Age, 23 years. Enlisted, August 20, 1862, at Thomson, to serve three years; mustered in as private, Co. D, October 8, 1862; discharged, January 24, 1863.

CAMPION, WILLIAM.—Age, 21 years. Enlisted, August 6, 1862, at Ithaca, to serve three years; mustered in as private, Co. D, October 8, 1862; deserted, October 14, 1862, at New York city.

CARR, GEHIAL.—Age, 36 years. Enlisted, August 6, 1862, at Ithaca, to serve three years; mustered in as private, Co. D, October 8, 1862; died of heart disease subsequent to June, 1863, at Tompkins County, N. Y.

COE, HENRY.—Age, 30 years. Enlisted, August 6, 1862, at Ithaca, to serve three years; mustered in as private, Co. D, October 8, 1862; transferred to Eighth Regiment, Veteran Reserve Corps, no date; mustered out, June 14, 1865, at Quincy, Ill.

COE, NELSON.—Age, 35 years. Enlisted at Ithaca, to serve three years, and mustered in as private, Co. D, February 17, 1864; absent, in hospital, at Jeffersonville, Ind., at muster-out of company.

COLLINS, JOHN.—Age, 22 years. Enlisted, August 16, 1862, at Lansing, to serve three years; mustered in as private, Co. D, October 8, 1862; mustered out with company, July 20, 1865, at Washington, D. C.

CONKLIN, FRANK.—Age, 18 years. Enlisted, August 6, 1862, at Ithaca, to serve three years; mustered in as private, Co. D, October 8, 1862; mustered out with company, July 20, 1865, at Washington, D. C.

CORKINS, ASA A.—Age, 37 years. Enlisted, August 20, 1862, at Lansing, to serve three years; mustered in as corporal, Co. D, October 8, 1862; transferred to Veteran Reserve Corps, June 16, 1864.

CORNELIUS, HORACE.—Age, 22 years. Enlisted, August 6, 1862, at Ithaca, to serve three years; mustered in as sergeant, Co. D, October 8, 1862; returned to ranks prior to April, 1863; captured, April 14, 1865; paroled, April 29, 1865; mustered out, June 28, 1865, at New York city.

CRIDDLE, WILLIAM H.—Age, 21 years. Enlisted, August 16, 1862, at Ithaca, to serve three years; mustered in as private, Co.

D, October 8, 1862; absent, recruiting at New York, since July 24, 1863, and at muster-out of company.

CRONCE, WILLIAM H.—Age, 18 years. Enlisted, August 6, 1862, at Ithaca, to serve three years; mustered in as private, Co. D, October 8, 1862; mustered out with company, July 20, 1865, at Washington, D. C.

CURTIS, EDWIN.—Age, 40 years. Enlisted, August 27, 1862, at Ithaca, to serve three years; mustered in as private, Co. D, October 8, 1862; mustered out with company ,July 20, 1865, at Washington, D. C.

DAVIS, JAMES W.—Age, 27 years. Enlisted, August 18, 1862, at Lansing, to serve three years; mustered in as private, Co. D, October 8, 1862; mustered out with company, July 20, 1865, at Washington, D. C.

DEPEW, ELIAS G.—Age, 18 years. Enlisted at Goshen, to serve one year, and mustered in as private, Co. D, September 9, 1864; mustered out, June 10, 1865, near Washington, D. C.

DESCHNER, THEODORE.—Age, 19 years. Enlisted, August 10, 1862, at Ithaca, to serve three years; mustered in as private, Co. D, October 8, 1862; promoted corporal prior to April 11, 1863; sergeant, no date; absent, on furlough, since June 24, 1865, and at muster-out of company.

DICKINSON, JOHN W.—Age, 21 years. Enlisted, August 21, 1862, at Ithaca, to serve three years; mustered in as private, Co. D, October 8, 1862; transferred to Co. I, Fifth Regiment, Veteran Reserve Corps, no date; discharged, July 19, 1865, at Burnside Barracks, Indianapolis, Ind.

DICKINSON, WILLET J.—Age, 18 years. Enlisted, August 15, 1862, at Ithaca, to serve three years; mustered in as private, Co. D, October 8, 1862; transferred to Co. G, Sixteenth Regiment, Veteran Reserve Corps, April 6, 1864; mustered out, July 23, 1865, at Camp Hinks, Harrisburg, Pa.

DODD, REUBEN W.—Age, 22 years. Enlisted, August 28, 1862, at Ithaca, to serve three years; mustered in as corporal, Co. D, October 8, 1862; promoted sergeant prior to April 11, 1863; first sergeant prior to October, 1864; returned to ranks, no date; mustered out with company, July 20, 1865, at Washington, D. C.

DUNLEAVY, DENNIS.—Age, 40 years. Enlisted, August 6, 1862, at Ithaca, to serve three years; mustered in as private, Co. D, October 8, 1862; transferred to Veteran Reserve Corps, March 7, 1864, as Dunleavey.

EGBERT, JAMES D.—Age, 44 years. Enlisted, August 20, 1862, at Lansing, to serve three years; mustered in as sergeant, Co. D, October 8, 1862; promoted first sergeant prior to April, 1863: discharged, December 28, 1863.

FRALICK, CLARK.—Age, 19 years. Enlisted, August 6, 1862, at Ithaca, to serve three years; mustered in as private, Co. D, October 8, 1862; promoted corporal prior to October, 1864; returned to ranks, no date; mustered out with company, July 20, 1865, at Washington, D. C.

FRALICK, EDWIN.—Age, 22 years. Enlisted, September 23, 1862, at Ithaca, to serve three years; mustered in as private, Co. D, October 8, 1862; mustered out with company, July 20, 1865, at Washington, D. C.

FRANCIS, JOHN.—Age, 45 years. Enlisted, August 29, 1862. at Thompson, to serve three years; mustered in as private, Co. D, October 8, 1862; discharged for disability, December 27, 1864, at hospital, David's Island, New York Harbor.

GARDNER, JOHN B.—Age, 40 years. Enlisted, August 21, 1862, at Ithaca, to serve three years; mustered in as corporal, Co. D, October 8, 1862; died of typhoid fever, January 25, 1863, at Upton's Hill, Va.

GROO, JOHN R.—Age, 23 years. Enrolled, September 15, 1862, at Monticello, to serve three years; mustered in as second lieutenant, Co. D, October 8, 1862; as first lieutenant, Co. C, March 26, 1864; discharged for disability to date, March 20, 1865. Commissioned second lieutenant, November 21, 1862, with rank from October 8, 1862, original; first lieutenant, April 18, 1864, with rank from January 25, 1864, vice N. C. Clark, discharged.

GUEST, CHARLES W.—Age, 22 years. Enlisted, August 17, 1862, at Lansing, to serve three years; mustered in as private, Co. D, October 8, 1862; promoted corporal, no date; died of typhoid fever, January 30, 1863, at Upton's Hill, Va.

HALLADAY, ADELBERT.—Age, 18 years. Enlisted, August 10, 1862, at Ithaca, to serve three years; mustered in as private, Co. D, October 8, 1862; transferred to Veteran Reserve Corps, March 7, 1864; also borne as Halliday.

HALLIDAY, DENSLOW.—Age, 39 years. Enlisted, August 20, 1862, at Ithaca, to serve three years; mustered in as sergeant, Co. D, October 8, 1862; absent on furlough since July 1, 1865, and at muster-out of company.

HARRINGTON, STEPHEN R.—Age, 28 years. Enlisted, August 4, 1862, at Ithaca, to serve three years; mustered in as private, Co. D, October 8, 1862; discharged, November 26, 1863.

HARRIS, RUSSELL.—Age, 35 years. Enlisted, August 20, 1862, at Lansing, to serve three years; mustered in as private, Co. D, October 8, 1862; mustered out with company, July 20, 1865, at Washington, D. C.

HAVENS, ANSEL B.—Age, 29 years. Enlisted, August 12, 1862, at Ithaca, to serve three years; mustered in as private, Co. D, October 8, 1862; mustered out with company, July 20, 1865, at Washington, D. C.

HENDERSHOT, CHARLES W.—Age, 21 years. Enlisted, August 6, 1862, at Ithaca, to serve three years; mustered in as corporal, Co. D, October 8, 1862; returned to ranks and transferred to Co. G, Twelfth Regiment, Veteran Reserve Corps, no dates; re-transferred to this regiment, April 5, 1864; deserted, July 6, 1865, near Alexandria, Va.

HIBBARD, GEORGE.—Age, 19 years. Enlisted, August 6, 1862, at Ithaca, to serve three years; mustered in as private, Co. D, October 8, 1862; deserted, October 14, 1862, at New York city.

HIGGINS, JOHN.—Age, 27 years. Enrolled, July 26, 1862, at Ithaca, to serve three years; mustered in as captain, Co. D, October 8, 1862; as major, January 9, 1864; discharged, May 16, 1865, for disability caused from wounds received in action. Commissioned captain, November 21, 1862, with rank from September 2, 1862, original; major, January 8, 1864, with rank from November 25, 1863, vice H. Watkins, promoted.

HITCHCOX, WILLIAM.—Age, 43 years. Enlisted, August 20, 1862, at Ithaca, to serve three years; mustered in as private, Co.

D, October 8, 1862; transferred to Veteran Reserve Corps, May 20, 1863.

HOLMES, WILLIAM.—Age, 36 years.   Enlisted, August 28, 1862, at Ithaca, to serve three years; mustered in as private, Co. D, October 8, 1862; promoted corporal prior to April, 1863; died of remittent fever, July 16, 1863, at hospital, Fortress Monroe, Va.

HOLLY, JOHN C.—Age, 43 years. Enlisted, August 6, 1862, at Ithaca, to serve three years; mustered in as private, Co. D, October 8, 1862; mustered out with company, July 20, 1865, at Washington, D. C.

HOUGHTALIN, JOHN.—Age, 34 years.   Enlisted, August 20, 1862, at Woodburn, to serve three years; mustered in as private, Co. D, October 8, 1862; mustered out with company, July 20, 1865, at Washington, D. C., as Houghtailing.

HOUGHTALIN, SANDS.—Age, 38 years. Enlisted, September 6, 1862, at Fallsburg, to serve three years; mustered in as private, Co. D, October 8, 1862; mustered out with company, July 20, 1865, at Washington, D. C., as Sands R. Houghtailing.

JACOBS, ALBERT L.—Age, 41 years. Enlisted, August 11, 1862, at Ithaca, to serve three years; mustered in as private, Co. D, October 8, 1862; discharged, July 1, 1865, at Carver Hospital, Washington, D. C.

JOHNSON, JR., NORMAN C.—Age, 18 years.   Enlisted, August 12, 1862, at Ithaca, to serve three years; mustered in as private, Co. D, October 8, 1862; captured, April 14, 1865; paroled, April 30, 1865; mustered out, June 30, 1865, at New York city.

LAYTON, CHARLES.—Age, 22 years. Enlisted, August 15, 1862, at Callicoon, to serve three years; mustered in as private, Co. D, October 8, 1862; mustered out, June 16, 1865, at hospital, Baltimore, Md.

LINDSAY, CHARLES W.—Age, 18 years.   Enlisted, August 6, 1862, at Ithaca, to serve three years; not mustered in as private, Co. D, and deserted, September 1, 1862.

LOGAN, CHARLES.—Age, 18 years. Enlisted, August 9, 1862, at Ithaca, to serve three years; mustered in as private, Co. D, October 8, 1862; deserted, July 15, 1863, near Hagerstown, Md.

LONGCOY, HARRISON.—Age, 21 years. Enlisted, August 6, 1862, at Ithaca, to serve three years; mustered in as private, Co. D, October 8, 1862; mustered out with company, July 20, 1865, at Washington, D. C.

LOOMIS, AMON.—Age, 18 years. Enlisted, August 17, 1862, at Lansing, to serve three years; mustered in as private, Co. D, October 8, 1862; wounded, July 23, 1864, near Atlanta, Ga.; died of his wounds, September 3, 1864, at hospital, Chattanooga, Tenn.

MACKEY, LINUS S.—Age, 24 years. Enlisted, August 6, 1862, at Ithaca, to serve three years; mustered in as private, Co. D, October 8, 1862; promoted sergeant prior to April, 1863; discharged, September 16, 1863.

MASTIN, ABRAM.—Age, 45 years. Enlisted, August 6, 1862, at Ithaca, to serve three years; mustered in as private, Co. D, October 8, 1862; transferred to Twelfth Regiment, Veteran Reserve Corps, September 1, 1863; mustered out with detachment, July 20, 1865, at Washington, D. C.

MATHEWS, JAMES H.—Age, 22 years. Enlisted, August 18, 1862, at Ithaca, to serve three years; mustered in as private, Co. D, October 8, 1862; mustered out with company, July 20, 1865, at Washington, D. C.

McWILLIAMS, WESLEY.—Age, 32 years. Enlisted, August 19, 1862, at Ithaca, to serve three years; mustered in as private, Co. D, October 8, 1862; mustered out with company, July 20, 1865, at Washington, D. C.

MEAD, JACOB.—Age, 37 years. Enlisted, August 20, 1862, at Lansing, to serve three years; mustered in as private, Co. D, October 8, 1862; transferred to Veteran Reserve Corps, March 16, 1864.

MERICLE, VAN GASBECK.—Age, 36 years. Enlisted, August 21, 1862, at Monticello, to serve three years; mustered in as private, Co. D, October 8, 1862; discharged, April 16, 1863, at Fairfax Seminary Hospital, Va.

MERNS, SAMUEL.—Age, 30 years. Enlisted, August 18, 1862, at Forestburg, to serve three years; mustered in as corporal, Co. D, October 8, 1862; promoted sergeant prior to October, 1864; mustered out with company, July 20, 1865, at Washington, D. C.

MELLEN, BARNEY.—Age, 32 years. Enlisted, August 19, 1862, at Ithaca, to serve three years; mustered in as private, Co. D, October 8, 1862; mustered out with company, July 20, 1865, at Washington, D. C., as Mellon.

MITCHELL, JOSEPH.—Age, 40 years. Enlisted, August 6, 1862, at Ithaca, to serve three years; mustered in as private, Co. D, October 8, 1862; absent, in hospital, at Chattanooga, Tenn., at muster-out of company.

MIX, HENRY.—Age, -- years. Enlisted at Ithaca, to serve three years, and mustered in as private, Co. D, February 16, 1864; died, July 14, 1864, in hospital, at Nashville, Tenn.

MORGAN, CHESTER S.—Age, 29 years. Enlisted, August 19, 1862, at Lansing, to serve three years; mustered in as corporal, Co. D, October 8, 1862; mustered out with company, July 20, 1865, at Washington, D. C.

MORRISON, EDWARD.—Age, 39 years. Enlisted, August 6, 1862, at Ithaca, to serve three years; mustered in as private, Co. D, October 8, 1862; died of chronic diarrhea, November 1, 1863, at hospital, Bridgeport, Ala.

MURPHY, EDMUND.—Age, 21 years. Enlisted, August 20, 1862, at Lansing, to serve three years; mustered in as private, Co. D, October 8, 1862; died, no date, in hospital, New York city, from injuries received in railroad accident.

MYERS, GEORGE.—Age, 28 years. Enlisted, August 19, 1862, at Lansing, to serve three years; mustered in as private, Co. D, October 8, 1862; mustered out with company, July 20, 1865, at Washington, D. C.

NORTH, CALEB HOWELL.—Age, 33 years. Enrolled, October 6, 1862, at Lansing, to serve three years; mustered in as first lieutenant, Co. D, October 8, 1862; as captain, Co. K, November 2, 1863; discharged for disability, July 15, 1864. Commissioned first lieutenant, November 21, 1862, with rank from October 8, 1862, original; captain, October 17, 1863, with rank from April 12, 1863, vice A. H. Bush, dismissed.

NORTON, JAMES.—Age, 21 years. Enlisted, August 6, 1862, at Ithaca, to serve three years; mustered in as private, Co. D, October 8, 1862; mustered out with company, July 20, 1865, at Washington, D. C.

NORTON, WILLIAM H.—Age, 28 years. Enlisted, August 6, 1862, at Ithaca, to serve three years; mustered in as corporal, Co. D, October 8, 1862; returned to ranks, no date; transferred to Veteran Reserve Corps, February 15, 1864.

ORMSBY, FLORIAN D.—Age, 26 years. Enlisted, August 17, 1862, at Lansing, to serve three years; mustered in as private, Co. D, October 8, 1862; promoted corporal prior to April 11, 1863; missing since October 27, 1863, while on march from Bridgeport, Ala., to Chattanooga, Tenn.; no further record.

OSBURN, ROBERT.—Age, 37 years. Enlisted, August 6, 1862, at Ithaca, to serve three years, as private, Co. D, and deserted, September 1, 1862.

PATTISON, JOHN.—Age, 44 years. Enlisted, August 6, 1862, at Ithaca, to serve three years; mustered in as private, Co. D, October 8, 1862; transferred to Co. B, Ninth Regiment, Veteran Reserve Corps, February 15, 1864; mustered out with detachment, July 8, 1865, at Washington. D. C.

PECK, JOHN P.—Age, 26 years. Enlisted, August 15, 1862, at Lansing, to serve three years; mustered in as private, Co. D, October 8, 1862; died, November 20, 1863, at Bridgeport, Ala.; also borne as John I.

PERSINIOUS, CORNELIUS B.—Age, 38 years. Enlisted, August 6, 1862, at Ithaca, to serve three years; mustered in as private, Co. D, October 8, 1862; promoted corporal, June 1, 1865; mustered out with company, July 20, 1865, at Washington, D. C.

PIFER, JACOB H.—Age, 30 years. Enlisted, August 6, 1862, at Ithaca, to serve three years; mustered in as private, Co. D, October 8, 1862; discharged, December 9, 1862, at Philadelphia, Pa.

POYER, AARON.—Age, 18 years. Enlisted, August 16, 1862, at Lansing, to serve three years; mustered in as private, Co. D, October 8, 1862; promoted corporal, June 1, 1865; mustered out with company, July 20, 1865, at Washington, D. C.

PRICE, SOLOMON.—Age, 43 years. Enlisted, August 20, 1862, at Lansing, to serve three years; mustered in as private, Co. D, October 8, 1862; discharged, February 16, 1863.

PRINGLE, JOHN.—Age, 24 years. Enlisted, August 6, 1862, at Ithaca, to serve three years; mustered in as corporal, Co. D, October 8, 1862; wounded in action, August 8, 1864, near Atlanta, Ga.; discharged for his wounds, February 27, 1865, at hospital, New York City.

QUICK, DE WITT.—Age, 19 years. Enlisted, August 9, 1862, at Ithaca, to serve three years; mustered in as private, Co. D, October 8, 1862; died of diarrhea, November 28, 1864, at hospital, Jeffersonville, Ind.

RANDOLPH, CHARLES.—Age, 28 years. Enlisted, August 22, 1862, at Ithaca, to serve three years; mustered in as private, Co. D, October 8, 1862; promoted corporal, June 1, 1865; mustered out with company, July 20, 1865, at Washington, D. C.

REYNOLDS, SAMUEL.—Age, 37 years. Enlisted, August 27, 1862, at Bridgeville, to serve three years; mustered in as private, Co. D, October 8, 1862; died of congestive fever, October 24, 1863, at hospital, Shelbyville, Tenn.

ROBBINS, DAVID B.—Age, 40 years. Enlisted, August 20, 1862, at Lansing, to serve three years; mustered in as private, Co. D, October 8, 1862; discharged, April 3, 1863, at camp hospital, near Fort Worth, Va.

ROBERTS, FRANCIS M.—Age, 18 years. Enlisted, August 18, 1862, at Lansing, to serve three years; mustered in as private, Co. D, October 8, 1862; transferred to Veteran Reserve Corps, March 7, 1864.

ROBERTS, JOHN W.—Age, 35 years. Enlisted, August 20, 1862, at Lansing, to serve three years; mustered in as private, Co. D, October 8, 1862; deserted, July 16, 1863, at Hagerstown, Md., as Robberts.

ROBINSON, DAVID.—Age, 35 years. Enlisted, August 22, 1862, at Lansing, to serve three years; mustered in as private, Co. D, October 8, 1862; mustered out with company, July 20, 1865, at Washington, D. C.

SCHRYVER, CHARLES H.—Age, 18 years. Enlisted, August 16, 1862, at Ithaca, to serve three years; mustered in as private, Co. D, October 8, 1862; mustered out with company, July 20, 1865, at Washington, D. C.

SHAW, HENRY.—Age, 27 years. Enlisted, August 21, 1862, at Ithaca, to serve three years; mustered in as private, Co. D, October 8, 1862; absent, at hospital, David's Island, New York Harbor, at muster-out of company.

SLOCUM, TRUXTON.—Age, 29 years. Enlisted, August 6, 1862, at Ithaca, to serve three years; mustered in as private, Co. D, October 8, 1862; mustered out with company, July 20, 1865, at Washington, D. C.

SNOW, WILLIAM G.—Age, 44 years. Enlisted, August 6, 1862, at Ithaca, to serve three years; mustered in as private, Co. D, October 8, 1862; discharged, February 16, 1863.

STEVENS, LEWIS.—Age, 31 years. Enlisted, August 16, 1862, at Ithaca, to serve three years; mustered in as private, Co. D, October 8, 1862; mustered out with company, July 20, 1865, at Washington, D. C.

STEWART, JAMES H.—Age, 20 years. Enlisted, August 6, 1862, at Ithaca, to serve three years; mustered in as private, Co. D, October 8, 1862; mustered out with company, July 20, 1865, at Washington, D. C.

STURDEVANT, LEGRAU.—Age, 44 years. Enlisted, August 16, 1862, at Monticello, to serve three years; mustered in as private, Co. D, October 8, 1862; discharged, September 12, 1863, as Legrand.

TRUE, GEORGE.—Age, 19 years. Enlisted, August 6, 1862, at Ithaca, to serve three years; mustered in as private, Co. D, October 8, 1862; mustered out with company, July 20, 1865, at Washington, D. C.

TWOMEY, TIMOTHY.—Age, 34 years. Enlisted, August 16, 1862, at Ithaca, to serve three years; mustered in as private, Co. D, October 8, 1862; mustered out with company, July 20, 1865, at Washington, D. C.

VAN ORDER, GEORGE.—Age, 19 years. Enlisted, August 13, 1862, at Ithaca, to serve three years; mustered in as private, Co. D, October 8, 1862; promoted corporal, no date; mustered out with company, July 20, 1865, at Washington, D. C.

VAN ORDER, MOSES.—Age, 44 years. Enlisted, August 6, 1862, at Ithaca, to serve three years; mustered in as private, Co. D, October 8, 1862; transferred to Co. C, Ninth Regiment, Veteran Reserve Corps, no date; retransferred to this regiment, February 14, 1865; mustered out with company, July 20, 1865, at Washington, D. C.

VAN ORMAN, GEORGE B.—Age, 21 years. Enlisted, August 6, 1862, at Ithaca, to serve three years; mustered in as private, Co. D, October 8, 1862; promoted corporal, no date; mustered out with company, July 20, 1865, at Washington, D. C.

VAN VAULKENBURG, OSCAR.—Age, 21 years. Enlisted, August 13, 1862, at Ithaca, to serve three years; mustered in as private, Co. D, October 8, 1862; mustered out with company, July 20, 1865, at Washington, D. C.

WEAVER, PHILIP A.—Age, 24 years. Enlisted, August 16, 1862, at Lansing, to serve three years; mustered in as private, Co. D, October 8, 1862; promoted corporal prior to April 11, 1863; sergeant prior to October, 1864; mustered out with company, July 20, 1865, at Washington, D. C.

WHITE, NELSON S.—Age, 18 years. Enlisted, August 12, 1862, at Ithaca, to serve three years; mustered in as private, Co. D, October 8, 1862; promoted corporal prior to April, 1863; mustered out with company, July 20, 1865, at Washington, D. C.

WOOD, SAMUEL.—Age, 21 years. Enlisted, August 29, 1862, at Ithaca, to serve three years; mustered in as private, Co. D, October 8, 1862; mustered out with company, July 20, 1865, at Washington, D. C.

KILLED IN ACTION.

None.

WOUNDED IN ACTION.

Bunnell, Luther G., no date given.
Higgins, John, no date given.
Pringle, John, Aug. 8, 1864, near Atlanta, Ga.

Died of Disease and Wounds.

Bunnell, Luther G., June 26, 1864, at Chattanooga, Tenn.
Carr, Gehial, subsequent to June, 1863, at Tompkins Co., N. Y.
Gardner, John B., Jan. 25, 1863, at Upton's Hill, Va.
Guest, Charles W., Jan. 30, 1863, at Upton's Hill, Va.
Hargin, Jefferson, July 27, 1863, at Fort Monroe, Va.
Holmes, William, July 16, 1863, at Fortress Monroe, Va.
Mix, Henry, July 14, 1864, at Nashville, Tenn.
Morrison, Edward, Nov. 1, 1863, at Bridgeport, Ala.
Murphy, Edmund, no date, at New York City.
Peck, John P., Nov. 20, 1863, at Bridgeport, Ala.
Quick, De Witt, Nov. 28, 1864, at Jeffersonville, Ind.
Reynolds, Samuel, Oct. 24, 1863, at Shelbyville, Tenn.
Robbins, David B., April 3, 1863, near Fort Worth, Va.

Discharged During Service.

Bickel, Adam, Dec. 22, 1862, for disability.
Bishop, Jeremiah, Feb. 16, 1863, cause not stated.
Egbert, James D., Dec. 28, 1863, cause not stated.
Francis, John, Dec. 27, 1864, for disability.
Groo, John R., Mar. 20, 1865, for disability.
Higgins, John, May 16, 1865, for disability.
Jacobs, Albert L., July 1, 1865, for disability.
Mackey, Linus S., Sept. 16, 1863, for disability.
Mericle, Van Gasbeck, April 16, 1863, for disability.
North, Caleb Howell, July 15, 1864, for disability.
Pifer, Jacob H., Dec. 19, 1862, for disability.
Price, Solomon, Feb. 16, 1863, for disability.
Pringle, John, Feb. 27, 1865, for disability.
Snow, William G., Feb. 16, 1863, for disability.
Sturdevant, Legrand, Sept. 12, 1863, for disability.

Transferred.

Apgar, Edgar K., Oct. 8, 1862, to Staff of 143d.
Coe, Henry, no date, to Veteran Reserve Corps.
Corkins, Asa A., June 16, 1864, to Veteran Reserve Corps.
Dickinson, Willet J., April 6, 1864, to Veteran Reserve Corps.

Dunleavy, Dennis, Mar. 7, 1864, to Veteran Reserve Corps.
Halladay, Adelbert, Mar 7, 1864, to Veteran Reserve Corps.
Hitchcox, William, May 20, 1863, to Veteran Reserve Corps.
Mastin, Abram, Sept. 1, 1863, to Veteran Reserve Corps.
Mead, Jacob, Mar. 16, 1864, to Veteran Reserve Corps.
Norton, William H., no date, to Veteran Reserve Corps.
Roberts, Francis M., Mar. 7, 1864, to Veteran Reserve Corps.

Deserted.

Campion, William, Oct. 14, 1862, at New York City.
Hendershot, Charles W., July 6, 1865, at Alexandria, Va.
Lindsay, Charles W., Sept. 1, 1862.
Logan, Charles, July 15, 1863, at Hagerstown, Md.
Osburn, Robert, Sept. 1, 1862.
Roberts, John W., July 16, 1863, at Hagerstown, Md.

Captured.

Cornelius, Horace, April 14, 1865, paroled April 29, 1865.
Johnson, Norman C., April 14, 1865, paroled April 30, 1865.

Missing.

Ormsby, Florian D., since Oct. 27, 1863, near Bridgeport, Ala.

COMPANY E.

CAPTAINS.

Ira Dorrance, original; resigned Mar. 30, 1863.

John F. Anderson, from Nov. 1, 1863; resigned Feb. 1, 1865.

DeWitt C. Apgar, from April 1, 1865, to muster-out of Regt. (Bvt. Major N. Y. V.)

FIRST LIEUTENANTS.

William R. Bennett, original; promoted to Captain Co. C.

Peter L. Waterbury, from Nov. 2, 1863; died of wounds.

Charles A. Smith, from Aug. 29, 1864, to muster-out of Regt.

James A. Eichenburgh, from April 27, 1865; not mustered.

SECOND LIEUTENANTS.

Peter L. Waterbury, original; promoted to First Lieutenant.

James A. Eichenburg, from Mar. 7, 1865; not mustered.

Foster F. Bennett, from July 24, 1865; not mustered.

RECORD OF MEMBERS OF COMPANY E—ORIGINAL.

ADAMS, HIRAM.—Age, 18 years. Enlisted, August 21, 1862, at Bridgeville, to serve three years; mustered in as private, Co. E, October 8, 1862; promoted corporal, prior to October, 1864; mustered out with company, July 20, 1865, at Washington, D. C.

ADAMS, WILLIAM.—Age, 20 years. Enlisted, August 21, 1862, at Bridgeville, to serve three years; mustered in as private, Co. E, October 8, 1862; died of disease, March 25, 1865, at hospital, Dennison, Ohio.

BARBER, THEODORE.—Age, 18 years. Enlisted, August 13, 1862, at Wurtsboro, to serve three years; mustered in as private, Co. E, October 8, 1862; mustered out with company, July 20, 1865, at Washington, D. C.

BENEDICK, WILLIAM F.—Age, 19 years. Enlisted, August 15, 1862, at Wurtsboro, to serve three years; mustered in as private, Co. E, October 8, 1862; discharged for disability, June 15, 1864.

BENNETT, FOSTER F.—Age, 19 years. Enrolled, August 13, 1862, at Wurtsboro, to serve three years; mustered in as corporal, Co. E, October 8, 1862; promoted sergeant prior to April 10, 1863; first sergeant, no date; mustered out with company, July 20, 1865, at Washington, D. C. Commissioned, not mustered, second lieutenant, July 24, 1865, with rank from May 16, 1865, vice D. C. Apgar, promoted.

BENNETT, ISAAC J.—Age, 29 years. Enlisted, August 20, 1862, at Wurtsboro, to serve three years; mustered in as private, Co. E, October 8, 1862; killed in action, March 19, 1865, near Bentonville, N. C.

BENNETT, JACOB.—Age, 26 years. Enlisted, August 15, 1862, at Wurtsboro, to serve three years; mustered in as private, Co. E, October 8, 1862; captured, April 14, 1865, near Raleigh, N. C.; paroled, April 29, 1865; mustered out, June 29, 1865, at New York city.

BENNETT, WILLIAM R.—Age, 24 years. Enrolled, August 16, 1862, at Wurtsboro, to serve three years; mustered in as first lieutenant, Co. E, September 6, 1862; as captain, Co. C, March 6, 1863; mustered out with company, July 20, 1865, near Alexandria, Va. Commissioned first lieutenant, November 21, 1862, with rank from September 6, 1862, original; captain, October 17, 1863, with rank from March 5, 1863, vice J. C. French, resigned.

BISHOP, CHARLES.—Age, 22 years. Enlisted, August 22, 1862, at Wurtsboro, to serve three years; mustered in as private, Co. E, October 8, 1862; deserted, November 18, 1862, at Upton's Hill, Va.

BODLE, WILLIAM.—Age, 23 years. Enlisted, August 16, 1862, at Wurtsboro, to serve three years; mustered in as private, Co. E, October 8, 1862; deserted, October 9, 1862, at Monticello, N. Y.

BOWERS, EDWIN L.—Age, 23 years. Enlisted, August 22, 1862, at Monticello, to serve three years; mustered in as private, Co. E, October 8, 1862; mustered out with company, July 20, 1865, at Washington, D. C.

BREEN, CHARLES L.—Age, 24 years. . Enlisted, August 15, 1862, at Wurtsboro, to serve three years; mustered in as private, Co. E, October 8, 1862; mustered out with company, July 20, 1865, at Washington, D. C.

BROWN, ALEXANDER H.—Age, 25 years. Enrolled, August 13, 1862, at Wurtsboro, to serve three years; mustered in as first sergeant, Co. E, October 8, 1862; as second lieutenant, Co. I, May 24, 1863; transferred to Co. H, May 1, 1864; mustered out, May 15, 1865. Commissioned second lieutenant, October 17, 1863, with rank from May 24, 1863, vice W. S. Moffatt, promoted.

CLARK, ELISHA.—Age, 19 years. Enlisted, August 14, 1862, at Wurtsboro, to serve three years; mustered in as private, Co. E, October 8, 1862; mustered out with company, July 20, 1865, at Washington, D. C.

CLARK, MILES.—Age, 30 years. Enlisted, August 13, 1862, at Wurtsboro, to serve three years; mustered in as corporal, Co. E, October 8, 1862; returned to ranks, no date; mustered out with company, July 20, 1865, at Washington, D. C.

CLEMENCE, BENJAMIN T.—Age, 32 years. Enlisted, August 21, 1862, at Bridgeville, to serve three years; mustered in as private, Co. E, October 8, 1862; discharged for disability, May 20, 1864.

COLE, MOSES B.—Age, 45 years. Enlisted, August 22, 1862, at Phillipsport, to serve three years; mustered in as musician, Co. E, October 8, 1862; discharged for disability, September 25, 1863, at Washington, D. C.

COLE, PHILIP D.—Age, 31 years. Enlisted, August 13, 1862, at Wurtsboro, to serve three years; mustered in as sergeant, Co. E, October 8, 1862; discharged for disability, September 10, 1863.

CRAWFORD, CHARLES N.—Age, 21 years. Enlisted, August 30, 1862, at Monticello, to serve three years; mustered in as private, Co. E, October 8, 1862; discharged for disability, August 17, 1863.

CUDDINGTON, JAMES.—Age, 31 years. Enlisted at Goshen, to serve one year, and mustered in as private, Co. E. September 8, 1864; mustered out, June 10, 1865, near Washington, D. C.

DAVED, JAMES B.—Age, 21 years. Enlisted, August 20, 1862, at Wurtsboro, to serve three years; mustered in as sergeant, Co. E, October 8, 1862; discharged for disability, December 14, 1863, at hospital, New York city; also borne as Deved.

DAVIS, WILLIAM.—Age, 41 years. Enlisted, August 22, 1862, at Wurtsboro, to serve three years; mustered in as private, Co. E, October 8, 1862; mustered out with company, July 20, 1865, at Washington, D. C.

DECKER, PETER.—Age, 29 years. Enlisted, August 22, 1862, at Phillipsport, to serve three years; mustered in as private, Co. E, October 8, 1862; discharged for disability, August 17, 1863.

DECKER, SELAR.—Age, 19 years. Enlisted, August 13, 1862, at Wurtsboro, to serve three years; mustered in as private, Co. E, October 8, 1862; promoted corporal, no date; killed in action, May 15, 1864, at Resaca, Ga.

DEGROOT, CHARLES.—Age, 35 years. Enlisted, August 20, 1862, at Wurtsboro, to serve three years; mustered in as private, Co. E, October 8, 1862; absent, on furlough, at muster-out of company.

DORRANCE, IRA.—Age, — years. Enrolled, August 16, 1862, at Wurtsboro, to serve three years; mustered in as captain, Co. E, September 6, 1862; resigned, March 30, 1863. Commissioned captain, November 21, 1862, with rank from September 6, 1862, original.

DUNLAP, JOHN.—Age, 24 years. Enlisted, August 13, 1862, at Wurtsboro, to serve three years; mustered in as corporal, Co. E, October 8, 1862; discharged for disability, June 13, 1865, at Albany, N. Y.

DUNLAP, WILLIAM.—Age, 21 years. Enlisted, August 20, 1862, at Wurtsboro, to serve three years; mustered in as private, Co. E, October 8, 1862; promoted corporal, May 30, 1865; mustered out with company, July 20, 1865, at Washington, D. C.

EICHENBURGH, JAMES A.—Age, 21 years. Enrolled, August 15, 1862, at Wurtsboro, to serve three years; mustered in as sergeant, Co. E, October 8, 1862; promoted first sergeant, no date; sergeant-major, April 26, 1865; mustered out with regiment, July 20, 1865, at Washington, D. C.; prior service in Twentieth Militia. Com-

:missioned, not mustered, second lieutenant, May 31, 1865, with rank from March 7, 1865, vice G. C. Pinney, promoted; first lieutenant, not mustered, July 24, 1865, with rank from May 16, 1865, vice W. Hill, promoted.

FRANTZ, GEORGE C.—Age, 29 years. Enlisted, August 13, 1862, at Wurtsboro, to serve three years; mustered in as private, Co. E, October 8, 1862; transferred to Co. G, Fifteenth Regiment, Veteran Reserve Corps, December 21, 1864; mustered out, July 13, 1865, at Springfield, Ill.

GALLOWAY, MARCUS B.—Age, 21 years. Enlisted, August 21, 1862, at Wurtsboro, to serve three years; mustered in as private, Co. E, October 8, 1862; mustered out, May 22, 1865, at Foster Hospital, New Berne, N. C.

GORDON, JAMES H.—Age, 22 years. Enlisted, August 21, 1862, at Wurtsboro, to serve three years; mustered in as private, Co. E, October 8, 1862; mustered out, May 25, 1865, at Ladies' Home Hospital, New York city.

GRAHAM, SAMUEL G.—Age, 44 years. Enlisted, August 22, 1862, at Phillipsport, to serve three years; mustered in as private, Co. E, October 8, 1862; mustered out with company, July 20, 1865, at Washington, D. C., as Samuel S.

HARDENBERGH, ALEX.—Age, 21 years. Enlisted, August 13, 1862, at Wurtsboro, to serve three years; mustered in as private, Co. E, October 8, 1862; discharged for disability, March 15, 1864.

HARDENBURGH, JOHN C.—Age, 24 years. Enrolled at Mamakating, to serve three years, and mustered in as private, Co. E, August 14, 1862; promoted hospital steward to date September 3, 1862; mustered out with regiment, July 20, 1865, at Washington, D. C.

HAWLEY, DANIEL G.—Age, 50 years. Enlisted, August 13, 1862, at Mamakating, to serve three years; mustered in as private, Co. E, October 8, 1862; discharged for disability, April 8, as Daniel S.

HOWARD, GEORGE.—Age, 20 years. Enlisted, August 13, 1862, at Wurtsboro, to serve three years; mustered in as private, Co. E, October 8, 1862; died of disease, November 19, 1863, in hospital, at Lookout Valley, Tenn.

HOYT, JONATHAN M.—Age, 23 years.   Enlisted, August 21, 1862, at Monticello, to serve three years; mustered in as private, Co. E, October 8, 1862; discharged for disability, February 27, 1864, at hospital, New York city.

KNAPP, JOHN L.—Age, 19 years.   Enlisted, August 20, 1862, at Wurtsboro, to serve three years; mustered in as private, Co. E, October 8, 1862; mustered out with company, July 20, 1865, at Washington, D. C.

KNIFFEN, JAMES H.—Age, 33 years.   Enlisted, August 14, 1862, at Wurtsboro, to serve three years; mustered in as private, Co. E, October 8, 1862; died of bronchitis, September 7, 1864, at Cumberland Hospital, Nashville, Tenn.

LEONARD, LEVI.—Age, 33 years.   Enlisted, August 15, 1862, at Wurtsboro, to serve three years; mustered in as private, Co. E, October 8, 1862; died of disease, February 11, 1864, at Wurtsboro, N. Y.

MASTEN, DAVID W.—Age, 24 years.   Enlisted, August 22, 1862, at Wurtsboro, to serve three years; mustered in as musician, Co. E, October 8, 1862; grade changed to private, no date; mustered out with company, July 20, 1865, at Washington, D. C.

McGOVERN, PATRICK.—Age, 29 years.   Enlisted, August 13, 1862, at Wurtsboro, to serve three years; mustered in as private, Co. E, October 8, 1862; mustered out with company, July 20, 1865, at Washington, D. C.

McLAUGHLIN, HENRY C.—Age, 21 years.   Enlisted, August 13, 1862, at Wurtsboro, to serve three years; mustered in as private, Co. E, October 8, 1862; mustered out with company, July 20, 1865, at Washington, D. C.

MEDLER, ZACHARIAH.—Age, 24 years.   Enlisted, August 14, 1862, at Wurtsboro, to serve three years; mustered in as corporal, Co. E, October 8, 1862; promoted sergeant prior to April 11, 1863; returned to ranks, April 17, 1863; promoted corporal and sergeant, no dates; mustered out with company, July 20, 1865, at Washington, D. C.

MUIR, DAVID.—Age, 43 years.   Enlisted, August 20, 1862, at Monticello, to serve three years; mustered in as private, Co. E,

October 8, 1862; mustered out with company, July 20, 1865, at Washington, D. C.

NATION, JOSEPH W.—Age, 19 years. Enlisted, August 20, 1862, at Wurtsboro, to serve three years; mustered in as private, Co. E, October 8, 1862; died of disease, January 18, 1863, at Upton's Hill, Va.

PIATT, JOHN M.—Age, 23 years. Enlisted, August 13, 1862, at Wurtsboro, to serve three years; mustered in as private, Co. E, October 8, 1862; died of disease, January 22, 1864, at hospital, Nashville, Tenn.; also borne as Pratt.

PIERCE, JOHN W.—Age, 21 years. Enlisted, August 13, 1862, at Wurtsboro, to serve three years; mustered in as private, Co. E, October 8, 1862; wounded in action, May 15, 1864, at Resaca, Ga.; mustered out, June 7, 1865, at Louisville, Ky.

PRICE, HENRY R.—Age, 41 years. Enlisted, August 15, 1862, at Wurtsboro, to serve three years; mustered in as corporal, Co. E, October 8, 1862; discharged for disability, January 5, 1864.

RACE, AUSTIN.—Age, 27 years. Enlisted at Bridgeville, to serve three years; mustered in as corporal, Co. E, October 8, 1862; promoted sergeant prior to October, 1864; absent, on furlough, at muster-out of company.

RACE, MORTIMER W.—Age, 19 years. Enlisted, August 21, 1862, at Bridgeville, to serve three years; mustered in as private, Co. E, October 8, 1862; promoted corporal prior to April 30, 1863; sergeant, May 30, 1865; mustered out with company, July 20, 1865, at Washington, D. C.

REED, SAMUEL.—Age, 36 years. Enlisted, August 17, 1862, at Wurtsboro, to serve three years; mustered in as private, Co. E, October 8, 1862; mustered out with company, July 20, 1865, at Washington, D. C.

REYNOLDS, HEZEKIAH I.—Age, 27 years. Enlisted, August 21, 1862, at Bridgeville, to serve three years; mustered in as private, Co. E, October 8, 1862; promoted corporal prior to April 11, 1863; sergeant, May 30, 1865; mustered out with company, July 20, 1865, at Washington, D. C.

RICHARD, JOHN.—Age, 31 years. Enlisted, August 20, 1862, at Wurtsboro, to serve three years; mustered in as private, Co. E, October 8, 1862; died, June 16, 1863, at Regimental Hospital, Yorktown, Va.

ROOVES, JOHN.—Age, 31 years. Enlisted, August 21, 1862, at Wurtsboro, to serve three year; mustered in as private, Co. E, October 8, 1862; deserted, September 28, 1863, at Bellair, Md.

SARINE, IRA.—Age, 26 years. Enlisted, August 14, 1862, at Wurtsboro, to serve three years; mustered in as private, Co. E, October 8, 1862; mustered out, June 5, 1865, at Augur Hospital, Washington, D. C., as Surine.

SARINE, JACOB.—Age, 21 years. Enlisted, August 13, 1862, at Wurtsboro, to serve three years; mustered in as private, Co. E, October 8, 1862; wounded in action, July 31, 1864, near Atlanta, Ga.; died of his wounds, September 3, 1864, at hospital, Nashville, Tenn.

SCHOONMAKER, ELIJAH.—Age, 21 years. Enlisted, August 13, 1862, at Wurtsboro, to serve three years; mustered in as corporal, Co. E, October 8, 1862; mustered out with company, July 20, 1865, at Washington, D. C.

SCOTT, GEORGE W.—Age, 24 years. Enlisted, August 13, 1862, at Wurtsboro, to serve three years; mustered in as private, Co. E, October 8, 1862; mustered out with company, July 20, 1865, at Washington, D. C.

SHAW, LEVI.—Age, 35 years. Enlisted, August 20, 1862, at Wurtsboro, to serve three years; mustered in as private, Co. E, October 8, 1862; mustered out with company, July 20, 1865, at Washington, D. C.

SHAW, SAMUEL C.—Age, 31 years. Enlisted, August 20, 1862, at Wurtsboro, to serve three years; mustered in as corporal, Co. E, October 8, 1862; returned to ranks, no date; mustered out with company, July 20, 1865, at Washington, D. C.

SHAW, THOMAS J.—Age, 19 years. Enlisted, August 22, 1862, at Bloomingburg, to serve three years; mustered in as private, Co. E, October 8, 1862; died of disease, February 3, 1864, at Murfreesboro, Tenn.

SIMPSON, ANDREW J.—Age, 27 years. Enlisted, August 14, 1862, at Wurtsboro, to serve three years; mustered in as private, Co. E, October 8, 1862; transferred to Veteran Reserve Corps, January 10, 1865.

SINSABAUGH, JACOB H.—Age, 21 years. Enlisted, August 21, 1862, at Wurtsboro, to serve three years; mustered in as private. Co. E, October 8, 1862; promoted corporal, no date; mustered out, July 22, 1865, at New York city.

SKINNER, BENJAMIN A.—Age, 34 years. Enlisted, August 22, 1862, at Wurtsboro, to serve three years; mustered in as private, Co. E, October 8, 1862; died of disease, October 27, 1863, at hospital, Bridgeport, Ala.

SKINNER, LEWIS.—Age, 25 years. Enlisted, August 13, 1862, at Wurtsboro, to serve three years; mustered in as private, Co. E, October 8, 1862; promoted corporal, May 30, 1865; mustered out with company, July 20, 1865, at Washington, D. C.

SKINNER, SAMUEL H.—Age, 30 years. Enlisted, August 20, 1862, at Wurtsboro, to serve three years; mustered in as private, Co. E, October 8, 1862; transferred to Veteran Reserve Corps, September 30, 1863; also borne as Samuel W.

SKINNER, SAMUEL L.—Age, 24 years. Enlisted, August 13, 1862, at Wurtsboro, to serve three years; mustered in as private, Co. E, October 8, 1862; discharged for disability, February 25, 1863, at Fairfax Seminary Hospital, Alexandria, Va.

SKINNER, THEODORE.—Age, 21 years. Enlisted, August 13, 1862, at Wurtsboro, to serve three years; mustered in as private, Co. E, October 8, 1862; mustered out with company, July 20, 1865, at Washington, D. C.

SMITH, CHARLES A.—Age, 27 years. Enlisted, August 20, 1862, at Wurtsboro, to serve three years; mustered in as private, Co. E, October 8, 1862; mustered out, June 8, 1865, at Madison, Ind.

SPENCER, ELIJAH.—Age, 19 years. Enlisted, August 13, 1862, at Wurtsboro, to serve three years; mustered in as private, Co. E, October 8, 1862; discharged for disability, May 24, 1863, at Fairfax Seminary Hospital, Alexandria, Va.

St. John, William J.—Age, 18 years. Enlisted, August 13, 1862, at Wurtsboro, to serve three years; mustered in as private, Co. E, October 8, 1862; died of measles, January 21, 1864, at Lookout Valley, Tenn.

Sweet, John D.—Age, 43 years. Enlisted, August 21, 1862, at Wurtsboro, to serve three years; mustered in as private, Co. E, October 8, 1862; transferred to Seventh Regiment, Veteran Reserve Corps, September 30, 1863; mustered out with detachment, July 14, 1865, at Washington, D. C.

Tarket, Dewitt C.—Age, 24 years. Enlisted, August 13, 1862, at Wurtsboro, to serve three years; mustered in as private, Co. E, October 8, 1862; discharged for disability, January 12, 1863, at Washington, D. C.

Tarket, Levi W.—Age, 21 years. Enlisted, August 20, 1862, at Wurstboro, to serve three years; mustered in as private, Co. E, October 8, 1862; captured, April 14, 1865, near Raleigh, N. C.; paroled, April 29, 1865; mustered out, June 30, 1865, at New York city.

Terwilliger, Aaron.—Age, 19 years. Enlisted, August 15, 1862, at Wurtsboro, to serve three years; mustered in as private, Co. E, October 8, 1862; mustered out with company, July 20, 1865, at Washington, D. C.

Thompson, James H.—Age, 21 years. Enlisted, August 18, 1862, at Wurtsboro, to serve three years; mustered in as private, Co. E, October 8, 1862; died of disease, July 11, 1863, at Fort Monroe, Va.

Tice, Horton.—Age, 19 years. Enlisted, August 15, 1862, at Wurtsboro, to serve three years; mustered in as private, Co. E, October 8, 1862; mustered out with company, July 20, 1865, at Washington, D. C.

Tillson, Jesse.—Age, 27 years. Enlisted, August 20, 1862, at Wurtsboro, to serve three years; mustered in as private, Co. E, October 8, 1862; discharged for disability, October 30, 1863.

Tompkins, Daniel D.—Age, 27 years. Enlisted, August 21, 1862, at Bridgeville, to serve three years; mustered in as private, Co. E, October 8, 1862; discharged for disability, March 18, 1863, at hospital, Philadelphia, Pa.

TOMPKINS, JEHIEL C.—Age, 23 years. Enlisted, August 22, 1862, at Wurtsboro, to serve three years; mustered in as private, Co. E, October 8, 1862; deserted, July 13, 1863, at Frederick City, Md.

TRAVISSE, WILLIAM.—Age, 45 years. Enlisted, August 22, 1862, at Phillipsport, to serve three years; mustered in as private, Co. E, October 8, 1862; killed in action, May 25, 1864, near Dallas, Ga.

VAN LUVEN, JOACHIN.—Age, 36 years. Enlisted, August 22, 1862, at Phillipsport, to serve three years; mustered in as private, Co. E, October 8, 1862; died of disease, January 14, 1864, at Murfreesboro, Tenn.

VAN LUVEN, JOHN.—Age, 31 years. Enlisted, August 21, 1862, at Wurtsboro, to serve three years; mustered in as private, Co. E, October 8, 1862; mustered out with company, July 20, 1865, at Washington, D. C.

WADE, JACOB S.—Age, 22 years. Enlisted, August 16, 1862, at Wurtsboro, to serve three years; mustered in as sergeant, Co. E, October 8, 1862; returned to ranks, no date; mustered out with company, July 20, 1865, at Washington, D. C.

WATERBURY, PETER L.—Age, 24 years. Enrolled, August 16, 1862, at Wurtsboro, to serve three years; mustered in as second lieutenant, Co. E, October 8, 1862; as first lieutenant, November 2, 1863; wounded in action, July 20, 1864, and died of his wounds, July 24, 1864, at Peach Tree Ridge, Ga. Commissioned second lieutenant, November 21, 1862, with rank from September 6, 1862, original; first lieutenant, October 17, 1863, with rank from April 12, 1863, vice C. H. North, promoted.

WHITMORE, ANDREW J.—Age, 26 years. Enlisted, August 16, 1862, at Wurtsboro, to serve three years; mustered in as private, Co. E, October 8, 1862; died of disease, July 1, 1864, at hospital, Lookout Valley, Tenn.

YOUNGS, MATHEW.—Age, 28 years. Enlisted, August 13, 1862, at Wurtsboro, to serve three years; mustered in as private, Co. E, October 8, 1862; died by suicide, March 18, 1863, at camp near Alexandria, Va.

Killed in Action.

Bennett, Isaac J., Mar. 19, 1865, near Bentonville, N. C.
Decker, Selar, May 15, 1864, at Resaca, Ga.
Travisse, William, May 25, 1864, near Dallas, Ga.

Wounded in Action.

Pierce, John W., May 15, 1864, at Resaca, Ga.
Sarine, Jacob, July 31, 1864, at Atlanta, Ga.
Waterbury, Peter L., July 20, 1864, at Peach Tree Creek, Ga.

Died of Disease and Wounds.

Adams, William, Mar. 25, 1865, at Dennison, Ohio.
Howard, George, Nov. 19, 1863, at Lookout Valley, Tenn.
Kniffen, James H., Sept. 7, 1864, at Nashville, Tenn.
Leonard, Levi, Feb. 11, 1864, at Wurtsboro, N. Y.
Nation, Joseph W., Jan. 18, 1863, at Upton's Hill, Va.
Piatt, John M., Jan. 22, 1864, at Nashville, Tenn.
Richard, John, June 16, 1863, at Yorktown, Va.
Sarine, Jacob, Sept. 3, 1864, at Nashville, Tenn.
Shaw, Thomas J., Feb. 3, 1863, at Murfreesboro, Tenn.
Skinner, Benjamin A., Oct. 27, 1863, at Bridgeport, Ala.
Thompson, James H., July 11, 1863, at Fort Monroe, Va.
Van Luven, Joachin, Jan. 14, 1864, at Murfreesboro, Tenn.
Waterbury, Peter L., July 24, 1864, at Peach Tree Creek, Ga.
Youngs, Mathew, Mar. 18, 1863, suicide, near Alexandria, Va.

Discharged During Service.

Benedict, William F., June 15, 1864, for disability.
Clemence, Benjamin T., May 20, 1864, for disability.
Cole, Moses B., Sept. 25, 1863, for disability.
Cole, Philip D., Sept. 10, 1863, for disability.
Crawford, Charles N., Aug. 17, 1863, for disability.
Daved, James B., Dec. 14, 1863, for disability.
Decker, Peter, Aug. 17, 1863, for disability.
Dorance, Ira, Mar. 30, 1863, resigned.
Dunlap, John, June 13, 1865, for disability.
Galloway, Marcus B., May 22, 1865, for disability.

Gordon, James H., May 25, 1865, for disability.
Hardenbeigh, Alex., Mar. 15, 1864, for disability.
Hawley, Daniel G., April 8, ——, for disability.
Hoyt, Jonathan M., Feb. 27, 1864, for disability.
Pierce, John W., June 7, 1865, for disability.
Price, Henry R., Jan. 5, 1864, for disability.
Sarine, Ira, June 5, 1865, for disability.
Skinner, Samuel L., Feb. 25, 1863, for disability.
Smith, Charles A., June 8, 1865, for ————.
Spencer, Elijah, May 24, 1863, for disability.
Tarket, Dewitt C., Jan. 12, 1863, for disability.
Tillson, Jesse, Oct. 30, 1863, for disability.
Tompkins, Daniel D., Mar. 18, 1863, for disability.

TRANSFERRED.

Frantz, George C., Dec. 21, 1864, to Veteran Reserve Corps.
Simpson, Andrew J., Jan. 10, 1865, to Veteran Reserve Corps.
Skinner, Samuel H., Sept. 30, 1863, to Veteran Reserve Corps.
Sweet, John D., Sept. 30, 1863, to Veteran Reserve Corps.

CAPTURED.

Bennett, Jacob, April 14, 1865, paroled April 29, 1865.
Tarkett, Levi W., April 14, 1865, paroled April 29, 1865.

DESERTED.

Bishop, Charles, Nov. 18, 1862, at Upton's Hill, Va.
Bodle, William, Oct. 9, 1862, at Monticello, N. Y.
Rooves, John, Sept. 28, 1863, at Bellair, Md.
Tompkins, Jehiel C., July 13, 1863, at Frederick City, Md.

COMPANY F.

CAPTAINS.

Edward H. Pinney, original, to muster-out of Regt.
Dwight Divine, from May 16, 1865; not mustered.

FIRST LIEUTENANTS.

John F. Anderson, original; promoted to Captain Co. E.
Dwight Divine, from April 17, 1863; promoted to Captain.
David A. Wasim, from March 16, 1865; not mustered.

SECOND LIEUTENANTS.

· Marcus J. Fraser, Jr., original; died Nov. 20, 1862.
Frank Buckley, from Nov. 21, 1862; resigned, Mar. 26, 1863.
Peter E. Palen, from Mar. 27, 1863; promoted to First Lieutenant, Co. K.

RECORD OF MEMBERS OF COMPANY F—ORIGINAL.

ALBEE, GEORGE.—Age, 24 years. Enlisted, August 21, 1862, at Callicoon, from Colchester, Del. Co., to serve three years; mustered in as private, Co. F, October 8, 1862; promoted corporal, prior to October, 1864; mustered out with company, July 20, 1865, at Washington, D. C.

ALBEE, LORENZO.—Age, 24 years. Enlisted, August 21, 1862, at Colchester, to serve three years; mustered in as private, Co. F, October 8, 1862; promoted corporal, no date; transferred to Veteran Reserve Corps, April 10, 1864.

ANDERSON, GEORGE.—Age, 20 years. Enrolled, August 21, 1862, at Fremont, to serve three years; mustered in as private, Co. F, October 8, 1862; promoted sergeant, April 17, 1863; first sergeant, September 1, 1864; mustered out with company, July 20, 1865, at Washington, D. C.

ANDERSON, JOHN F.—Age, 35 years. Enrolled, August 14, 1862, at Callicoon, to serve three years; mustered in as first lieutenant, Co. F, October 8, 1862; as captain, Co. E, November 1, 1863; discharged for disability, February 1, 1865, at Robertsville, S. C. Commissioned first lieutenant, November 21, 1862, with rank from September 6, 1862, original; captain, October 17, 1863, with rank from March 30, 1863, vice I. Dorrance, resigned.

BAIRD, OTIS.—Age, 18 years. Enlisted, August 19, 1862, at Callicoon, to serve three years; mustered in as private, Co. F, October 8, 1862; mustered out with company, July 20, 1865, at Washington, D. C.

BEATTIE, JAMES S.—Age, 23 years. Enlisted, August 19, 1862, at Liberty, to serve three years; mustered in as corporal, Co. F, October 8, 1862; promoted sergeant, May 1, 1864; mustered out with company, July 20, 1865, at Washington, D. C.

BENEDICT, JAMES M.—Age, 21 years. Enlisted, August 5, 1862, at Callicoon, to serve three years; mustered in as corporal, Co. F, October 8, 1862; returned to ranks, subsequent to June, 1863; promoted corporal, June 14, 1864; mustered out with company, July 20, 1865, at Washington, D. C.

BIFFAR, FRANCIS A.—Age, 18 years. Enlisted, August 22, 1862, at Callicoon, to serve three years; mustered in as private, Co. F, October 8, 1862; promoted corporal, no date; mustered out with company, July 20, 1865, at Washington, D. C.

BRADY, ANDREW.—Age, 26 years. Enlisted, August 20, 1862, at Fremont, to serve three years; mustered in as private, Co. F, October 8, 1862; mustered out with company, July 20, 1865, at Washington, D. C.

BREINER, JOHN.—Age, 25 years. Enlisted, August 21, 1862, at Callicoon, to serve three years; mustered in as private, Co. F, October 8, 1862; mustered out with company, July 20, 1865, at Washington, D. C., as Briner.

BROWN, WILLIAM.—Age, 26 years. Enlisted, August 21, 1862, at Fremont, to serve three years; mustered in as private, Co. F, October 8, 1862; mustered out with company, July 20, 1865, at Washington, D. C.

BUCKLEY, FRANK.—Age, 21 years. Enrolled, August 20, 1862, at Fremont, to serve three years; mustered in as first sergeant, Co. F, October 8, 1862; as second lieutenant, November 21, 1862; discharged, March 26, 1863. Commissioned second lieutenant, November 26, 1862, with rank from November 21, 1862, vice M. Fraser, deceased.

BUCKSBEE, JEREMIAH.—Age, 23 years. Enlisted, August 22, 1862, at Callicoon, to serve three years; mustered in as private, Co. F, October 8, 1862; appointed wagoner prior to April 11, 1863; mustered out with company, July 20, 1865, at Washington, D. C.

BURY, FREDERICK.—Age, 20 years. Enlisted, August 22, 1862, at Fremont, to serve three years; mustered in as private, Co. F, October 8, 1862; mustered out with company, July 20, 1865, at Washington, D. C., as Buri.

COLE, ASA.—Age, 28 years. Enlisted, August 21, 1862, at Callicoon, to serve three years; mustered in as private, Co. F, October 8, 1862; discharged for disability, February 18, 1864, at Bridgeport, Ala.

CONKLIN, JAMES A.—Age, 44 years. Enlisted, August 14, 1862, at Fremont, to serve three years; mustered in as private, Co. F, October 8, 1862; mustered out with detachment, July 1, 1865, at Carver Hospital, Washington, D. C.

COOK, ENOCH R.—Age, 26 years. Enlisted, August 20, 1862, at Colchester, to serve three years; mustered in as private, Co. E, October 8, 1862; mustered out with company, July 20, 1865, at Washington, D. C.

COONS, HENRY.—Age, 40 years. Enlisted, August 15, 1862, at Fremont, to serve three years; mustered in as private, Co. F, October 8, 1862; mustered out, June 5, 1865, at Albany, N. Y., while in hospital, Troy, N. Y.

DAVIS, JOSEPH D.—Age, 25 years. Enlisted, August 22, 1862, at Liberty, to serve three years; mustered in as private, Co. F, October 8, 1862; mustered out with company, July 20, 1865, at Washington, D. C.

DUSENBURY, LANCASTER B.—Age, 32 years. Enlisted, August 22, 1862, at Callicoon, to serve three years; mustered in as ser geant, Co. F, October 8, 1862; transferred to Veteran Reserve Corps, September 1, 1863.

EDLINE, EUGENE.—Age, 18 years. Enlisted, August 14, 1862, at Callicoon, to serve three years; mustered in as private, Co. F, October 8, 1862; died, January 6, 1864, at Eleventh Army Corps Hospital, Lookout Valley, Tenn.; also borne as Edelim.

FERDON, JOHN D.—Age, 18 years. Enlisted, August 21, 1862, at Callicoon, to serve three years; mustered in as private, Co. F, October 8, 1862; mustered out with company, July 20, 1865, at Washington, D. C., as Furdon.

FERDON, WILLIAM S.—Age, 45 years. Enlisted, August 22, 1862, at Callicoon, to serve three years; mustered in as private, Co. F, October 8, 1862; discharged for disability, August 29, 1863, at Convalescent Camp, Alexandria, Va., as Furdon.

FRASER, DAVID.—Age, 23 years. Enlisted, August 8, 1862, at Callicoon, to serve three years; mustered in as corporal, Co. F, October 8, 1862; promoted sergeant prior to October, 1864; mus- tered out with company, July 20, 1865, at Washington, D. C.

FRASER, JR., MARCUS J.—Age, 26 years. Enrolled, September 6, 1862, at Monticello, to serve three years; mustered in as second lieutenant, Co. F, October 8, 1862; died, November 20, 1862, at St. Aloysius Hospital, Washington, D. C. Commissioned second lieutenant, November 21, 1862, with rank from September 6, 1862, original.

FULLER, CYRENUS M.—Age, 21 years. Enlisted, August 15, 1862, at Fremont, to serve three years; mustered in as private, Co. F, October 8, 1862; died, January 6, 1864, at Eleventh Army Corps Hospital, Lookout Valley, Tenn.

FULLER, ORLANDO D.—Age, 27 years. Enlisted at Norwich, to serve one year, and mustered in as private, Co. F, September 5, 1864; mustered out with detachment, June 10, 1865, near Wash- ington, D. C.

GILBERT, JOHN.—Age, 18 years. Enlisted, August 9, 1862, at Callicoon, to serve three years; mustered in as private, Co. F, October 8, 1862; mustered out with company, July 20, 1865, at Washington, D. C.

GLEICHAUF, ALBERT.—Age, 32 years. Enlisted at Goshen, to serve one year, and mustered in as private, Co. F, September 22, 1864; mustered out with detachment, June 10, 1865, near Washington, D. C.

HANCHEN, ANDREW.—Age, 29 years. Enlisted, August 15, 1862, at Callicoon, to serve three years; mustered in as private, Co. F, October 8, 1862; killed in action, July 20, 1864, at Peach Tree Creek, Ga.; also borne as Hanschen.

HANFORD, CHARLES H.—Age, 33 years. Enlisted, August 15, 1862, at Callicoon, to serve three years; mustered in as private, Co. F, October 8, 1862; discharged for disability, April 27, 1865, at Elmira, N. Y.

HARDIE, CHARLES.—Age, 28 years. Enlisted, August 22, 1862, at Rockland, to serve three years; mustered in as private, Co. F, October 8, 1862; mustered out with company, July 20, 1865, at Washington, D. C.; also borne as Harden.

HARTMAN, BENJAMIN.—Age, 26 years. Enlisted, August 22, 1862, at Callicoon, to serve three years; mustered in as private, Co. F, October 8, 1862; transferred to Veteran Reserve Corps, March 15, 1864.

HAUSEE, EDWARD A.—Age, 18 years. Enlisted, August 21, 1862, at Fremont, to serve three years; mustered in as private, Co. F, October 8, 1862; mustered out with company, July 20, 1865, at Washington, D. C.; also borne as Hauser.

HECTOR, ALBERT.—Age, 33 years. Enlisted, August 20, 1862, at Liberty, to serve three years; mustered in as private, Co. F, October 8, 1862; died, November 30, 1863, in hospital, at Murfreesboro, Tenn.

HILL, FILLMORE.—Age, 19 years. Enlisted, August 21, 1862, at Fremont, to serve three years; mustered in as private, Co. F, October 8, 1862; died, January 17, 1864, at Eleventh Army Corps Hospital, Lookout Valley, Tenn.

HILL, GRANGER.—Age, 20 years. Enlisted, August 11, 1862, at Fremont, to serve three years; mustered in as private, Co. F,

October 8, 1862; mustered out with company, July 20, 1865, at Washington, D. C.

HITT, IRA F.—Age, 31 years. Enlisted at Norwich, to serve one year, and mustered in as private, Co. F, September 2, 1864; mustered out with detachment, June 10, 1865, near Washington, D. C.

HITT, LEWIS.—Age, 22 years. Enlisted at Norwich, to serve one year, and mustered in as private, Co. F, September 2, 1864; mustered out with detachment, June 10, 1865, near Washington, D. C.

HOAGLAND, AARON.—Age, 28 years. Enlisted, August 7, 1862, at Callicoon, to serve three years; mustered in as sergeant, Co. F, October 8, 1862; promoted first sergeant, no date; wounded in action, July 20, 1864, at Peach Tree Creek, Ga.; died of his. wounds, July 21, 1864; also borne as Hoaglen.

HOFER, JOHN.—Age, 20 years. Enlisted, August 22, 1862, at Callicoon, to serve three years; mustered in as private, Co. F, October 8, 1862; mustered out with company, July 20, 1865, at Washington, D. C.

HUBER, NICHOLAS.—Age, 21 years. Enlisted at Callicoon to serve one year and mustered in as private, Co. F, September 14, 1864; mustered out, June 10, 1865, with detachment, near Washington, D. C.

HUBER, ULRICH.—Age, 26 years. Enlisted at Goshen, to serve one year, and mustered in as private, Co. F, September 22, 1864; mustered out with detachment, June 10, 1865, near Washington, D. C.

HUFF, LEWIS.—Age, 21 years. Enlisted, August 20, 1862, at Callicoon, to serve three years, as private, Co. F; absent, at muster-in of company; was mustered in November 17, 1863; mustered out with company, July 20, 1865, at Washington, D. C.

JACKSON, ALEXANDER.—Age, 29 years. Enlisted, August 22, 1862, at Liberty, to serve three years; mustered in as private, Co. F, October 8, 1862; discharged for disability, December 17, 1862, at Washington, D. C.

JACKSON, CHARLES.—Age, 23 years. Enlisted at Goshen, to serve one year, and mustered in as private, Co. F, October 5, 1864; mustered out, May 30, 1865, at New York city.

JACOBY, ROBERT E.—Age, 25 years. Enlisted, August 18, 1862, at Callicoon, to serve three years; mustered in as private, Co. F, October 8, 1862; wounded in action, July 20, 1864, at Peach Tree Creek, Ga.; mustered out with company, July 20, 1865, at Washington, D. C.

KIMBALL, HERMAN.—Age, 18 years. Enlisted, August 22, 1862, at Fremont, to serve three years; mustered in as private, Co. F, October 8, 1862; discharged, September 22, 1863, at Washington, D. C.; also borne at Kimble.

LAMB, ALFRED.—Age, 23 years. Enlisted, August 22, 1862, at Callicoon, to serve three years; mustered in as private, Co. F, October 8, 1862; mustered out with company, July 20, 1865, at Washington, D. C.

LEWIS, EDWARD A.—Age, 22 years. Enlisted, August 22, 1862, at Callicoon, to serve three years; mustered in as private, Co. F, October 8, 1862; died of disease, June 21, 1863, at Nelson Hospital, Yorktown, Va.

LIEB, THEODORE.—Age, 21 years. Enlisted, August 22, 1862, at Callicoon, to serve three years; mustered in as private, Co. F, October 8, 1862; mustered out with company, July 20, 1865, at Washington, D. C., as Leib.

LONG, JOHN.—Age, 21 years. Enlisted, August 21, 1862, at Callicoon, to serve three years; mustered in as private, Co. F, October 8, 1862; wounded in action, June 16, 1864, at Golgotha, Ga.; absent, sick in hospital, at Camp Dennison, Ohio, since October, 1864, and at muster-out of company.

LYNSON, JOHN.—Age, 40 years. Enlisted, August 18, 1862, at Callicoon, to serve three years; mustered in as private, Co. F, October 8, 1862; deserted, July 17, 1863, near Berlin, Md.

MALTBY, MARCUS.—Age, 24 years. Enlisted, August 18, 1862, at Cochecton, to serve three years; mustered in as private, Co. F, October 8, 1862; transferred to Co. C, March 1, 1863; died, May 20, 1863, at Regimental Hospital, West Point, Va.

MILLER, GEORGE.—Age, 28 years. Enlisted, August 22, 1862, at Callicoon, to serve three years; mustered in as corporal, Co. F, October 8, 1862; promoted sergeant, July 22, 1864; wounded, no date; mustered out with company, July 20, 1865, at Washington, D. C.

MILLER, HENRY.—Age, 25 years. Enlisted, August 22, 1862, at Fremont, to serve three years; mustered in as private, Co. F, October 8, 1862; promoted corporal prior to October, 1864; mustered out with company, July 20, 1865, at Washington, D. C.

MILLER, JOHN.—Age, 23 years. Enlisted, August 22, 1862, at Callicoon, to serve three years; mustered in as private, Co. F, October 8, 1862; mustered out with company, July 20, 1865, at Washington, D. C.

MILLS, GEORGE H.—Age, 27 years. Enlisted, August 21, 1862, at Monticello, to serve three years; mustered in as private, Co. F, October 8, 1862; mustered out with company, July 20, 1865, at Washington, D. C.

MILLS, SETH B.—Age, 42 years. Enlisted, August 22, 1862, at Liberty, to serve three years; mustered in as private, Co. F, October 8, 1862; transferred to Veteran Reserve Corps, no date.

MISNER, GEORGE R.—Age, 23 years. Enlisted, August 21, 1862, at Fremont, to serve three years; mustered in as corporal, Co. F, October 8, 1862; died, July 25, 1863, in hospital near Williamsburg, Va.; also borne as Misren.

MITCHELL, WILLIAM H.—Age, 44 years. Enlisted, August 22, 1862, at Cochecton, to serve three years; mustered in as private, Co. F, October 8, 1862; promoted corporal, no date; mustered out with company, July 20, 1865, at Washington, D. C.

MORGAN, WILLIAM T.—Age, 18 years. Enrolled, August 21, 1862, at Monticello, to serve three years; mustered in as sergeant, Co. F, October 8, 1862; promoted first sergeant, July 23, 1864; sergeant-major, September 1, 1864, and mustered in as first lieutenant Co. G, April 26, 1865; mustered out with company, July 20, 1865, near Alexandria, Va. Commissioned first lieutenant, April 15, 1865, with rank from March 18, 1865, vice R. M. J. Hardenburgh, killed in action.

Muller, George.—Age, 42 years. Enlisted, August 14, 1862, at Callicoon, to serve three years; mustered in as private, Co. F. October 8, 1862; died, August 28, 1864, at Hospital No. 1, Chattanooga, Tenn.; also borne as Miller.

Murray, George.—Age, 27 years. Enlisted, August 20, 1862, at Fremont, to serve three years; mustered in as private, Co. F, October 8, 1862; promoted corporal, no date; wounded in action, July 20, 1864, at Peach Tree Creek, Ga.; promoted sergeant, September 1, 1864; mustered out, June 5, 1865, at Albany, N. Y.

Murray, William.—Age, 21 years. Enlisted in Tenth Congressional District, to serve three years, and mustered in as private, Co. F, March 7, 1864; wounded in action, May 14, 1864, at Resaca, Ga.; died of his wounds, May 26, 1864.

Norton, Edward J.—Age, 25 years. Enlisted, August 14, 1862, at Fremont, to serve three years; mustered in as corporal, Co. F, October 8, 1862; transferred to Fifth Artillery, from which he deserted, January 15, 1864; discharged, June 29, 1865, at Fort McHenry, Baltimore, Md.

Norton, John.—Age, 28 years. Enlisted, August 15, 1862, at Fremont, to serve three years; mustered in as private, Co. F, October 8, 1862; discharged for disability, February, 1864, at Nashville, Tenn.

Norton, Willis.—Age, 41 years. Enlisted, August 15, 1862, at Fremont, to serve three years; mustered in as private, Co. F, October 8, 1862; discharged for disability, December 14, 1863, at Evansville, Ind.

Palmatier, Abraham.—Age, 32 years. Enlisted, August 21, 1862, at Callicoon, to serve three years; mustered in as private, Co. F, October 8, 1862; transferred to Co. A, Fourteenth Regiment, Veteran Reserve Corps, July 1, 1863; mustered out with detachment, July 14, 1865, at Washington, D. C.

Parker, George W.—Age, 21 years. Enlisted, August 21, 1862, at Highland, to serve three years; mustered in as private, Co. F, October 8, 1862; promoted corporal, September 1, 1864; mustered out with company, July 20, 1865, at Washington, D. C.

Pendell, Sydney T.—Age, 22 years. Enlisted, August 7, 1862, at Callicoon, to serve three years; mustered in as private,

Co. F, October 8, 1862; mustered out, July 10, 1865, at Washington, D. C.

POLLOCK, ROBERT.—Age, 25 years. Enlisted, August 20, 1862, at Wurtsboro, to serve three years; mustered in as wagoner, Co. E, October 8, 1862; mustered out with company, July 20, 1865, at Washington, D. C.

PINNEY, EDWARD H.—Age, 39 years. Enrolled, August 14, 1862, at Callicoon, to serve three years; mustered in as captain, Co. F, October 8, 1862; mustered out with company, July 20, 1865, at Washington, D. C. Commissioned captain, November 21, 1862, with rank from September 6, 1862, original; major, not mustered, July 24, 1865, with rank from May 16, 1865, vice J. Higgins, discharged.

PINNEY, GEORGE C.—Age, 29 years. Enrolled, August 19, 1862, at Liberty, to serve three years; mustered in as first sergeant, Co. F, October 8, 1862; as second lieutenant, Co. I, May 1, 1864; as first lieutenant, Co. H, June 19, 1865; mustered out with company, July 20, 1865, at Washington, D. C. Commissioned second lieutenant, October 17, 1863, with rank from April 12, 1863, vice P. L. Waterbury, promoted; first lieutenant, May 31, 1865, with rank from March 7, 1865, vice J. I. Young, promoted.

PRIESTLY, JOHN.—Age, 25 years. Enlisted, July 27, 1862, at Fremont, to serve three years; mustered in as private, Co. F, October 8, 1862; mustered out with company, July 20, 1865, at Washington, D. C.

PRIME, GEORGE C.—Age, 29 years. Enlisted, August 21, 1862, at Jeffersonville, to serve three years; mustered in as private, Co. F, October 8, 1862; no further record.

QUICK, CYRUS J.—Age, 38 years. Enlisted, August 22, 1862, at Callicoon, to serve three years; mustered in as corporal, Co. F, October 8, 1862; returned to ranks, no date; mustered out with company, July 20, 1865, at Washington, D. C.

REYNOLDS, JOHN W.—Age, 30 years. Enlisted, August 15, 1862, at Fremont, to serve three years; mustered in as private, Co. F, October 8, 1862; died, December 13, 1863, at Charleston, Tenn.

ROBERTSON, CLARK J.—Age, 20 years. Enlisted, August 13, 1862, at Monticello, to serve three years; mustered in as private, Co. F, October 8, 1862; died, July 5, 1864, at Cumberland Hospital, Nashville, Tenn.

ROSE, CALEB G.—Age, 25 years. Enlisted at Goshen, to serve three years, and mustered in as private, Co. F, February 9, 1864; discharged, July 20, 1865, at Washington, D. C.

ROSE, JR., JAMES.—Age, 21 years. Enlisted, August 9, 1862, at Callicoon, to serve three years; mustered in as private, Co. F, October 8, 1862; mustered out with company, July 20, 1865, at Washington, D. C.

ROSE, WILLIAM M.—Age, 26 years. Enlisted at Goshen, to serve three years, and mustered in as private, Co. F, December 18, 1863; mustered out with company, July 20, 1865, at Washington, D. C.

RUMSEY, GEORGE.—Age, 25 years. Enlisted, August 21, 1862, at Callicoon, to serve three years; mustered in as private, Co. F, October 8, 1862; died, October 18, 1863, at Third Division Hospital, Alexandria, Va.

RYAN, MICHAEL.—Age, 21 years. Enlisted, August 21, 1862, at Fremont, to serve three years; mustered in as private, Co. F, October 8, 1862; deserted, October 13, 1862, at New York city.

SHORT, LEWIS H.—Age, 21 years. Enlisted, August 22, 1862, at Callicoon, to serve three years; mustered in as private, Co. F, October 8, 1862; transferred to Co. H, Seventeenth Regiment, Veteran Reserve Corps, January 10, 1865; mustered out, June 30, 1865.

SIEBECKER, LEWIS.—Age, 22 years. Enlisted, August 22, 1862, at Callicoon, to serve three years; mustered in as private, Co. F, October 8, 1862; mustered out with company, July 20, 1865, at Washington, D. C., as Serbicker.

SMITH, EDWARD P.—Age, 30 years. Enlisted, August 14, 1862, at Fremont, to serve three years; mustered in as sergeant, Co. F, October 8, 1862; promoted first sergeant, April 17, 1863; discharged for disability, January 12, 1864, at Nashville, Tenn.

SMITH, GEORGE H.—Age, 42 years. Enlisted, August 18, 1862, at Fremont, to serve three years; mustered in as private, Co. F, October 8, 1862, and discharged, same day, at Monticello, N. Y.

SMITH, WILLIAM C.—Age, 26 years. Enlisted, August 22, 1862, at Callicoon, to serve three years; mustered in as private, Co. F, October 8, 1862; discharged for disability, January 2, 1863, at Philadelphia, Pa.

SWARTWOUT, GEORGE W.—Age, 31 years. Enlisted, August 21, 1862, at Fremont, to serve three years; mustered in as corporal, Co. F, October 8, 1862; returned to ranks, no date; promoted corporal, June 14, 1864; mustered out with company, July 20, 1865, at Washington, D. C.

TEED, ALONZO D.—Age, 20 years. Drafted at Norwich, to serve three years, and mustered in as private, Co. F, September 4, 1863; transferred to Forty-eighth Company, Second Battalion, Veteran Reserve Corps, no date; mustered out with detachment, September 12, 1865, at Washington, D. C.

THOMPSON, ANDREW J.—Age, 26 years. Enlisted at Norwich, to serve one year, and mustered in as private, Co. F, September 5, 1864; mustered out with detachment, June 10, 1865, near Washington, D. C. From Colchester, Del. Co.

TRIMPER, JOHN.—Age, 29 years. Enlisted, August 22, 1862, at Liberty, to serve three years; mustered in as private, Co. F, October 8, 1862; absent, on furlough, since July 3, 1865, and at muster-out of company.

VAN TASSAL, PHILIP.—Age, 30 years. Enlisted at Callicoon, to serve one year, and mustered in as private, Co. F, September 14, 1864; mustered out with detachment, June 10, 1865, near Washington, D. C.

VON ARX, HERMAN.—Age, 32 years. Enlisted, August 11, 1862, at Callicoon, to serve three years; mustered in as private, Co. F, October 8, 1862; mustered out with company, July 20, 1865, at Washington, D. C.

VON ARX, RUDOLPH.—Age, 26 years. Enlisted, August 13, 1862, at Callicoon, to serve three years; mustered in as private, Co. F, October 8, 1862; discharged for disability, September 5, 1863, at convalescent camp, Alexandria, Va.

WALKER, JAMES.—Age, 30 years. Enlisted, August 21, 1862, at Jeffersonville, to serve three years; mustered in as private, Co. F, October 8, 1862; transferred to Forty-eighth Company, Second Battalion, Veteran Reserve Corps, May 26, 1863; mustered out with detachment, September 12, 1865, at Washington, D. C.

WHITMARSH, CHAUNCEY.—Age, 34 years. Enlisted, August 22, 1862, at Callicoon, to serve three years; mustered in as private, Co. F, October 8, 1862; discharged for disability, December 22, 1862, at Washington, D. C.

WILLIAMS, HENRY H.—Age, 21 years. Enlisted, August 8, 1862, at Callicoon, to serve three years; mustered in as private, Co. F, October 8, 1862; mustered out with company, July 20, 1865, at Washington, D. C.

WILLIAMS, MARK L.—Age, 20 years. Enlisted, August 8, 1862, at Callicoon, to serve three years; mustered in as private, Co. F, October 8, 1862; promoted corporal, no date; died, November 20, 1863, at Hospital No. 3, Murfreesboro, Tenn.

WINGERT, JOHN.—Age, 25 years. Enlisted, August 21, 1862, at Callicoon, to serve three years; mustered in as private, Co. F, October 8, 1862; wounded in action, July 20, 1864, at Peach Tree Creek, Ga.; dicharged for disability, June 1, 1865, at Grant Hospital, Willett's Point, New York Harbor.

WINSLOW, JOSEPH.—Age, 36 years. Enlisted, August 21, 1862, at Fremont, to serve three years; mustered in as private, Co. F, October 8, 1862; discharged for disability, March 11, 1864, at hospital, Hampton, Va.

WORMUTH, ALFRED D.—Age, 19 years. Enlisted, August 15. 1862, at Callicoon, to serve three years; mustered in as private, Co. F, October 8, 1862; mustered out, May 22, 1865, at Hospital No. 3, Lookout Mountain, Tenn.

WORMUTH, ISAAC.—Age, 18 years. Enlisted, August 10, 1862, at Callicoon, to serve three years; mustered in as private, Co. F, October 8, 1862; died of typhoid fever, July 9, 1863, at hospital, Hampton, Va.

WORMUTH, STEPHEN.—Age, 38 years. Enlisted, August 14, 1862, at Callicoon, to serve three years; mustered in as private,

Co. F, October 8, 1862; mustered out with detachment, July 1, 1865, at Washington, D. C.

YAWKER, HENRY.—Age, 22 years. Enlisted, August 5, 1862, at Callicoon, to serve three years; mustered in as private, Co. F, October 8, 1862; mustered out with company, July 20, 1865, at Washington, D. C.; also borne as Yawkee.

KILLED IN ACTION.

Hanchen, Andrew, July 20, 1864, at Peach Tree Creek, Ga.
Wingert, John, July 20, 1864, at Peach Tree Creek, Ga.

WOUNDED IN ACTION.

Murray, George, July 20, 1864, at Peach Tree Creek, Ga.
Murray, William, May 14, 1864, at Resaca, Ga.

DIED OF DISEASE AND WOUNDS.

Edline, Eugene, Jan. 6, 1864, at Lookout Valley, Tenn.
Fraser, Marcus J., Jr., Nov. 20, 1862, at Washington, D. C.
Fuller, Cyrenus M.., Jan. 6, 1864, at Lookout Valley, Tenn.
Hector, Albert, Nov. 30, 1863, at Murfreesboro, Tenn.
Hill, Fillmore, Jan. 17, 1864, at Lookout Valley, Tenn.
Maltby, Marcus, May 20, 1863, at West Point, Va.
Misner, George B., July 25, 1863, at Williamsburg, Va.
Muller, George, Aug. 28, 1864, at Chattanooga, Tenn.
Murray, William, May 26, 1864, at ————.
Reynolds, John W., Dec. 13, 1863, at Charleston, Tenn.
Rumsey, George, Oct. 18, 1863, at Alexandria, Va.
Williams, Mark L., Nov. 20, 1863, at Murfreesboro, Tenn.
Wormuth, Isaac, July 9, 1863, at Hampton, Va.

DISCHARGED DURING SERVICE.

Anderson, John F., Feb. 1, 1865, for disability.
Buckley, Frank, Mar. 26, 1863, for disability.
Cole, Asa, Feb. 18, 1864, for disability.
Coons, Henry, June 5, 1865, for disability.
Ferdon, William S.. Aug. 29, 1863, for disability.

Hanford, Charles H., April 27, 1865, for disability.
Jackson, Alexander, Dec. 17, 1862, for disability.
Jackson, Charles, May 30, 1865, for disability.
Kimball, Herman, Sept. 22, 1863, for disability.
Murray, George, June 5, 1865, for disability.
Norton, John, Feb., 1864, for disability.
Norton, Willis, Dec. 14, 1863, for disability.
Smith, Edward P., Jan. 12, 1864, for disability.
Smith, George H., Oct. 8, 1862, cause not stated.
Smith, William C., Jan. 2, 1863, for disability.
Von Arx, Rudolph, Sept. 5, 1863, for disability.
Whitmarsh, Chauncey, Dec. 22, 1862, for disability.
Wingert, John, June 1, 1865, for disability.
Winslow, Joseph, Mar. 11, 1864, for disability.
Wormuth, Alfred D., May 22, 1865, for disability.

TRANSFERRED.

Albee, Lorenzo, April 10, 1864, to Veteran Reserve Corps.
Dusenbury, Lancaster B., Sept. 1, 1863, to Veteran Reserve Corps.
Hartman, Benjamin, Mar. 15, 1864, to Veteran Reserve Corps.
Maltby, Marcus, Mar. 1, 1863, to Co. C, 143d Regt.
Mills, Seth B., no date, to Veteran Reserve Corps.
Norton, Edward J., Jan. 15, 1862, to Fifth Artillery.
Palmatier, Abraham, July 1, 1863, to Veteran Reserve Corps.
Teed, Alonzo D., no date, to Veteran Reserve Corps.
Walker, James, May 26, 1863, to Veteran Reserve Corps.

DESERTED.

Lynson, John, July 17, 1863, near Berlyn, Md.
Ryan, Michael, Oct. 13, 1862, at New York City.

COMPANY G.

CAPTAINS.

Benjamin Reynolds, original, resigned May 5, 1865. (Bvt. Major N. Y. V.)

Jirah I. Young, from June 19, 1865, to muster out of Regt.

FIRST LIEUTENANTS.

Theron B. Luckey, original, resigned May 24, 1863.

Rensselaer Hammond, from May 1, 1864, promoted to Adjt.

Richard M. J. Hardenburgh, from Aug. 29, 1864, died of wounds.

William T. Moffat, from April 26, 1865, to muster-out of Regt. (Bvt. Capt. N. Y. V.)

SECOND LIEUTENANTS.

Alexander C. Kellam, original, resigned Mar. 17, 1863.

Wallace Hill, from Oct. 17, 1863, promoted to First Lieutenant, Co. I.

ROSTER OF MEMBERS OF COMPANY G—ORIGINAL.

ACHART, WILLIAM H.—Age, 43 years. Enlisted, August 20, 1862, at Bloomingburg, to serve three years; mustered in as corporal, Co. G, October 9, 1862; returned to ranks prior to April 11, 1863; transferred to Co. B, Ninth Regiment, Veteran Reserve Corps, September 26, 1863; mustered out with detachment, July 8, 1865, at Washington, D. C.

ALLEN, SIMPSON.—Age, 19 years. Enlisted, August 12, 1862, at Fremont, to serve three years; mustered in as private, Co. G, October 9, 1862; mustered out with company, July 20, 1865, near Alexandria, Va.

BABCOCK, GEORGE H.—Age, 45 years. Enlisted, August 12, 1862, at Bloomingburg, to serve three years; mustered in as corporal, Co. G, October 9, 1862; transferred to Fifty-eighth Company, Second Battalion, Veteran Reserve Corps, September 3, 1863; mustered out with detachment, June 17, 1865.

BABCOCK, JAMES H.—Age, 19 years. Enlisted, August 12, 1862, at Bloomingburg, to serve three years; mustered in as private, Co. G, October 9, 1862; wounded in action, March 16, 1865, at Averasboro, N. C.; mustered out, June 5, 1865, at Albany, N. Y.

BAKER, CHARLES H.—Age, 22 years. Enlisted, August 12, 1862, at Bloomingburg, to serve three years; mustered in as private, Co. G, October 9, 1862; wounded in action, July 20, 1864, at Peach Tree Creek, Ga.; transferred to Co. G, Sixteenth Regiment, Veteran Reserve Corps, no date; mustered out, July 29, 1865, at Harrisburg, Pa.

BILLINGS, PHILO C.—Age, 21 years. Enlisted, August 22, 1862, at Fremont, to serve three years; mustered in as private, Co. G, October 9, 1862; mustered out with company, July 20, 1865, near Alexandria, Va.

BOYLE, THOMAS E.—Age, 21 years. Enlisted, September 5, 1862, at Camp Holley, to serve three years; mustered in as private, Co. G, October 9, 1862; captured, April 14, 1865; paroled, April 29, 1865; mustered out, June 28, 1865, at New York city; see sergeant, Eighteenth Battery, U. S. Engineers.

BRAZEE, LEVI.—Age, 21 years. Enlisted, August 22, 1862, at Fremont, to serve three years; mustered in as private, Co. G, October 9, 1862; died, March 4, 1863, while on furlough at Fremont, N. Y.

BREWSTER, JOEL N.—Age, 18 years. Enlisted, August 15, 1862, at Bloomingburg, to serve three years; mustered in as private, Co. G, October 9, 1862; absent, on duty at Barracks No. 1, at Nashville, Tenn., at muster-out of company.

BREWSTER, WILLIAM H.—Age, 29 years. Enlisted, August 18, 1862, at Bloomingburg, to serve three years; mustered in as corporal, Co. G, October 9, 1862; returned to ranks prior to April 11, 1863; transferred to Veteran Reserve Corps, April 7, 1865.

BROWN, JAMES.—Age, 18 years. Enlisted, July 30, 1862, at Fremont, to serve three years; mustered in as private, Co. G, October 9, 1862; wounded in action, May 25, 1864, near Dallas, Ga.; discharged, May 26, 1865, at hospital, New Albany, Ind.

BUDD, ANDREW P.—Age, 23 years. Enlisted, September 1, 1862, at Monticello, to serve three years; mustered in as corporal, Co. G, October 9, 1862; mustered out with company, July 20, 1865, near Alexandria, Va.

CAIN, GEORGE S.—Age, 41 years. Enlisted, August 21, 1862, at Fremont, to serve three years; mustered in as private, Co. G, October 9, 1862; promoted corporal, February 10, 1863; wounded in action, October 29, 1863, at Lookout Valley, Tenn.; discharged for wounds, July 11, 1865, at hospital, Murfreesboro, Tenn.

CARNEY, BENJAMIN W.—Age, 30 years. Enlisted, September 4, 1862, at Monticello, to serve three years; mustered in as private, Co. G, October 9, 1862; died, January 27, 1864, at hospital, Nashville, Tenn.

CARPENTER, CHARLES.—Age, 18 years. Enlisted, August 12, 1862, at Bloomingburg, to serve three years; mustered in as private, Co. G, October 9, 1862; mustered out with company, July 20, 1865, near Alexandria, Va.

CHANDLER, ALVAH M.—Age, 21 years. Enlisted, August 14, 1862, at Fremont, to serve three years; mustered in as private, Co. G, October 9, 1862; promoted corporal, no date; mustered out with company, July 20, 1865, near Alexandria, Va.

CHANDLER, MARVIN.—Age, 28 years. Enlisted, August 14, 1862, at Fremont, to serve three years; mustered in as corporal, Co. G, October 9, 1862; promoted sergeant prior to October, 1864; absent, on furlough, since July 1, 1865, and at muster-out of company.

CLARK, JOSEPH W.—Age, 20 years. Enlisted, August 13, 1862, at Fremont, to serve three years; mustered in as private, Co. G, October 9, 1862; mustered out with company, July 20, 1865, near Alexandria, Va.

CONKLIN, GEORGE H.—Age, 43 years. Enlisted, August 4, 1862, at Cochecton, to serve three years; mustered in as private,

Co. G, October 9, 1862; transferred to Veteran Reserve Corps, May 16, 1863.

COOK, MATHIAS.—Age, 37 years. Enlisted, August 22, 1862, at Bloomingburg, to serve three years; mustered in as private, Co. G, October 9, 1862; mustered out with company, July 20, 1865, near Alexandria, Va.

CRANE, ADAM R.—Age, 35 years. Enlisted, September 2, 1862, at Bloomingburg, to serve three years; mustered in as private, Co. G, October 9, 1862; left sick in camp, near Williamsburg, Va., June 11, 1863; no further record.

CREAMER, JEREMIAH.—Age, 29 years. Enlisted, August 22, 1862, at Fremont, to serve three years; mustered in as private, Co. G, October 9, 1862; mustered out with company, July 20, 1865, near Alexandria, Va.

DAVIS, JOSEPH.—Age, 21 years. Enlisted, August 15, 1862, at Tusten, to serve three years; mustered in as private, Co. G, October 9, 1862; mustered out with company, July 20, 1865, near Alexandria, Va.

DAVIS, PROSPER P.—Age, 45 years. Enlisted, August 15, 1862, at Tusten, to serve three years; mustered in as private, Co. G, October 9, 1862; discharged for disability, February 16, 1863.

DELANEY, THOMAS.—Age, 26 years. Enlisted, July 24, 1862, at Fremont, to serve three years; mustered in as sergeant, Co. G, October 9, 1862; mustered out with company, July 20, 1865, near Alexandria, Va.

DEVENS, JAMES P.—Age, 39 years. Enlisted, August 19, 1862, at Bloomingburg, to serve three years; mustered in as private, Co. G, October 9, 1862; died of diarrhea, January 1, 1864, at Eleventh Corps Hospital, Lookout Valley, Tenn.; also borne as Debens.

DICKINSON, MARCELLAS.—Age, 18 years. Enlisted, August 13, 1862, at Fremont, to serve three years; mustered in as private, Co. G, October 9, 1862; discharged for disability, September 2, 1864, at Jeffersonville, Ind.

DOOLITTLE, TIMOTHY.—Age, 29 years. Enlisted, August 19, 1862, at Bloomingburg, to serve three years; mustered in as corporal, Co. G, October 9, 1862; mustered out with company, July 20, 1865, near Alexandria, Va.

FISH, HENRY S.—Age, 44 years. Enlisted, August 21, 1862, at Bloomingburg, to serve three years; mustered in as corporal, Co. G, October 9, 1862; died of diarrhea, December 8, 1863.

GORTON, DUBOIS.—Age, 28 years. Enlisted, August 22, 1862, at Neversink, to serve three years; mustered in as private, Co. G, October 9, 1862; mustered out with company, July 20, 1865, near Alexandria, Va.

GORTON, JOSEPH.—Age, 27 years. Enlisted at Goshen, to serve one year, and mustered in as private, Co. G, September 3, 1864; mustered out with detachment, June 10, 1865, at Washington, D. C.

GOULD, RICHARD.—Age, 23 years. Enlisted, August 22, 1862, at Fremont, to serve three years; mustered in as private, Co. G, October 9, 1862; wounded in action, July 28, 1864, near Atlanta, Ga.; mustered out with company, July 20, 1865, near Alexandria, Va.

HALL, AARON B.—Age, 24 years. Enlisted, August 13, 1862, at Fremont, to serve three years; mustered in as private, Co. G, October 9, 1862; mustered out with company, July 20, 1865, near Alexandria, Va.; also borne as Hull.

HAUK, CHRISTIAN.—Age, 18 years. Enlisted, August 22, 1862, at Rockland, to serve three years; mustered in as private, Co. G, October 9, 1862; transferred to Ninth Regiment, Veteran Reserve Corps, September 26, 1863; mustered out, July 19, 1865, at Washington, D. C.; also borne as Hank.

HAZEN, JEREMIAH.—Age, 19 years. Enlisted, August 30, 1862, at Bethel, to serve three years; mustered in as private, Co. G, October 9, 1862; promoted corporal, no date; mustered out with company, July 20, 1865, near Alexandria, Va.

HENDRICKSON, RICHARD C.—Age, 38 years. Enlisted, August 13, 1862, at Fremont, to serve three years; mustered in as private, Co. G, October 9, 1862; absent, on furlough, since July 1, 1865, and at muster-out of company.

HOTCHKIN, CHESTER D.—Age, 22 years. Enlisted, September 4, 1862, at Liberty, to serve three years; mustered in as private, Co. G, October 9, 1862; deserted, July 16, 1863, near Funkstown, Md.

HUGHS, WARREN —Age, 21 years. Enlisted, August 22, 1862, at Fremont, to serve three years; mustered in as private, Co. G, October 9, 1862; promoted corporal, February 10, 1863; transferred to Co. D, Seventeenth Regiment, Veteran Reserve Corps, April 8, 1865; discharged, July 20, 1865, at Indianapolis, Ind.

HULL, see Hall.

JOHNSON, DENNIS.—Age, 44 years. Enlisted, August 22, 1862, at Neversink, to serve three years; mustered in as private, Co. G, October 9, 1862; promoted corporal prior to October, 1864; sergeant, no date; killed in action, March 16, 1865, at Averasboro, N. C.

KELLAM, ALEXANDER C.—Age, 26 years. Enrolled at Washington, D. C., to serve three years; mustered in as second lieutenant, Co. G, September 8, 1862; discharged, March 17, 1863. Commissioned second lieutenant, November 21, 1862, with rank from September 6, 1862, original.

KELLAM, PETER.—Age, 32 years. Enlisted, July 24, 1862, at Fremont, to serve three years; mustered in as first sergeant, Co. G, October 9, 1862; absent, at hospital, David's Island, New York Harbor, since April 15, 1865, and at muster-out of company.

KELLAM, SANDWITH D.—Age, 21 years. Enlisted, August 22, 1862, at Fremont, to serve three years; mustered in as private, Co. G, October 9, 1862; transferred to Co. B, Eighteenth Regiment, Veteran Reserve Corps; promoted corporal, no dates; mustered out with detachment, July 19, 1865, at Washington, D. C.

KIMBALL, JAMES.—Age, 18 years. Enlisted, August 15, 1862, at Neversink, to serve three years; mustered in as private, Co. G, October 9, 1862; died subsequent to June, 1863, at Bridgeport, Ala.

KNAPP, NELSON P.—Age, 30 years. Enlisted, August 22, 1862, at Fremont, to serve three years; mustered in as private, Co. G, October 9, 1862; died of diarrhea, December 18, 1863, at Eleventh Corps Hospital, Lookout Valley, Tenn.

KNAPP, WILLIAM.—Age, 26 years. Enlisted, August 29, 1862, at Thompson, to serve three years; mustered in as private, Co. G, October 9, 1862; mustered out with company, July 20, 1865, near Alexandria, Va.

KRUM, PETER L.—Age, 23 years. Enlisted, August 21, 1862, at Neversink, to serve three years; mustered in as private, Co. G, October 9, 1862; discharged for disability, October 17, 1863.

KYRK, EPHRAIM E.—Age, 21 years. Enlisted, August 15, 1862, at Bloomingburg, to serve three years; mustered in as private, Co. G, October 9, 1862; mustered out with company, July 20, 1865, near Alexandria, Va.; also borne as Kirk.

LAESA, MARAANA.—Age, 30 years. Enlisted, August 16, 1862, at Fremont, to serve three years; mustered in as private, Co. G, October 9, 1862; deserted, March 12, 1863, near Alexandria, Va.

LAMBERT, ADAM.—Age, 18 years. Enlisted at Goshen, to serve one year, and mustered in as private, Co. G, September 9, 1864; mustered out with detachment, June 10, 1865, at Washington, D. C.

LANNING, STEPHEN.—Age, 21 years. Enlisted, September 1, 1862, at Bloomingburg, to serve three years; mustered in as private, Co. G, October 9, 1862; mustered out with company, July 20, 1865, near Alexandria, Va.

LUCKEY, THERON B.—Age, 21 years. Enrolled at Albany, to serve three years, and mustered in as first lieutenant, Co. G, September 8, 1862; discharged, May 24, 1863. Commissioned first lieutenant, November 21, 1862, with rank from September 6, 1862, original.

LUCKEY, WILLIAM V.—Age, 28 years. Enlisted, August 22, 1862, at Bloomingburg, to serve three years; mustered in as sergeant, Co. G, October 9, 1862; deserted, August 26, 1864.

McWILLIAMS, CHARLES S.—Age, 18 years. Enlisted, August 14, 1862, at Bloomingburg, to serve three years; mustered in as musician, Co. G, September 9, 1862; mustered out with company, July 20, 1865, near Alexandria, Va.

MILLER, VERDINE H.—Age, 20 years. Enlisted, August 13, 1862, at Bloomingburg, to serve three years; mustered in as private, Co. G, October 9, 1862; wounded in action, May 25, 1864, near Dallas, Ga.; absent, at Camp Deniston, Ohio, at muster-out of company.

MILLIGAN, WILLIAM G.—Age, 20 years. Enlisted, August 22, 1862, at Bloomingburg, to serve three years; mustered in as private, Co. G, October 9, 1862; died, January 5, 1864, at Convalescent Camp, Bridgeport, Ala.

MYERS, JR., JOHN.—Age, 24 years. Enlisted, August 19, 1862, at Bloomingburg, to serve three years; mustered in as private, Co. G, October 9, 1862; discharged for disability, June 14, 1864.

NEER, SAMUEL.—Age, 35 years. Enlisted, August 22, 1862, at Fremont, to serve three years; mustered in as private, Co. G, October 9, 1862; mustered out with company, July 20, 1865, near Alexandria, Va.

ODELL, JESSE H.—Age, 35 years. Enlisted, August 18, 1862, at Bloomingburg, to serve three years; mustered in as private, Co. G, October 9, 1862; mustered out with company, July 20, 1865, near Alexandria, Va.

OSTERHOUT, GEORGE W.—Age, 22 years. Enlisted, August 13, 1862, at Fremont, to serve three years; mustered in as private, Co. G, October 9, 1862; mustered out with company, July 20, 1865, near Alexandria, Va.

PRICE, PAUL P.—Age, 39 years. Enlisted, August 22, 1862, at Fremont, to serve three years; mustered in as corporal, Co. G, October 9, 1862; promoted sergeant, no date; mustered out with company, July 20, 1865, near Alexandria, Va.

REYNOLDS, BENJAMIN.—Age, 22 years. Enrolled at Albany, to serve three years; mustered in as captain, Co. G, September 8, 1862; captured, no date; paroled, March, 1865; discharged to date, May 5, 1865. Commissioned captain, November 21, 1862, with rank from September 6, 1862, original.

REYNOLDS, HIRAM T.—Age, 44 years. Enlisted, August 22, 1862, at Highland, to serve three years; mustered in as private, Co. G, October 9, 1862; died of diarrhea, subsequent to June, 1863, at Jeffersonville, Ind.

REYNOLDS, WILLIAM H.—Age, 21 years. Enlisted at Goshen, to serve one year, and mustered in as private, Co. G, October 10, 1864; mustered out with detachment, July 1, 1865, at Washington, D. C.

ROBINSON, WILLIAM.—Age, 18 years. Enlisted, August 22, 1862, at Rockland, to serve three years; mustered in as private,

Co. G, October 9, 1862; mustered out with company, July 20, 1865, near Alexandria, Va.

ROCKFELLOW, CHARLES B.—Age, 23 years. Enlisted, August 15, 1862, at Bloomingburg, to serve three years; mustered in as private, Co. G, October 9, 1862; discharged with detachment, June 2, 1865, at hospital, Camp Denison, Ohio.

ROSE, GEORGE W.—Age, 31 years. Enlisted, August 13, 1862, at Fremont, to serve three years; mustered in as private, Co. G, October 9, 1862; transferred to Veteran Reserve Corps, September 1, 1863.

ROSE, WILLIAM E.—Age, 23 years. Enlisted, August 13, 1862, at Fremont, to serve three years; mustered in as private, Co. G, October 9, 1862; died from amputation of arm, June 12, 1864, at Nashville, Tenn.

RYDER, JACOB T.—Age, 26 years. Enlisted, August 26, 1862, at Fremont, to serve three years; mustered in as private, Co. G, October 9, 1862; died of diarrhea, January 30, 1864, at Eleventh Corps Hospital; also borne as Rider.

SCOTT, ADAM.—Age, 36 years. Enlisted, August 22, 1862, at Fremont, to serve three years; mustered in as private, Co. G, October 9, 1862; died of diarrhea, November 10, 1863, at hospital, Alexandria, Va.

SEAMAN, JAMES H.—Age, 27 years. Enlisted, August 19, 1862, at Bloomingburg, to serve three years; mustered in as sergeant, Co. G, October 9, 1862; discharged, June 18, 1863, at Evansville, Ind.

SEELEY, JAMES L.—Age, 27 years. Enlisted, August 22, 1862, at Tusten, to serve three years; mustered in as private, Co. G, October 9, 1862; discharged for disability, January 7, 1865.

SEELEY, SANFORD S.—Age, 23 years. Enlisted, August 22, 1862, at Tusten, to serve three years; mustered in as private, Co. G, October 9, 1862; discharged for disability, July 2, 1863.

SHIELDS, CHARLES J.—Age, 26 years. Enlisted at Goshen, to serve one year, and mustered in as private, Co. G, September 8, 1864; mustered out with detachment, June 10, 1865, at Washington, D. C.

STEWART, LEVI.—Age, 26 years. Enlisted, August 14, 1862, at Neversink, to serve three years; mustered in as sergeant, Co. G, October 9, 1862; mustered out with company, July 20, 1865, near Alexandria, Va.

STURDEVANT, FRANKLIN.—Age, 18 years. Enlisted, August 18, 1862, at Forestburg, to serve three years; mustered in as private, Co. G, October 9, 1862; promoted corporal prior to October, 1864; mustered out with company, July 20, 1865, near Alexandria, Va.

TELLER, HORACE D.—Age, 18 years. Enlisted, September 4, 1862, at Neversink, to serve three years; mustered in as private, Co. G, October 9, 1862; killed in action, October 30, 1863, at Lookout Valley, Tenn.

THOMAS, NATHAN M.—Age, 35 years. Enlisted, August 22, 1862, at Fremont, to serve three years; mustered in as private, Co. G, October 9, 1862; promoted corporal, no date; wounded in action, May 15, 1864, near Resaca, Ga.; mustered out with company, July 20, 1865, near Alexandria, Va.

TODD, JOHN.—Age, 18 years. Enlisted, August 15, 1862, at Bloomingburg, to serve three years; mustered in as private, Co. G, October 9, 1862; transferred to Veteran Reserve Corps, April 30, 1864; mustered out, July 22, 1865, at St. Louis, Mo., as of One Hundred and Fifty-sixth Company, Second Battalion, Veteran Reserve Corps.

TOMPKINS, LEONARD.—Age, 18 years. Enlisted, August 12, 1862, at Bloomingburg, to serve three years; mustered in as private, Co. G, October 9, 1862; promoted corporal, no date; mustered out with company, July 20, 1865, near Alexandria, Va.

TURNER, HENRY.—Age, 18 years. Enlisted, August 22, 1862, at Fremont, to serve three years; mustered in as private, Co. G, October 9, 1862; captured, March 27, 1865, near Goldsboro, N. C.; paroled, May 5, 1865; discharged, June 30, 1865, at New York city.

TURNER, NATHANIEL.—Age, 21 years. Enlisted, August 22, 1862, at Fremont, to serve three years; mustered in as private, Co. G, October 9, 1862; died of diarrhea, December 20, 1863, at Eleventh Corps Hospital.

TYLER, WILLIAM.—Age, 18 years. Enlisted, August 16, 1862, at Fremont, to serve three years; mustered in as private, Co. G, October 9, 1862; discharged, June 6, 1865, at Madison, Ind.

VERWIMP, JOHN.—Age, 27 years. Enlisted, August 21, 1862, at Bloomingburg, to serve three years; mustered in as private, Co. G, October 9, 1862; mustered out with company, July 20, 1865, near Alexandria, Va.

WALKER, JOHN JACOB.—Age, 26 years. Enlisted, August 12, 1862, at Thompson, to serve three years; mustered in as private, Co. G, October 9, 1862; died of meningitis, October 7, 1864, at hospital, Atlanta, Ga.

WARING, STEPHEN.—Age, 35 years. Enlisted, August 20, 1862, at Thompson, to serve three years; mustered in as wagoner, Co. G, October 9, 1862; transferred to Thirty-eighth Company, Second Battalion, Veteran Reserve Corps, no date; mustered out with detachment, July 26, 1865, at Washington, D. C.

WATTS, THOMAS.—Age, 40 years. Enlisted, August 16, 1862, at Thompson, to serve three years; mustered in as private, Co. G, October 9, 1862; discharged for disability, March 26, 1864.

WORMSLEY, WARNER.—Age, 26 years. Enlisted, August 14, 1862, at Fremont, to serve three years; mustered in as private, Co. G, October 9, 1862; absent, without leave, since March 14, 1864, and at muster-out of company.

KILLED IN ACTION.

Johnson, Dennis, Mar. 16, 1865, at Averasboro, N. C.
Teller, Horace D., Oct. 30, 1863, at Lookout Valley, Tenn.

WOUNDED IN ACTION.

Babcock, James H., Mar. 16, 1865, at Averasboro, N. C.
Baker, Charles H., July 20, 1864, at Peach Tree Creek, Ga.
Brown, James, May 25, 1864, near Dallas, Ga.
Cain, George S., Oct. 20, 1863, at Lookout Valley, Tenn.
Gould, Richard, July 28, 1864, near Atlanta, Ga.
Thomas, Nathan M., May 15, 1864, at Resaca, Ga.

DIED OF DISEASE AND WOUNDS.

Brazee, Levi, Mar. 4, 1863, at Freemont, N. Y.
Carney, Benjamin W., Jan. 27, 1864, at Nashville, Tenn.
Devens, James P., Jan. 1, 1864, at Lookout Valley, Tenn.
Fish, Henry S., Dec. 8, 1863, at ————.
Kimball, James, before June, 1863, at Bridgeport, Ala.
Knapp, Nelson P., Dec. 18, 1863, at Lookout Valley, Tenn.
Milligan, William G. Jan. 5, 1864, at Bridgeport, Ala.
Reynolds, Hiram T., before June, 1863, at Jeffersonville, Ind.
Rose, William E., June 12, 1864, at Nashville, Tenn.
Ryder, Jacob T., Jan. 30, 1864, at 11th Corps Hospital.
Turner, Nathaniel, Dec. 20, 1863, at 11th Corps Hospital.
Walker, John Jacob, Oct. 6, 1864, at Atlanta, Ga.

DISCHARGED DURING SERVICE.

Babcock, James H., June 5, 1865, for disability.
Brown, James, May 26, 1865, for disability.
Cain, George S., July 11, 1865, for disability.
Davis, Prosper P., Feb. 16, 1863, for disability.
Dickinson, Marcellas, Sept. 2, 1864, for disability.
Kellam, Alexander C., Mar. 17, 1863, for disability.
Krum, Peter L., Oct. 17, 1863, for disability.
Luckey, Theron B., May 24, 1863, for disability.
Myers, John, Jr., June 14 1864, for disability.
Seaman, James H., June 18, 1863, for disability.
Seeley, James L., Jan. 7, 1865, for disability.
Seeley, Sanford S., July 2, 1863, for disability.
Tyler, William, June 6, 1865, for disability.
Watts, Thomas, Mar. 26, 1864, for disability.

TRANSFERRED.

Achart, William H., Sept. 26, 1863, to Veteran Reserve Corps.
Babcock, George H., Sept. 3, 1863, to Veteran Reserve Corps.
Baker, Charles H., no date, to Veteran Reserve Corps.
Brewster, William H., April 7, 1865, to Veteran Reserve Corps.
Conklin, George H., May 16, 1863, to Veteran Reserve Corps.
Hank, Christian, Sept. 26, 1863, to Veteran Reserve Corps.

Hughs, Warren, April 8, 1865, to Veteran Reserve Corps.
Rose, George W., Sept. 1, 1863, to Veteran Reserve Corps.
Todd, John, April 30, 1864, to Veteran Reserve Corps.
Waring, Stephen, no date, to Veteran Reserve Corps.

DESERTED.

Hotchkin, Chester D., July 16, 1863, near Funkstown, Md.
Laesa, Maraana, Mar. 12, 1863, near Alexandria, Va.
Luckey, William V., Aug. 26, 1864.
Wormsley, Warner, absent without leave since Mar. 14, 1864.

CAPTURED.

Boyle, Thomas H., April 14, 1865, paroled April 29, 1865.
Reynolds, Benjamin, no date, paroled Mar., 1865.
Turner, Henry, Mar. 27, 1865, paroled May 5, 1865.
Crane, Adam R., left sick near Williamsburg, Va.; no further record.

COMPANY H.

CAPTAINS.

George H. Decker, original, to muster out of Regt. (Bvt. Major N. Y. V.)

FIRST LIEUTENANTS.

Jirah I. Young, original, promoted to Captain Co. G.

George C. Pinney, from June 19, 1865, to muster out of Regt.

SECOND LIEUTENANTS.

Rensselaer Hammond, original, promoted to First Lieut. Co. G.

Alexander H. Brown, May 1, 1864, resigned May 15, 1865.

Henry Ward, July 24, 1865, not mustered.

RECORD OF MEMBERS OF COMPANY H—ORIGINAL.

ANNIS, WILLIAM D.—Age, 20 years. Enlisted, August 15, 1862, at Liberty, to serve three years; mustered in as corporal, Co. H, October 8, 1862; mustered out with company, July 20, 1865, at Washington, D. C.

ARMSTRONG, STEPHEN.—Age, 17 years. Enlisted at Goshen, to serve one year, and mustered in private, Co. H, September 9, 1864; mustered out with detachment, June 10, 1865, near Washington, D. C.

ATWELL, SELAH.—Age, 18 years. Enlisted, August 16, 1862, at Rockland, to serve three years; mustered in as private, Co. H, October 8, 1862; wounded in action, July 20, 1864, at Peach Tree Creek, Ga.; died of his wounds, July 22, 1864, near Atlanta, Ga.

BARKER, EDWARD.—Age, 28 years. Enlisted at Goshen, to serve one year, and mustered in as private, Co. H, October 5, 1864; mustered out with company, July 20, 1865, at Washington, D. C.

BARNHART, GEORGE.—Age, 37 years. Enlisted at Goshen, to serve one year, and mustered in as private, Co. H, September 20,

1864; mustered out with detachment, June 10, 1865, near Washington, D. C.

BARNHART, STEPHEN C.—Age, 26 years. Enlisted, August 15, 1862, at Liberty, to serve three years; mustered in as private, Co. H, October 8, 1862; mustered out with company, July 20, 1865, at Washington, D. C.

BEACH, ERASTUS D.—Age, 35 years. Enlisted, August 21, 1862, at Monticello, to serve three years; mustered in as sergeant, Co. H, October 8, 1862; discharged for disability, March 9, 1863, at Trinity Hospital, Washington, D. C.

BEACH, HIRAM.—Age, 23 years. Enlisted, August 21, 1862, at Liberty, to serve three years; mustered in as private, Co. H, October 8, 1862; discharged, February 17, 1864, at Camp Distribution, Va.

BEASMER, DE WITT CLINTON.—Age, 26 years. Enlisted, August 16, 1862, at Rockland, to serve three years; mustered in as private, Co. H, October 8, 1862; died, November 2, 1863, at Hospital No. 14, Nashville, Tenn.; also borne as DeWitt Beesimer.

BECKER, ANTHONY.—Age, 26 years. Enlisted, August 22, 1862, at Monticello, to serve three years; mustered in as private, Co. H, October 8, 1862; deserted, October 14, 1862; reported June, 1863, as having joined the One Hundred and Sixty-eighth Infantry.

BENSON, GARRETT W.—Age, 38 years. Enlisted at Goshen, to serve one year, and mustered in as private, Co. H, September 9, 1864; mustered out with detachment, June 10, 1865, near Washington, D. C.

BENTON, JAMES H.—Age, 18 years. Enlisted at Goshen, to serve one year, and mustered in as private, Co. H, September 9, 1864; mustered out with detachment, June 10, 1865, near Washington, D. C.

BILLINGTON, GEORGE.—Age, 23 years. Enlisted, August 20, 1862, at Dryden, to serve three years; mustered in as private, Co. H, October 8, 1862; discharged for disability, April 11, 1863, at hospital, Philadelphia, Pa.

BORDEN, HIRAM.—Age, 22 years. Enlisted, August 16, 1862, at Liberty, to serve three years; mustered in as private, Co. H, October 8, 1862; captured, April 14, 1865; paroled, April 29, 1865; mustered out, June 28, 1865, at New York city.

BRACE, ISAAC.—Age, 30 years. Enlisted, August 16, 1862, at Rockland, to serve three years; mustered in as private, Co. H, October 8, 1862; mustered out with company, July 20, 1865, at Washington, D. C.

BRADLEY, WALTER.—Age, 23 years. Enlisted, August 21, 1862, at Monticello, to serve three years; mustered in as private, Co. H, October 8, 1862; mustered out with company, July 20, 1865, at Washington, D. C.

BURTON, GEORGE W.—Age, 24 years. Enlisted at Rockland, to serve three years, and mustered in as private, Co. H, January 10, 1864; mustered out with company, July 20, 1865, at Washington, D. C.

CALKINS, GEORGE H.—Age, 27 years. Enlisted, August 21, 1862, at Liberty, to serve three years; mustered in as private, Co. H, October 8, 1862; mustered out with company, July 20, 1865, at Washington, D. C.

CALKINS, JOHN.—Age, 23 years. Enlisted, August 21, 1862, at Liberty, to serve three years; mustered in as private, Co. H, October 8, 1862; promoted corporal, May 27, 1865; mustered out with company, July 20, 1865, at Washington, D. C.

CAMPBELL, BENJAMIN F.—Age, 19 years. Enlisted, August 20, 1862, at Liberty, to serve three years; mustered in as private, Co. H, October 8, 1862; mustered out with company, July 20, 1865, at Washington, D. C.

CAMPBELL, WILLIAM H.—Age, 27 years. Enlisted, August 20, 1862, at Rockland, as private, Co. H; deserted, September 2, 1862, before muster-in; arrested, charge of desertion removed, returned to company, and mustered in to date March 6, 1864; mustered out June 9, 1865, at Washington, D. C., while in Sickel Hospital, Alexandria, Va.

CARRIER, ADELBERT A.—Age, 20 years. Enlisted, August 15, 1862, at Liberty, to serve three years; mustered in as private, Co. H, October 8, 1862; mustered out, May 18, 1865, at Hospital No. 15, Nashville, Tenn.

CHAPMAN, AMOS M.—Age, 21 years. Enlisted, August 15,. 1862, at Liberty, to serve three years; mustered in as private, Co. H, October 8, 1862; wounded in action, July 20, 1864, at Peach Tree Creek, Ga.; died of his wounds, July 22, 1864, at Vining's Station, Ga.

CLARK, GEORGE.—Age, 25 years. Enlisted at Jamaica, to serve one year, and mustered in as private, Co. H, October 8, 1864;. mustered out with company, July 20, 1865, at Washington, D. C.

CLARK, WILLIAM H. H.—Age, 22 years. Enlisted, August 21,. 1862, at Monticello, to serve three years; mustered in as private, Co. H, October 8, 1862; promoted corporal, March 7, 1863; returned to ranks, November 14, 1864; discharged, August 8, 1865.

COCHRAN, ARCHIBALD.—Age, 19 years. Enlisted, August 16, 1862, at Liberty, to serve three years; mustered in as private, Co H, October 8, 1862; mustered out with company, July 20, 1865, at Washington, D. C.

COLE, JR., WILLIAM.—Age, 23 years. Enlisted, August 21, 1862, at Liberty, to serve three years; mustered in as private, Co. H, October 8, 1862; promoted corporal, March 7, 1863; mustered out with company, July 20, 1865, at Washington, D. C.

COLLINS, THOMAS D.—Age, 18 years. Enlisted, August 16, 1862, at Liberty, to serve three years; mustered in as private, Co. H, October 8, 1862; detailed as scout at Corps Headquarters, and made sergeant; discharged at Washington, D. C. Awarded a medal of honor.

CONKLIN, DAVID D.—Age, 23 years. Enlisted, August 14,. 1862, at Monticello, to serve three years; mustered in as corporal,. Co. H, October 8, 1862; transferred to First Battalion, Veteran Reserve Corps, no date; mustered out, August 5, 1865, at Nashville, Tenn.

CONKLIN, LEVI.—Age, 29 years. Enlisted, August 21, 1862, at Liberty, to serve three years; mustered in as private, Co. H, October 8, 1862; mustered out with company, July 20, 1865, at Washington, D. C.

CONKLIN, MANNINGS.—Age, 19 years. Enlisted, August 19,. 1862, at Liberty, to serve three years; mustered in as private, Co.

H, October 8, 1862; mustered out with company, July 20, 1865, at Washington, D. C.

CRARY, JERRY.—Age, 21 years. Enlisted, August 15, 1862, at Liberty, to serve three years; mustered in as corporal, Co. H, October 8, 1862; promoted sergeant, March 7, 1863; wounded in action, May 15, 1864, at Resaca, Ga.; absent, in hospital, at Jeffersonville, Ind., since, and at muster-out of company.

CURRY, RICHARD C.—Age, 36 years. Enlisted at Goshen, to serve one year, and mustered in as private, Co. H, September 9, 1864; mustered out with detachment, June 10, 1865, near Washington, D. C.

DAWSON, DAVID L.—Age, 32 years. Enlisted, August 21, 1862, at Monticello, to serve three years; mustered in as private, Co. H, October 8, 1862; mustered out with company, July 20, 1865, at Washington, D. C.

DECKER, GEORGE H.—Age, 27 years. Enrolled, August 22, 1862, at Monticello, to serve three years; mustered in as captain, Co. H, September 12, 1862; mustered out with company, July 20, 1865, at Washington, D. C. Commissioned captain, November 21, 1862, with rank from September 12, 1862, original.

DECKER, GIDEON W.—Age, 25 years. Enlisted, August 16, 1862, at Rockland, to serve three years; mustered in as private, Co. H, October 8, 1862; mustered out with company, July 20, 1865, at Washington, D. C.

DECKER, JOHN D. W.—Age, 21 years. Enlisted, August 16, 1862, at Rockland, to serve three years; mustered in as private, Co. H, October 8, 1862; transferred to Co. F, Ninth Regiment, Veteran Reserve Corps, no date; mustered out, October 9, 1865, at Washington, D. C..

DECKER, MATHEW.—Age, 19 years. Enlisted, August 16, 1862, at Rockland, to serve three years; mustered in as corporal, Co. H, October 8, 1862; mustered out with company, July 20, 1865, at Washington, D. C.

DECKER, WILLIAM.—Age, 27 years. Enlisted, August 21, 1862. at Liberty, to serve three years; mustered in as private, Co. H, October 8, 1862; died, December 13, 1863, at Eleventh Corps Hospital, Lookout Valley, Tenn.

DONALDSON, CORNELIUS.—Age, 42 years. Enlisted at Goshen, to serve one year, and mustered in as private, Co. H, September 9, 1864; mustered out with detachment, June 10, 1865, near Washington, D. C.

DORAN, JAMES.—Age, 20 years. Enlisted, August 21, 1862, at Monticello, to serve three years; mustered in as private, Co. H, October 8, 1862; mustered out with company, July 20, 1865, at Washington, D. C.

DRENNON, ROBERT.—Age, 40 years. Enlisted, September 6, 1862, at Monticello, to serve three years; mustered in as private, Co. H, October 8, 1862; discharged for disability, March 13, 1863, at hospital, Fort Schuyler, New York Harbor.

DUDLEY, AARON.—Age, 21 years. Enlisted, August 16, 1862, at Rockland, to serve three years; mustered in as private, Co. H, October 8, 1862; mustered out with company, July 20, 1865, at Washington, D. C.

ECKERT, AUGUSTUS O.—Age, 40 years. Enlisted at Goshen, to serve one year, and mustered in as private, Co. H, September 9, 1864; mustered out with detachment, June 10, 1865, near Washington, D. C.

EDWARD, JAMES H.—Age, 18 years. Enlisted, August 21, 1862, at Monticello, to serve three years; mustered in as private, Co. H, October 8, 1862; died, December 20, 1863, while on furlough at Liberty, N. Y.; also borne as Edwards.

ELLIS, GEORGE W.—Age, 18 years. Enlisted, August 19, 1862, at Rockland, to serve three years; mustered in as private, Co. H, October 8, 1862; mustered out with company, July 20, 1865, at Washington, D. C.

ELLIS, SUEL.—Age, 44 years. Enlisted, August 20, 1862, at Monticello, to serve three years; mustered in as private, Co. H, October 8, 1862; died, December 21, 1863, at Eleventh Army Corps Hospital, Lookout Valley, Tenn.

FALKERSON, SEYMOUR J.—Age, 18 years. Enlisted, August 21, 1862, at Liberty, to serve three years; mustered in as private, Co. H, October 8, 1862; wounded in action, July 20, 1864, at Peach Tree Creek, Ga.; died of his wounds, July 21, 1864, near Atlanta, Ga.

FISK, CHANCY S.—Age, 19 years. Enlisted, August 15, 1862, at Liberty, to serve three years; mustered in as sergeant, Co. H, October 8, 1862; absent, on furlough, since July 1, 1865, and at muster-out of company.

FORCE, WILLIAM.—Age, 19 years. Enlisted at Goshen, to serve one year, and mustered in as private, Co. H, September 12, 1864; mustered out with detachment, June 10, 1865, near Washington, D. C.

FOSTER, MOSES H.—Age, 31 years. Enlisted, August 22, 1862, at Liberty, to serve three years; mustered in as private, Co. H, October 8, 1862; died, November 10, 1863, at hospital, Stevenson, Ala.

FRENCH, JONATHAN.—Age, 28 years. Enlisted, August 13, 1862, at Purvis, to serve three years; mustered in as private, Co. H, October 8, 1862; wounded in action, July 20, 1864, at Peach Tree Creek, Ga.; promoted corporal, July 23, 1864; absent, in hospital, since wounded, and at muster-out of company.

FRENCH, WILLIAM H.—Age, 25 years. Enlisted, August 21, 1862, at Monticello, to serve three years; mustered in as musician, Co. H, October 8, 1862; discharged for disability, May 19, 1863, at Fairfax Seminary Hospital, Va.

GEROW, WILLIAM J.—Age, 21 years. Enlisted, August 15, 1862, at Liberty, to serve three years; mustered in as sergeant, Co. H, October 9, 1862; discharged, March 7, 1864, at Hospital No. 1, Murfreesboro, Tenn.

GILDERSLEVE, JOHN A.—Age, 30 years. Enlisted, August 20, 1862, at Liberty, to serve three years; mustered in as private, Co. H, October 8, 1862; transferred to Veteran Reserve Corps, no date.

GILLETT, LUTHER W.—Age, 18 years. Enlisted, August 14, 1862, at Liberty, to serve three years; mustered in as private, Co. H, October 8, 1862; mustered out with company, July 20, 1865, at Washington, D. C.

GORTON, WILLIAM.—Age, 33 years. Enlisted at Goshen, to serve one year; mustered in as private, Co. H, September 9, 1864; mustered out with detachment, June 10, 1865, near Washington, D. C.

GRANT, JOHN H.—Age, 21 years. Enlisted, August 14, 1862, at Liberty, to serve three years; mustered in as private, Co. H, October 8, 1862; promoted corporal, no date; mustered out with company, July 20, 1865, at Washington, D. C.

GRANT, LEWIS.—Age, 20 years. Enlisted, August 15, 1862, at Liberty, to serve three years; mustered in as private, Co. H, October 8, 1862; mustered out with company, July 20, 1865, at Washington, D. C.

GRAY, BENJAMIN.—Age, 21 years. Enlisted, August 21, 1862, at Rockland, to serve three years; mustered in as private, Co. H, October 8, 1862; discharged, September 13, 1863, at Portsmouth Hospital, Fort Monroe, Va.

HAMILTON, WILLIAM.—Age, 24 years. Enlisted, August 19, 1862, at Rockland, to serve three years; mustered in as private, Co. H, October 8, 1862; transferred to Veteran Reserve Corps, May 20, 1863.

HAMMOND, RENSSELAER.—Age, 21 years. Enrolled, August 22, 1862, at Monticello, to serve three years; mustered in as second lieutenant, Co. H, October 8, 1862; as first lieutenant, Co. G, May 1, 1864; as adjutant, September 1, 1864; mustered out with regiment, July 20, 1865, at Washington, D. C. Commissioned second lieutenant, November 21, 1862, with rank from September 12, 1862, original; first lieutenant, April 18, 1864, with rank from April 2, 1864, vice E. K. Apgar, dismissed; adjutant, August 12, 1864, with rank from July 20, 1864, vice W. M. Ratcliff, killed in action; captain, not mustered, July 24, 1865, with rank from May 16, 1865, vice G. Young, discharged.

HAVENS, SAMUEL H.—Age, 45 years. Enlisted, August 14, 1862, at Monticello, to serve three years; mustered in as private, Co. H, October 8, 1862; mustered out with company, July 20, 1865, at Washington, D. C.

HECTOR, HIRAM.—Age, 27 years. Enlisted at Goshen, to serve one year, and mustered in as private, Co. H, October 5, 1864; mustered out with detachment, June 20, 1865, at Mower Hospital, Philadelphia, Pa.

HILL, GEORGE.—Age, 23 years. Enlisted, August 21, 1862, at Cochecton, to serve three years; mustered in as private, Co. H, October 8, 1862; discharged, July 30, 1864, at Indianapolis, Ind.

HODGE, LEANDER A.—Age, 23 years. Enlisted, August 15, 1862, at Liberty, to serve three years; mustered in as private, Co. H, October 8, 1862; deserted, April 7, 1863, on expiration of furlough, from Mower Hospital, Philadelphia, Pa.

HOWARD, JOHN M.—Age, 23 years. Enlisted, August 21, 1862, at Monticello, to serve three years; mustered in as wagoner, Co. H, October 8, 1862; discharged, August 8, 1863, at Convalescent Camp, near Alexandria, Va.

HUNTINGTON, EDWARD H.—Age, 18 years. Enlisted, August 14, 1862, at Liberty, to serve three years; mustered in as private, Co. H, October 8, 1862; mustered out, June 6, 1865, at David's Island, New York Harbor, also borne as Hundington.

HURLEY, JR., ELISHA.—Age, 44 years. Enlisted, August 14, 1862, at Dryden, to serve three years; mustered in as corporal, Co. H, October 8, 1862; transferred to Veteran Reserve Corps, May 15, 1864.

IRONS, GEORGE H.—Age, 21 years. Enlisted, August 14, 1862. at Liberty, to serve three years; mustered in as corporal, Co. H, October 8, 1862; returned to ranks, November 14, 1864; absent, without leave, since April 8, 1865, and at muster-out of company.

KILE, GEORGE W.—Age, 19 years. Enlisted, August 16, 1862, at Liberty, to serve three years; mustered in as private, Co. H, October 8, 1862; deserted, no date, on expiration of furlough, from Harewood Hospital, Washington, D. C.

KNIFFIN, BENJAMIN.—Age, 21 years. Enlisted, August 21, 1862, at Liberty, to serve three years; mustered in as private, Co. H, October 8, 1862; mustered out with company, July 20, 1865, at Washington, D. C.

LAIR, JAMES D.—Age, 17 years. Enlisted at Goshen, to serve one year, and mustered in as private, Co. H, September 20, 1864; mustered out with detachment, June 10, 1865, near Washington, D. C.

LAYMON, ALSTON.—Age, 29 years. Enlisted, August 14, 1862, at Liberty, to serve three years; mustered in as private, Co. H, October 8, 1862; mustered out with company, July 20, 1865, at Washington, D. C.

LEWIS, CHARLES W.—Age, 27 years. Enlisted, August 22, 1862, at Monticello, to serve three years; mustered in as private, Co. H, October 8, 1862; discharged with detachment, July 1, 1865, at Carver Hospital, Washington, D. C.

LEWIS, JOSEPH P.—Age, 18 years. Enlisted at Goshen, to serve one year, and mustered in as private, Co. H, October 5, 1864; mustered out with company, July 20, 1865, at Washington, D. C.

LEWIS, SAMUEL A.—Age, 18 years. Enlisted at Goshen, to serve one year, and mustered in as private, Co. H, October 5, 1864; mustered out with company, July 20, 1865, at Washington, D. C.

MARVIN, JOHN B.—Age, 21 years. Enlisted, August 14, 1862, at Liberty, to serv : three years; mustered in as private, Co. H, October 8, 1862; mustered out with company, July 20, 1865, at Washington, D. C.

McKELLIPS, ENOS C.—Age, 18 years. Enlisted, August 16, 1862, at Rockland, to serve three years; mustered in as musician, Co. H, October 8, 1862; grade changed to private, no date; mustered out with company, July 20, 1865, at Washington, D. C.

McLYNN, JAMES.—Age, 19 years. Enlisted at Goshen, to serve one year, and mustered in as private, Co. H, October 11, 1864; assigned to company, November 11, 1864; never reported.

McPHELOMY, ROBERT.—Age, 19 years. Enlisted, August 15, 1862, at Liberty, to serve three years; mustered in as private, Co. H, October 8, 1862; absent, in hospital, at Nashville, Tenn., since May 2, 1864, and at muster-out of company.

MOFFITT, FERRIS.—Age, 21 years. Enlisted, August 22, 1862, at Liberty, to serve three years; mustered in as private, Co. H, October 8, 1862; transferred to Co. I, Seventh Regiment, Veteran Reserve Corps, no date; transferred to this regiment, October 25, 1864; mustered out with company, July 20, 1865, at Washington, D. C.

MORGAN, PATRICK.—Age, 39 years. Enlisted, August 17, 1862, at Liberty, to serve three years; mustered in as private, Co. H, October 8, 1862; transferred to Co. H, Sixth Regiment, Veteran Reserve Corps, April 26, 1864; mustered out with detachment, August 5, 1865, at Johnson's Island, Ohio.

MORSE, JOHN W.—Age, 45 years. Enlisted, August 20, 1862, at Liberty, to serve three years; mustered in as private, Co. H, October 8, 1862; mustered out with company, July 20, 1865, at Washington, D. C.

MURRY, ADOLPHUS E.—Age, 21 years. Enlisted, August 21, 1862, at Monticello, to serve three years; mustered in as private, Co. H, October 8, 1862; discharged, November 21, 1863, at hospital, Louisville, Ky.

MURRY, ANDREW.—Age, 25 years. Enlisted, September 1, 1862, at Neversink, to serve three years; mustered in as private, Co. H, October 8, 1862; promoted coropral, no date; mustered out with company, July 20, 1865, at Washington, D. C.

MYERS, WILLIAM.—Age, 20 years. Date of enlistment and muster-in as private, Co. H, not stated; deserted, no date, and enlisted in Thirteenth Cavalry, November 14, 1864; never returned to this regiment.

O'BRIAN, JOHN.—Age, 21 years. Enlistde at Goshen, to serve one year, and mustered in as private, Co. H, October 11, 1864; assigned to company, November 11, 1864; never reported.

OSTERHOUT, GIDEON.—Age, 21 years. Enlisted, August 21, 1862, at Grahamville, to serve three years; mustered in as private, Co. H, October 8, 1862; died, November 2, 1863, at Hospital No. 14, Nashville, Tenn.

PARLIMAN, WILLIAM H.—Age, 22 years. Enlisted, August 14, 1862, at Liberty, to serve three years; mustered in as private, Co. H, October 8, 1862; absent, at hospital, Annapolis, Md., since July 18, 1863, and at muster-out of company.

PORTER, HENRY W.—Age, 18 years. Enlisted, August 21, 1862, at Liberty, to serve three years; mustered in as private, Co. H, October 8, 1862; discharged, September 29, 1864, at Atlanta, Ga.

PORTER, ORSON.—Age, 16 years. Enlisted at Poughkeepsie, to serve one year, and mustered in as private, Co. H, October 13, 1864; mustered out with company, July 20, 1865, at Washington, D. C.

PORTER, RUFUS W.—Age, 22 years. Enlisted, August 14, 1862, at Liberty, to serve three years; mustered in as first sergeant, Co. H, October 8, 1862; wounded in action, July 20, 1864, at Peach Tree Creek, Ga.; mustered out, May 19, 1865, at Indianapolis, Ind.

REESE, CHARLES G.—Age, 18 years. Enlisted, August 15, 1862, at Liberty, to serve three years; mustered in as corporal, Co. H, October 8, 1862; returned to ranks, no date; promoted corporal, March 7, 1863; wounded in action, July 20, 1864, at Peach Tree Creek, Ga.; died, February 19, 1865, at Hospital No. 11, Nashville, Tenn.

ROOSA, WILLIAM M.—Age, 25 years. Enlisted at Goshen, to serve one year, and mustered in as private, Co. H, October 13, 1864; mustered out with company, July 20, 1865, at Washington, D. C.

ROSE, GARRETT.—Age, 31 years. Enlisted at Goshen, to serve one year, and mustered in as private, Co. H, October 5, 1864; mustered out with company, July 20, 1865, at Washington, D. C.

ROSE, GUSTAVUS.—Age, 25 years. Enlisted at Goshen, to serve one year, and mustered in as private, Co. H, October 5, 1864; mustered out with company, July 20, 1865, at Washington D. C.

ROSE, HIRAM E.—Age, 18 years. Enlisted, August 16, 1862, at Liberty, to serve three years; mustered in as private, Co. H, October 8, 1862; mustered out with company, July 20, 1865, at Washington, D. C.

ROSE, SETH B.—Age, 25 years. Enlisted at Goshen, to serve one year, and mustered in as private, Co. H, September 3, 1864; mustered out with detachment, June 10, 1865, near Washington, D. C.

SHAFER, JACOB E.—Age, 33 years. Enlisted, August 15, 1862, at Liberty, to serve three years; mustered in as private, Co. H, October 8, 1862; mustered out with company, July 20, 1865, at Washington, D. C.

SHEELY, CALVIN.—Age, 18 years. Enlisted at Goshen, to serve one year, and mustered in as private, Co. H, September 3, 1864; mustered out with detachment, June 10, 1865, near Washington, D. C.

SHERWOOD, ROSEVELT F.—Age, 22 years. Enlisted, August 21, 1862, at Liberty, to serve three years; mustered in as private, Co. H, October 8, 1862; discharged, August 17, 1863, at Convalescent Camp, near Alexandria, Va.

SLATER, STEPHEN.—Age, 19 years. Enlisted at Goshen, to serve one year, and mustered in as private, Co. H, September 9. 1864; mustered out with detachment, June 10, 1865, near Washington, D. C.

SMITH, WILLIAM J.—Age, 24 years. Enlisted at Goshen, to serve one year, and mustered in as private, Co. H, September 9, 1864; mustered out, July 7, 1865, at Hick's Hospital, Baltimore, Md., as William G.

SPRAGUE, LAFAYETTE.—Age, 18 years. Enlisted, August 16, 1862, at Liberty, to serve three years; mustered in as private, Co. H, October 8, 1862; mustered out with company, July 20, 1865, at Washington, D. C.

STICKELS, ANDREW.—Age, 23 years. Enlisted, August 16, 1862, at Monticello, to serve three years; mustered in as corporal, Co. H, October 8, 1862; wounded in action, July 20, 1864, at Peach Tree Creek, Ga.; mustered out, May 27, 1865, at Louisville, Ky.

STOTARD, WILLIAM.—Age, 21 years. Enlisted, August 16, 1862, at Monticello, to serve three years; mustered in as sergeant, Co. H, October 8, 1862; mustered out with company, July 20, 1865, at Washington, D. C., as Stoddard.

TRAVIS, CHARLES W.—Age, 22 years. Enlisted, August 21, 1862, at Liberty, to serve three years; mustered in as private, Co. H, October 8, 1862; mustered out, July 22, 1865, at New York city.

WAGER, ENOS.—Age, 45 years. Enlisted, August 21, 1862, at Parksville, to serve three years; mustered in as private, Co. H, October 8, 1862; discharged, December 12, 1862, at Columbia College Hospital, Georgetown, D. C.

WARD, HENRY.—Age, 29 years. Enrolled, August 22, 1862, at Liberty, to serve three years; mustered in as corporal, Co. H, October 8, 1862; promoted sergeant, July 23, 1864; mustered out with company, July 20, 1865, at Washington, D. C., as Harry Ward. Commissioned, not mustered, second lieutenant, July 24, 1865, with rank from May 16, 1865, vice R. Hammond, promoted.

WARD, JR., JOSEPH.—Age, 26 years. Enlisted, August 18, 1862, at Monticello, to serve three years; mustered in as private, Co. H, October 8, 1862; mustered out with company, July 20, 1865, at Washington, D. C.

WARRING, GRAHAM.—Age, 18 years. Enlisted at Goshen, to serve one year, and mustered in as private, Co. H, September 9, 1864; mustered out, June 5, 1865, at Albany, N. Y., while in hospital at Troy, N. Y.

WHIPPLE, CHARLES C.—Age, 19 years. Enlisted, August 16, 1862, at Rockland, to serve three years; mustered in as private, Co. H, October 8, 1862; mustered out with company, July 20, 1865, at Washington, D. C.

WHITMARSH, SANFORD.—Age, 23 years. Enlisted, August 14, 1862, at Liberty, to serve three years; mustered in as private, Co. H, October 8, 1862; deserted, October 14, 1862.

WINNER, SOLOMON.—Age, 19 years. Enlisted, August 16, 1862, at Rockland, to serve three years; mustered in as private, Co. H, October 8, 1862; mustered out with company, July 20, 1865, at Washington, D. C.

WOODWARD, ARCHIBALD.—Age, 18 years. Enlisted at Goshen, to serve one year, and mustered in as private, Co. H, October 5, 1864; mustered out, July 19, 1865, at New York city.

YOUNG, EBEN C.—Age, 22 years. Enlisted, August 21, 1862, at Liberty, to serve three years; mustered in as private, Co. H, October 8, 1862; promoted corporal, March 29, 1865; absent, in hospital, at Washington, D. C., since June 15, 1865, and at muster-out of company.

YOUNG, JIRAH I.—Age, 21 years. Enrolled, August 22, 1862, at Monticello, to serve three years, and mustered in as first lieutenant, Co. H, October 8, 1862; as captain, Co. G, June 19, 1865;

mustered out with company, July 20, 1865, near Alexandria, Va.. Commissioned first lieutenant, November 21, 1862, with rank from September 12, 1862, original; captain, May 31, 1865, with rank from March 7, 1865, vice B. Reynolds, discharged.

YOUNG, ROBERT.—Age, 22 years. Enlisted, August 13, 1862, at Liberty, to serve three years; mustered in as private, Co. H, October 8, 1862; transferred to Co. H, Eleventh Regiment, Veteran Reserve Corps, April 10, 1864; mustered out, July 22, 1865, at Albany, N. Y.

MEDAL OF HONOR.

Collins, Thomas D., for bravery at Resaca, Ga.

WOUNDED IN ACTION.

Atwell, Selah, July 20, 1864, at Peach Tree Creek, Ga.
Chapman, Amos M., July 20, 1864, at Peach Tree Creek, Ga. .
Falkerson, Seymour J., July 20, 1864, at Peach Tree Creek, Ga..
French, Jonathan, July 20, 1864, at Peach Tree Creek, Ga.
Reese, Charles G., July 20, 1864, at Peach Tree Creek, Ga.
Stickels, Andrew, July 20, 1864, at Peach Tree Creek, Ga.

DIED OF DISEASE AND WOUNDS.

Atwell, Selah, July 22, 1864, near Atlanta, Ga.
Beasmer, DeWitt C., Nov. 2, 1863, at Nashville, Tenn.
Chapman, Amos M., July 22, 1864, at Vining's Station, Ga.
Decker, William, Dec. 13, 1863, at Lookout Valley, Tenn.
Edward, James H., Dec. 20, 1863, at Liberty, N. Y.
Ellis, Suel, Dec. 21, 1863, at Lookout Valley, Tenn.
Falkerson, Seymour J., July 21, 1864, near Atlanta, Ga..
Foster, Moses H., Nov. 10, 1863, at Stevenson, Ala.
Osterhout, Gideon, Nov. 2, 1863, at Nashville, Tenn.
Reese, Charles G., Feb. 19, 1865, at Nashville, Tenn.

DISCHARGED DURING SERVICE.

Beach, Erastus D., Mar. 9, 1863, for disability.
Beach, Hiram, Feb. 17, 1864, for disability.
Billington, George, April 11, 1863, for disability.
Campbell; William H., June 9, 1865, for disability.

Carrier, Adelbert A., May 18, 1865, for disability.
Drennon, Robert, Mar. 13, 1863, for disability.
French, William H., May 19, 1863, for disability.
Gerow, William J., Mar. 7, 1864, for disability.
Gray, Benjamin, Sept. 13, 1863, for disability.
Hill, George, July 30, 1864, for disability.
Howard, John M., Aug. 8, 1863, for disability.
Huntington, Edward H., June 6, 1865, ————?
Murry, Adolphus E., Nov. 21, 1863, for disability.
Porter, Henry W., Sept. 29, 1864, for disability.
Porter, Rufus W., May 19, 1865, for disability.
Sherwood, Rosevelt F., Aug. 17, 1863, for disability.
Smith, William J., July 7, 1865, for disability.
Stickels, Andrew, May 27, 1865, for disability.
Wager, Enos, Dec. 12, 1862, for disability.
Waring, Graham, June 5, 1865, for disability.

TRANSFERRED.

Conklin, David D., no date, to Veteran Reserve Corps.
Decker, John D. W., no date, to Veteran Reserve Corps.
Gildersleve, John A., no date, to Veteran Reserve Corps.
Hamilton, William, May 20, 1863, to Veteran Reserve Corps.
Hurley, Elisha, Jr., May 15, 1864, to Veteran Reserve Corps.
Young, Robert, April 10, 1864, to Veteran Reserve Corps.

DESERTED.

Becker, Anthony, Oct. 14, 1862.
Hodge, Leander A., April 7, 1863, at Philadelphia, Pa.
Kile, George W., no date, at Washington, D. C.
Myers, William, no date, enlisted in cavalry.
Whitmarsh, Sanford, Oct. 14, 1862.
Irons, George H., absent without leave since April 8, 1865.

COMPANY I.

CAPTAINS.

Harrison Marvin, original, to muster-out of Regt.

FIRST LIEUTENANTS.

William T. George, original, promoted to Capt. Co. A.
Wallace Hill, from May 1, 1864, to muster-out of Regt.

SECOND LIEUTENANTS.

William T. Moffat, original, promoted to First Lieut. Co. G.
Alexander H. Brown, from May 24, 1863, transferred to Co. H.
Elihu Hildebrandt, July 24, 1865, not mustered.

RECORD OF MEMBERS OF COMPANY I—ORIGINAL.

ARMSTRONG, THOMAS.—Age, 20 years. Enlisted at Goshen, to serve one year, and mustered in as private, Co. I, February 28, 1865; deserted, June 22, 1865, near Washington, D. C.

ARNOLD, CHEDDIAH.—Age, 23 years. Enlisted, August 14, 1862, at Dryden, to serve three years; mustered in as private, Co. I, October 8, 1862; mustered out with company, July 20, 1865, near Washington, D. C.

BAILEY, BYRON.—Age, 18 years. Enlisted at Dryden, to serve one year, and mustered in as private, Co. I, August 9, 1864; mustered out, November 2, 1865, at Elmira, N. Y.

BALDWIN, WILLIAM.—Age, 30 years. Enlisted August, 17, 1862, at Dryden, to serve three years; mustered in as private, Co. I, October 8, 1862; mustered out with company, July 20, 1865, near Washington, D. C.

BALLARD, GABRIEL R.—Age, 19 years. Enlisted, August 15, 1862, at Dryden, to serve three years; mustered in as private, Co.

I, October 8, 1862; mustered out with company, July 20, 1865, near Washington, D. C.

BATES, OTIS A.—Age, 21 years. Enlisted, August 21, 1862, at Dryden, to serve three years; mustered in as private, Co. I, October 8, 1862; promoted corporal, prior to April, 1863; sergeant, June 1, 1865; mustered out with company, July 20, 1865, near Washington, D. C.

BESSEY, PETER.—Age, 25 years. Enlisted, August 21, 1862, at Dryden, to serve three years; mustered in as private, Co. I, October 8, 1862; died, February 27, 1864, at hospital, Louisville, Ky.

BLACKMAN, ARCHIBALD H.—Age, 25 years. Enlisted, August 21, 1862, at Fremont, to serve three years; mustered in as private, Co. I, October 8, 1862; promoted corporal, September 1, 1864; mustered out with company, July 20, 1865, at Washington, D. C.

BLOOMFIELD, EDWARD.—Age, 44 years. Enlisted, August 18, 1862, at Cochecton, to serve three years; mustered in as private, Co. I, October 8, 1862; died, February 14, 1864, at hospital, Murfreesboro, Tenn.

BRIGHAM, NEWTON.—Age, 26 years. Enlisted, August 16, 1862, at Dryden, to serve three years; mustered in as private, Co. I, October 8, 1862; discharged for disability, December 29, 1862.

BROWN, ORSON C.—Age, 22 years. Enlisted, August 21, 1862, at Dryden, to serve three years; mustered in as private, Co. I, October 8, 1862; discharged for disability, August 27, 1864, at Elmira, N. Y.

CAMPBELL, JOHN.—Age, 24 years. Enlisted at New York city, to serve three years, and mustered in as private, Co. I, March 1, 1865; deserted, June 9, 1865, near Washington, D. C.

CHAMBERS, AMOS.—Age, 18 years. Enlisted, August 19, 1862, at Dryden, to serve three years; mustered in as private, Co. I, October 8, 1862; absent, sick in hospital, at Mound City, Ill., at muster-out of company.

COLE, ROBERT.—Age, 39 years. Enlisted, August 21, 1862, at Dryden, to serve three years; mustered in as private, Co. I, October 8, 1862; discharged for disability, April 1, 1864, at Nashville, Tenn.

CONKLIN, HARRISON.—Age, 22 years. Enlisted, July 30, 1862. at Cochecton, to serve three years; mustered in as private, Co. I, October 8, 1862; wounded in action, May 15, 1864, and died of wounds, May 19, 1864, near Resaca, Ga.

COOK, ENOS.—Age, 42 years. Enlisted, August 20, 1862, at Dryden, to serve three years; mustered in as private, Co. I, October 8, 1862; died, December 18, 1863, in camp, at Lookout Valley, Tenn.

COPLEY, JOHN W.—Age, 43 years. Enlisted, August 14, 1862, at Dryden, to serve three years; mustered in as first sergeant, Co. I, October 8, 1862; transferred to Co. D, Twelfth Regiment, Veteran Reserve Corps, September 1, 1863; mustered out with detachment, July 20, 1865, at Washington, D. C.

COYKENDALL, HARRISON.—Age, 21 years. Enlisted at Goshen, to serve one year, and mustered in as priavte, Co. I, February 28, 1865; deserted, June 22, 1865, near Washington, D. C.

DAVENPORT, DANIEL D.—Age, 35 years. Enlisted, August 20, 1862, at Dryden, to serve three years; mustered in as private, Co. I, October 8, 1862; promoted corporal, June 1, 1865; mustered out with company, July 20, 1865, near Washington, D. C.

DECKER, RUFUS.—Age, 27 years. Enlisted, August 16, 1862, at Dryden, to serve three years; mustered in as private, Co. I, October 8, 1862; died, August 14, 1864, at hospital, Nashville, Tenn.

DEUEL, JAMES M.—Age, 18 years. Enlisted, August 21, 1862, at Dryden, to serve three years; mustered in as private, Co. I, October 8, 1862; died, March 25, 1863, at camp near Fairfax Seminary, Va.

DEVANEY, GILBERT.—Age, 35 years. Enlisted, August 18, 1862, at Dryden, to serve three years; mustered in as sergeant, Co. I, October 8, 1862; discharged for disability, December 24, 1864, at hospital, Indianapolis, Ind.

DODGE, LEVI.—Age, 21 years. Enlisted, August 14, 1862, at Dryden, to serve three years; mustered in as private, Co. I, October 8, 1862; mustered out with company, July 20, 1865, near Washington, D. C.

DONAHOE, PATRICK.—Age, 27 years. Enlisted at Goshen, to serve one year, and mustered in as private, Co. I, February 13, 1865; mustered out with company, July 20, 1865, near Washington, D. C.

EDSALL, WILLIAM.—Age, 35 years. Enlisted, August 21, 1862, at Dryden, to serve three years; mustered in as private, Co. I, October 8, 1862; mustered out with company, July 20, 1865, near Washington, D. C.

FAHRENKRUB, JOHN F.—Age, 39 years. Enlisted at Goshen, to serve three years, and mustered in as private, Co. I, February 7, 1865; mustered out with company, July 20, 1865, near Washington, D. C.; also borne as Fahunking.

FARRELL, ANDREW.—Age, 22 years. Enlisted, August 16, 1862, at Dryden, to serve three years; mustered in as private, Co. I, October 8, 1862; deserted, October 14, 1862, near New York city.

FERRIS, DAVID.—Age, 18 years. Enlisted, August 15, 1862, at Dryden, to serve three years; mustered in as private, Co. I, October 8, 1862; deserted, October 14, 1862, near New York city.

FERRIS, JOHN.—Age, 29 years. Enlisted, August 17, 1862, at Dryden, to serve three years; mustered in as private, Co. I, October 8, 1862; discharged for disability, January 28, 1863, at Upton Hill, Va.

FISHER, WILLET.—Age, 21 years. Enlisted, August 16, 1862, at Dryden, to serve three years; mustered in as private, Co. I, October 8, 1862; mustered out, June 23, 1865, at Washington, D. C., while in Fairfax Seminary Hospital, Va.

FITTS, HENRY W.—Age, 18 years. Enlisted, August 21, 1862, at Dryden, to serve three years; mustered in as private, Co. I, October 8, 1862; died, January 11, 1864, in camp at Lookout Valley, Tenn.

FOGARTY, JOHN.—Age, 44 years. Enlisted, August 20, 1862, at Dryden, to serve three years; mustered in as private, Co. I, October 8, 1862; transferred to Co. D, Seventeenth Regiment, Veteran Reserve Corps, no date; discharged for disability, April 18, 1865, at Indianapolis, Ind.

Fox, Merritt B.—Age, 41 years. Enlisted, August 18, 1862, at Dryden, to serve three years; mustered in as wagoner, Co. I, October 8, 1862; discharged for disability, August 26, 1863, at Convalescent Camp, Va.

Freeman, Charles D.—Age, 37 years. Enlisted, August 14, 1862, at Dryden, to serve three years; mustered in as private, Co. I, October 8, 1862; missing since November 28, 1863; no further record.

George, William T.—Age, 39 years. Enrolled, August 14, 1862, at Dryden, to serve three years; mustered in as first lieutenant, Co. I, September 13, 1862; as captain, Co. A, November 25, 1863; mustered out with company, July 20, 1865, at Washington, D. C. Commissioned first lieutenant, November 21, 1862, with rank from September 13, 1862, original; captain, April 18, 1864. with rank from November 25, 1863, vice H. Watkins, promoted.

Harned, George.—Age, 18 years. Enlisted, August 14, 1862, at Dryden, to serve three years; mustered in as private, Co. I, October 8, 1862; died, September 28, 1863, at hospital, Fortress Monroe, Va.

Hartsough, Thomas J.—Age, 23 years. Enlisted, August 21, 1862, at Dryden, to serve three years; mustered in as private, Co. I, October 8, 1862; promoted corporal prior to April, 1863; died, December 6, 1863, in Field Hospital, Lookout Valley, Tenn.

Hathaway, William H.—Age, 18 years. Enlisted at Cortland, to serve one year, and mustered in as private, Co. I, August 8, 1864; mustered out with detachment, June 10, 1865, near Washington, D. C.

Haviland, Abbot.—Age, 18 years. Enlisted, August 16, 1862, at Dryden, to serve three years; mustered in as private, Co. I, October 8, 1862; wounded, February, 1863; discharged for disability, April 17, 1863, at Fairfax Seminary Hospital, Va.

Hayes, Michael.—Age, 23 years. Enlisted, September 10, 1864, at Goshen, to serve one year; mustered in as private, Co. I, September 13, 1864; mustered out with detachment, June 10, 1865, at Washington, D. C.

HEMINGWAY, CHAUNCY.—Age, 36 years. Enlisted, August 16, 1862, at Dryden, to serve three years; mustered in as private, Co. I, October 8, 1862; discharged, June 19, 1865, at Washington, D. C., while in Fairfax Seminary Hospital, Va.

HEMINGWAY, HENRY H.—Age, 28 years. Enrolled, August, 8, 1862, at Dryden, to serve three years; mustered in as sergeant, Co. I, October 8, 1862; promoted first sergeant prior to October, 1864; mustered in as first lieutenant, Co. C, April 15, 1865; mustered out with company, July 20, 1865, near Alexandria, Va. Commissioned first lieutenant, May 17, 1865, with rank from April 15, 1865, vice J. R. Groo, discharged.

HEMINGWAY, ORLANDO.—Age, 25 years. Enlisted, August 21, 1862, at Dryden, to serve three years; mustered in as sergeant, Co. I, October 8, 1862; died, October 15, 1863, at hospital, Alexandria, Va.

HILDEBRANT, ELIHU.—Age, 19 years. Enrolled, August 14, 1862, at Dryden, to serve three years; mustered in as corporal, Co. I, October 8, 1862; promoted sergeant, September 1, 1864; first sergeant, June 1, 1865; mustered out with company, July 20, 1865, at Washington, D. C. Commissioned, not mustered, second lieutenant, July 24, 1865, with rank from May 16, 1865, vice W. Hill, promoted.

HOLLENSHEAD, DANIEL B.—Age, 42 years. Enlisted, August 21, 1862, at Dryden, to serve three years; mustered in as corporal, Co. I, October 8, 1862; discharged for disability, January 28, 1863, as Hollinshead.

HOWE, JAMES T.—Age, 41 years. Enlisted, August 14, 1862, at Dryden, to serve three years; mustered in as private, Co. I, October 8, 1862; discharged, September 1, 1863.

HULSLANDER, WILLIAM.—Age, 19 years. Enlisted, August 16, 1862, at Dryden, to serve three years; mustered in as private, Co. I, October 8, 1862; discharged, December 30, 1862, at Columbia College Hospital, Washington, D. C.

HURD, JOHN.—Age, 33 years. Enlisted, August 19, 1862, at Dryden, to serve three years; mustered in as private, Co. I, October 8, 1862; transferred to Veteran Reserve Corps, September 1, 1863.

JAGGER, FRANK.—Age, 18 years. Enlisted, August 16, 1862, at Dryden, to serve three years; mustered in as private, Co. I, October 8, 1862; mustered out, July 22, 1865, at New York city.

KIZER, ALBERT A.—Age, 20 years. Enlisted, August 14, 1862, at Dryden, to serve three years; mustered in as private, Co. I, October 8, 1862; wounded in action, July 20, 1864, at Peach Tree Creek, Ga.; died of his wounds, September 1, 1864, at hospital, Chattanooga, Tenn.

KIZER, JACOB.—Age, 36 years. Enlisted at Owego, to serve three years, and mustered in as private, Co. I, February 10, 1864; mustered out with company, July 20, 1865, near Washington, D. C.

KNICKERBOCKER, CLAY.—Age, 18 years. Enlisted, August 16, 1862, at Dryden, to serve three years; mustered in as private, Co. I, October 8, 1862; discharged, December 22, 1862, at Camp Bliss, Upton's Hill, Va.

LAMBERSON, JAMES.—Age, 20 years. Enlisted, August 14, 1862, at Dryden, to serve three years; mustered in as private, Co. I, October 8, 1862; discharged, August 26, 1863, at Convalescent Camp, Va., as James E.

LAMBERSON, WILLIAM.—Age, 25 years. Enlisted, August 14, 1862, at Dryden, to serve three years; mustered in as private, Co. I, October 8, 1862; discharged, April 2, 1863, at hospital, West Philadelphia, Pa.

MARVIN, HARRISON.—Age, 34 years. Enrolled, August 21, 1862, at Dryden, to serve three years; mustered in as captain, Co. I, October 8, 1862; mustered out with company, July 20, 1865, at Washington, D. C. Commissioned captain, November 21, 1862, with rank from September 13, 1862, original.

MATSON, JOHN C.—Age, 18 years. Enlisted, August 21, 1862, at Dryden, to serve three years; mustered in as private, Co. I, October 8, 1862; transferred to Co. D, Nineteenth Regiment, Veteran Reserve Corps, May, 1863; mustered out with detachment, July 13, 1865, at Elmira, N. Y.

MAXWELL, EDWARD.—Age, 32 years. Enlisted, August 18, 1862, at Dryden, to serve three years; mustered in as private, Co. I, October 8, 1862; transferred to Sixth Company, Second Battalion, Veteran Reserve Corps, July 1, 1863; mustered out, July 6, 1865, at Elmira, N. Y.

McDermott, James.—Age, 30 years. Enlisted, August 16, 1862, at Dryden, to serve three years, as corporal, Co. I, and de-serted, September 29, 1862, prior to muster-in at Bethel, N. Y.

McWhorter, John T.—Age, 30 years. Enlisted, August 14, 1862, at Dryden, to serve three years; mustered in as sergeant, Co. I, October 8, 1862; discharged for disability, July 11, 1864, at Elmira, N. Y.

Moffat, William T.—Age, 43 years. Enrolled, August 21, 1862, at Dryden, to serve three years; mustered in as second lieu-tenant, Co. I, October 8, 1862; as first lieutenant, Co. G, May 24, 1863; transferred to Co. D, January 1, 1864; discharged, February 13, 1864. Commissioned second lieutenant, November 21, 1862, with rank from September 13, 1862, original; first lieutenant, Octo-ber 17, 1863, with rank from May 24, 1863, vice T. B. Luckey, resigned.

Morey, William Alfred.—Age, 19 years. Enlisted, August 21, 1862, at Dryden, to serve three years; mustered in as private, Co. I, October 8, 1862; died, June 25, 1864, in hospital at Chat-tanooga, Tenn.

Mosher, Philip D.—Age, 30 years. Enlisted, August 19, 1862, at Dryden, to serve three years; mustered in as private, Co. I, October 8, 1862; died, January 11, 1863, in hospital at Alexan-dria, Va.

Nash, David.—Age, 38 years. Enlisted, August 16, 1862, at Dryden, to serve three years; mustered in as private, Co. I, Octo-ber 8, 1862; mustered out with company, July 20, 1865, at Wash-ington, D. C.

Nugent, John.—Age, 38 years. Enlisted, August 15, 1862, at Dryden, to serve three years; mustered in as private, Co. I, and deserted, September 29, 1862, at Bethel, N. Y.

Overacker, Isaac.—Age, 37 years. Enlisted, August 16, 1862, at Dryden, to serve three years; mustered in as private, Co. I, Oc-tober 8, 1862; died, April 4, 1864, at Dryden, N. Y.

PLATTINGILL, FLAVELL.—Age, 21 years. Enlisted, August 20, 1862, at Dryden, to serve three years; mustered in as corporal, Co. I, October 8, 1862; died, December 5, 1862, at Columbia College Hospital, Washington, D. C.

PAYNE, JOHN.—Age, 24 years. Enlisted, August 14, 1862, at Dryden, to serve three years; mustered in as private, Co. I, October 8, 1862; discharged for disability, July 20, 1863.

PEAS, ALMOND.—Age, 43 years. Enlisted, August 21, 1862, at Dryden, to serve three years; mustered in as private, Co. I, October 8, 1862; mustered out with company, July 20, 1865, near Washington, D. C.

PERRIGO, CHARLES M.—Age, 23 years. Enlisted, August 17, 1862, at Dryden, to serve three years; mustered in as private, Co. I, October 8, 1862; discharged for disability, September 17, 1863, at Elmira, N. Y.

PRATT, SAMUEL.—Age, 49 years. Enlisted, August 20, 1862, at Dryden, to serve three years; mustered in as private, Co. I, October 8, 1862; deserted, April 29, 1863, at hospital, New York city.

PUDEDBAUGH, THEODORE.—Age, 24 years. Enlisted at Cortland, to serve one year, and mustered in as private, Co I, August 8, 1864; mustered out with detachment, June 10, 1865, at Washington, D. C.

RIDER, WILLIAM.—Age, 18 years. Enlisted, August 14, 1862, at Dryden, to serve three years; mustered in as private, Co. I, October 8, 1862; mustered out with company, July 20, 1865, near Washington, D. C., as Ryder.

ROBINSON, LANGLAN.—Age, 24 years. Enlisted, August 21, 1862, at Dryden, to serve three years; mustered in as private, Co. I, October 8, 1862; promoted corporal, September 1, 1864; sergeant, June 1, 1865; mustered out with company, July 20, 1865, near Washington, D. C.; also borne as Robison.

ROE, WILLIAM M.—Age, 28 years. Enlisted, August 14, 1862, at Dryden, to serve three years; mustered in as corporal, Co. I, October 8, 1862; wounded in action, July 20, 1864, at Peach Tree Creek, Ga.; promoted sergeant, June 1, 1865; mustered out with company, July 20, 1865, at Washington, D. C.

SCOTT, SOCRATES.—Age, 37 years. Enlisted, August 15, 1862, at Dryden, to serve three years; mustered in as private, Co. I, October 8, 1862; died, April 6, 1863, at Kalorama Hospital, Washington, D. C.

SEAMON, PETER.—Age, 22 years. Enlisted, August 14, 1862, at Dryden, to serve three years; mustered in as corporal, Co. I, October 8, 1862; promoted sergeant prior to October, 1864; mustered out, May 17, 1865, at Louisville, Ky.

SHAVER, JOHN W.—Age, 18 years. Enlisted, August 21, 1862, at Dryden, to serve three years; mustered in as private, Co. I, October 8, 1862; promoted corporal, June 1, 1865; returned to ranks, July 7, 1865; mustered out with company, July 20, 1865, near Washington, D. C.

SHAW, HENRY.—Age, 34 years. Enlisted, August 14, 1862, at Dryden, to serve three years; mustered in as private, Co. I, October 8, 1862; discharged with detachment, June 20, 1865, at Mower Hospital, Philadelphia, Pa.

SHAW, WILLIAM.—Age, 45 years. Enlisted, August 21, 1862, at Dryden, to serve three years; mustered in as private, Co. I, October 8, 1862; deserted, October 11, 1862, at Paterson, N. J.

SHERWOOD, JOHN.—Age, 56 years. Enlisted, August 21, 1862, at Dryden, to serve three years; mustered in as private, Co. I, October 8, 1862; discharged, April 30, 1863, at Fairfax Seminary Hospital, Alexandria, Va.

SHERWOOD, MORGAN.—Age, 44 years. Enlisted, August 14, 1862, at Dryden, to serve three years; mustered in as private, Co. I, October 8, 1862; died, November 15, 1863, at hospital, Nashville, Tenn.

SHERWOOD, WILLIAM P.—Age, 22 years. Enlisted, August 18, 1862, at Dryden, to serve three years; mustered in as private, Co. I, October 8, 1862; died, November 4, 1863, at field hospital, Bridgeport, Ala.

SKILLMAN, JAMES M.—Age, 32 years. Enlisted, August 21, 1862, at Dryden, to serve three years; mustered in as private, Co. I, October 8, 1862; discharged, April 30, 1863, at Fairfax Seminary Hospital, Alexandria, Va.

SMITH, LAWRENCE D.—Age, 21 years. Enlisted, August 14, 1862, at Dryden, to serve three years; mustered in as private, Co. I, October 8, 1862; killed in action, July 30, 1864, near Atlanta, Ga.

SMITH, THOMAS.—Age, 19 years. Enlisted at Goshen, to serve three years, and mustered in as private, Co. I, February 17, 1865; mustered out with company, July 20, 1865, at Washington, D. C.

SNYDER, HENRY J.—Age, 34 years. Enlisted, August 19, 1862, at Dryden, to serve three years; mustered in as private, Co. I, October 8, 1862; discharged, April 1, 1864, at Camp Dennison, Ohio.

STARR, BIELBY P.—Age, 24 years. Enlisted, August 15, 1862, at Dryden, to serve three years; mustered in as private, Co. I, October 8, 1862; promoted corporal prior to April, 1863; returned to ranks, August 10, 1864; promoted corporal, June 1, 1865; mustered out with company, July 20, 1865, near Washington, D. C.

SUTTON, JOHN L.—Age, 30 years. Enlisted at Goshen, to serve one year, and mustered in as private, Co. I, February 16, 1865; mustered out with company, July 20, 1865, near Washington, D. C.

SWAIN, WILLIAM H.—Age, 30 years. Enlisted at Goshen, to serve one year, and mustered in as private, Co. I, February 13, 1865; deserted, June 25, 1865, near Alexandria, Va.

TANNER, GARRET.—Age, 19 years. Enlisted at Dryden, to serve three years, and mustered in as private, Co. I, August 5, 1864; mustered out with company, July 20, 1865, near Washington, D. C.

TERWILLIGER, CHARLES.—Age, 18 years. Enlisted, August 19, 1862, at Dryden, to serve three years; mustered in as musician, Co. I, October 8, 1862; grade changed to private prior to April, 1863; mustered out, June 7, 1865, at Elmira, N. Y., as Charles O. Twilleger.

TOMLINSON, ROBERT.—Age, 22 years. Enlisted, August 19, 1862, at Dryden, to serve three years; mustered in as private, Co. I, and deserted, September 29, 1862, at Bethel, N. Y.

TOMPKINS, NICHOLAS.—Age, 44 years. Enlisted, August 9, 1862, at Thompson, to serve three years; mustered in as private,

Co. I, October 8, 1862; deserted, April 15, 1863, near Alexandria, Va.

WAIT, ANDREW.—Age, 23 years. Enlisted, August 14, 1862, at Dryden, to serve three years; mustered in as private, Co. I, October 8, 1862; discharged, December 12, 1862, at hospital, Georgetown, D. C.

WAIT, HENRY B.—Age, 35 years. Enlisted, August 14, 1862, at Dryden, to serve three years; mustered in as private, Co. I, October 8, 1862; mustered out with company, July 20, 1865, near Washington, D. C.

WAIT, JAMES.—Age, 21 years. Enlisted, August 14, 1862, at Dryden, to serve three years; mustered in as private, Co. I, October 8, 1862; deserted, October 9, 1862, at Monticello, N. Y.

WARD, AI.—Age, 29 years. Enlisted, August 21, 1862, at Dryden, to serve three years; mustered in as private, Co. I, October 8, 1862; discharged, January 28, 1863, at Upton's Hill, Va.

WEBSTER, CYRUS.—Age, place, date of enlistment and muster-in as private, Co. I, not stated; absent, at Lincoln Hospital, Washington, D. C., since June 8, 1865; no further record.

WELCH, JAMES.—Age, 30 years. Enlisted, August 16, 1862, at Dryden, to serve three years as private, Co. I, and deserted, September 29, 1862, at Bethel, N. Y.

WICKHAM, GEORGE.—Age, 18 years. Enlisted at Dryden, to serve three years, and mustered in as private, Co. I, August 5, 1864; mustered out with company, July 20, 1865, at Washington, D. C.

WILCOX, LYMAN.—Age, 54 years. Enlisted, August 21, 1862, at Dryden, to serve three years; mustered in as private, Co. I, October 8, 1862; deserted, October 14, 1862, at New York city.

WILSON, EDWARD B.—Age, 43 years. Enlisted, August 21, 1862, at Highland, to serve three years; mustered in as private, Co. I, October 8, 1862; transferred to Veteran Reserve Corps, August 10, 1864; discharged, June 27, 1865.

WOODMANEY, GEORGE.—Age, 22 years. Enlisted, August 21, 1862, at Dryden, to serve three years; mustered in as private, Co.

I, October 8, 1862; promoted corporal, no date; absent, on furlough, at muster-out of company.

WRIGHT, GEORGE W.—Age, 21 years.   Enlisted, August 18,.
1862, at Dryden, to serve three years; mustered in as private, Co.
I, October 8, 1862; deserted, October 9, 1862, at Monticello, N. Y.

KILLED IN ACTION.

Smith, Lawrence D., July 30, 1864, near Atlanta, Ga.

WOUNDED IN ACTION.

Conklin, Harrison, May 15, 1864, at Resaca, Ga.
Haviland, Abbot, Feb., 1863, ————?
Kizer, Albert A., July 20, 1864, at Peach Tree Creek, Ga.

DIED OF DISEASE AND WOUNDS.

Bessey, Peter, Feb. 27, 1864, at Louisville, Ky.
Bloomfield, Edward, Feb. 14, 1864, at Murfreesboro, Tenn.
Conklin, Harrison, May 19, 1864, near Resaca, Ga.
Cook, Enos, Dec. 18, 1863, at Lookout Valley, Tenn.
Decker, Rufus, Aug. 14, 1864, at Nashville, Tenn.
Deuel, James M., Mar. 25, 1863, near Fairfax Seminary, Va.
Fitts, Henry W., Jan. 11, 1864, at Lookout Valley, Tenn.
Harned, George, Sept. 28, 1863, at Fortress Monroe, Va.
Hartsough, Thomas J., Dec. 9, 1863, at Lookout Valley, Tenn.
Hemingway, Orlando, Oct. 15, 1863, at Alexandria, Va.
Kizer, Albert A., Sept. 1, 1864, at Chattanooga, Tenn.
Morey, William Alfred, June 25, 1864, at Chattanooga, Tenn.
Mosher, Philip D., Jan. 11, 1863, at Alexandria, Va.
Overacker, Isaac, April 4, 1864, at Dryden, N. Y.
Pattingill, Flavell, Dec. 5, 1862, at Washington, D. C.
Scott, Socrates, April 6, 1863, at Washington, D. C.
Sherwood, Morgan, Nov. 15, 1863, at Nashville, Tenn.
Sherwood, William P., Nov. 4, 1863, at Bridgeport, Ala.

DISCHARGED DURING SERVICE.

Brigham, Newton, Dec. 29, 1862, for disability.
Brown, Orson C., Aug. 27, 1864, for disability.

Devaney, Gilbert, Dec. 24, 1864, for disability.
Ferris, John, Jan. 28, 1863, for disability.
Fisher, Willet, June 23, 1865, for disability.
Fox, Merrit B., Aug. 26, 1863, for disability.
Haviland, Abbot, April 17, 1863, for disability.
Hemingway, Chauncy, June 19, 1865, for disability.
Hollenshead, Daniel B., Jan. 28, 1863, for disability.
Howe, James T., Sept. 1, 1863, for disability.
Hulslander, William, Dec. 30, 1862, for disability.
Knickerbocker, Clay, Dec. 22, 1862, for disability.
Lamberson, James, Aug. 26, 1863, for disability.
Lamberson, William, April 2, 1863, for disability.
McWhorter, John T., July 11, 1864, for disability.
Moffat, William T., Feb. 13, 1864, resigned.
Payne, John, July 20, 1863, for disability.
Perrigo, Charles M., Sept. 17, 1863, for disability.
Seamon, Peter, May 17, 1865, for disability.
Sherwood, John, April 30, 1863, for disability.
Skillman, James M., April 30, 1863, for disability.
Snyder, Henry J., April 1, 1864, for disability.
Wait, Andrew, Dec. 12, 1862, for disability.
Ward, Ai, Jan. 28, 1863, for disability.

TRANSFERRED.

Copley, John W., Sept. 1, 1863, to Veteran Reserve Corps.
Fogarty, John, no date, to Veteran Reserve Corps.
Matson, John C., May, 1863, to Veteran Reserve Corps.
Maxwell, Edward, July 1, 1863, to Veteran Reserve Corps.
Wilson, Edward B., Aug. 10, 1864, to Veteran Reserve Corps.

DESERTED.

Armstrong, Thomas, June 22, 1865, near Washington, D. C.
Campbell, John, June 9, 1865, near Washington, D. C.
Coykendall, Harrison, June 22, 1865, near Washington, D. C.
Farrell, Andrew, Oct. 14, 1862, near New York city.
Ferris, David, Oct. 44, 862, near New York city.
Freeman, Charles D., missing since Nov. 28, 1863.
McDermot, James, Sept. 29, 1862, at Bethel, N. Y.

Nugent, John, Sept. 29, 1862, at Bethel, N. Y.
Swain, William H., June 25, 1865, near Alexandria, Va.
Tomlinson, Robert, Sept. 29, 1862, at Bethel, N. Y.
Tompkins, Nicholas, April 15, 1863, near Alexandria, Va.
Wait, James, Oct. 9, 1862, at Monticello, N. Y.
Welch, James, Sept. 29, 1862, at Bethel, N. Y.
Wilcox, Lyman, Oct. 14, 1862, at New York city.
Wright, George W., Oct. 9, 1862, at Monticello, N. Y.

COMPANY K.

CAPTAINS.

Anthony H. Bush, original, dismissed, Mar. 31, 1863.

C. Howell North, from Nov. 2, 1863, resigned, July 15, 1864.

Edwin Bruen, from Oct. 17, 1864, not mustered.

FIRST LIEUTENANTS.

Lewis N. Stanton, original, promoted to Captain, Co. D.

Peter E. Palen, from May 1, 1864, to muster-out of Regt. (Bvt. Capt. N. Y. V.)

SECOND LIEUTENANTS.

Willett T. Embler, original, to muster-out of Regt.

Isaac Jelliff, from April 17, 1863, promoted to First Lieutenant, Co. B.

Daniel A. Bedford, July 24, 1865, not mustered.

RECORD OF MEMBERS OF COMPANY K—ORIGINAL.

AKERS, JOHN.—Age, 23 years. Enlisted, August 21, 1862, at Cochecton, to serve three years; mustered in as private, Co. K, October 9, 1862; promoted corporal, prior to October, 1864; absent on duty, at Exchange Barracks, Nashville, Tenn., at muster-out of company.

ANGEL, RICHARD.—Age, 18 years. Enlisted, September 5, 1862, at Cochecton, to serve three years; mustered in as private, Co. K, October 9, 1862; deserted, October 14, 1862, at New York city.

APPLEY, GILBERT.—Age, 23 years. Enlisted, August 6, 1862, at Cochecton, to serve three years; mustered in as private, Co. K, October 9, 1862; died of chronic diarrhea, January 2, 1864, at Lookout Valley, Tenn.

ARCH, EBERHART.—Age, 23 years. Enlisted, August 4, 1862, at Callicoon, to serve three years; mustered in as private, Co. K, October 9, 1862; mustered out with company, July 20, 1865, at Washington, D. C.

BAIRD, ANDREW J.—Age, 35 years. Enlisted, August 22, 1862, at Callicoon, to serve three years; mustered in as corporal, Co. K, October 9, 1862; returned to ranks, no date; mustered out with company, July 20, 1865, at Washington, D. C.; also borne as Beard.

BAIRD, CLINTON L.—Age, 21 years. Enlisted, August 21, 1862, at Tusten, to serve three years; mustered in as private, Co. K, October 9, 1862; promoted corporal, April 17, 1863; sergeant, May 1, 1864; wounded in action, no date; died of his wounds, April 16, 1865, at hospital, New Berne, N. C.; also borne as Beard.

BAMPER, GARRET L.—Age, 39 years. Enlisted, August 20, 1862, at Cochecton, to serve three years; mustered in as private, Co. K, October 9, 1862; mustered out with company, July 20, 1865. at Washington, D. C.

BARRETT, JOHN H.—Age, 45 years. Enlisted, July 21, 1862, at Cochecton, to serve three years; mustered in as private, Co. K, October 9, 1862; transferred to Veteran Reserve Corps, September 1, 1863.

BAUERNFEIND, CHRISTOPHER.—Age, 21 years. Enlisted, August 12, 1862, at Cochecton, to serve three years; mustered in as private, Co. K, October 9, 1862; discharged for disability, February 1, 1864, at Indianapolis, Ind.; also borne as Beaurnfiend.

BEDFORD, DANIEL A.—Age, 20 years. Enlisted, August 21, 1862, at Tusten, to serve three years; mustered in as corporal, Co. K, October 9, 1862; promoted sergeant, January 16, 1864; first sergeant, no date; mustered out with company, July 20, 1865, at Washington, D. C. Commissioned, not mustered, second lieutenant, July 24, 1865, with rank from May 16, 1865, vice A. H. Brown, discharged.

BENTLEY, WILLIAM C.—Age, 21 years. Enlisted, August 21, 1862, at Tusten, to serve three years; mustered in as private, Co. K, October 9, 1862; died of typhoid fever, June 18, 1863, at Nelson Hospital, Yorktown, Va.

BESSMER, MICHAEL.—Age, 22 years. Enlisted, August 19, 1862, at Fremont, to serve three years; mustered in as private, Co. K, October 9, 1862; promoted corporal, September 1, 1864; mustered out, June 5, 1865, at Albany, N. Y., while in hospital, at Troy, N. Y.

BOUETS, BENJAMIN.—Age, 23 years. Enlisted, August 28, 1862, at Cochecton, to serve three years; mustered in as wagoner, Co. K, October 9, 1862; died, May 22, 1865, at DeCamp Hospital, David's Island, New York Harbor.

BRINNING, JAMES.—Age, 22 years. Enlisted, August 18, 1862, at Cochecton, to serve three years; mustered in as private, Co. K, October 9, 1862; mustered out with company, July 20, 1865, at Washington, D. C.

BRUEN, EDWIN.—Commissioned, not mustered, captain, October 19, 1864, with rank from October 17, 1864, vice C. H. North, discharged.

BUSH, ANTHONY H.—Age, 25 years. Enrolled, August 7, 1862, at Cochecton, to serve three years; mustered in as captain, Co. K, October 9, 1862; dismissed, March 31, 1863. Commissioned captain, November 21, 1862, with rank from October 9, 1862, original.

CALKINS, JAMES R.—Age, 28 years. Enlisted, August 6, 1862, at Cochecton, to serve three years; mustered in as sergeant, Co. K, October 9, 1862; returned to ranks prior to October, 1864; promoted corporal, no date; mustered out with company, July 20, 1865, at Washington, D. C.

CHITTENDEN, ALBERT W.—Age, 20 years. Enlisted, August 9, 1862, at Callicoon, to serve three years; mustered in as sergeant, Co. K, October 9, 1862; died of typhoid fever, May 11, 1863, at Chesapeake Hospital, Va.

CONKLIN, WILLIAM.—Age, 39 years. Enlisted, August 4, 1862, at Cochecton, to serve three years; mustered in as private, Co. K, October 9, 1862; mustered out with company, July 20, 1865, at Washington, D. C.

CONNELL, PATRICK.—Age, 23 years. Enlisted, August 21, 1862, at Tusten, to serve three years; mustered in as private, Co. K, October 9, 1862; mustered out with company, July 20, 1865, at Washington, D. C.

CONNOR, JR., PATRICK.—Age, 22 years. Enlisted, August 7, 1862, at Cochecton, to serve three years; mustered in as private, Co. K, October 9, 1862; mustered out with company, July 20, 1865, at Washington, D. C.

CORNISH, NEWTON.—Age, 22 years. Enlisted, August 22, 1862, at Cochecton, to serve three years; mustered in as corporal, Co. K, October 9, 1862; discharged for disability, December 29, 1863, at Fairfax Seminary Hospital, Va.

DAVENPORT, GEORGE W.—Age, 26 years. Enlisted, August 21, 1862, at Tusten, to serve three years; mustered in as private, Co. K, October 9, 1862; promoted corporal, September 1, 1864; mustered out with company, July 20, 1865, at Washington, D. C.

DEATRICH, JOHN.—Age, 18 years. Enlisted, August 20, 1862, at Highland, to serve three years; mustered in as private, Co. K, October 9, 1862; mustered out with company, July 20, 1865, at Washington, D. C.; also borne as Detrich.

DEATRICH, LAWRENCE.—Age, 26 years. Enlisted, August 21, 1862, at Tusten, to serve three years; mustered in as private, Co. K, October 9, 1862; discharged for disability, April 2, 1863, at hospital, Fort Columbus, New York Harbor; also borne as Detrich.

DECKER, GEORGE L.—Age, 26 years. Enlisted, August 21, 1862, at Highland, to serve three years; mustered in as private, Co. K, October 9, 1862; died of chronic diarrhea, November 28, 1863, at New Albany, Ind.

DEXTER, BENJAMIN D.—Age, 30 years. Enlisted, August 21, 1862, at Tusten, to serve three years; mustered in as private, Co. K, October 9, 1862; mustered out with company, July 20, 1865, at Washington, D. C.

DIBBLE, DAVID N.—Age, 20 years. Enlisted, August 21, 1862, at Cochecton, to serve three years; mustered in as private, Co. K, October 9, 1862; promoted corporal, no date; killed in action, July 20, 1864, at Peach Tree Creek, Ga.

DODGE, CYRENUS.—Age, 46 years. Enlisted, July 26, 1862, at Cochecton, to serve three years; not mustered in as private, Co. K; absent, sick in Hospital No. 2, Murfreesboro, Tenn.; April,

1864; assigned to company as recruit, May 29, 1865; never joined company.

ELBERT, NICHOLAS.—Age, 21 years. Enlisted, August 15, 1862, at Cochecton, to serve three years; mustered in as private, Co. K, October 9, 1862; left sick near Hagerstown, Md., July 14, 1863; deserted, no date.

ELFREY, JOHN.—Age, 18 years. Enlisted, August 28, 1862, at Cochecton, to serve three years; mustered in as private, Co. K, October 9, 1862; absent, on sick furlough, since January 24, 1864, and at muster-out of company.

ELFREY, PETER.—Age, 22 years. Enlisted, August 25, 1862, at Cochecton, to serve three years; mustered in as private, Co. K, October 9, 1862; died of diarrhea, December 20, 1863, at Chattanooga, Tenn.

EMBLER, WILLETT T.—Age, 41 years. Enrolled, August 21, 1862, at Cochecton, to serve three years; mustered in as second lieutenant, Co. K, October 9, 1862; mustered out with company, July 20, 1865, at Washington, D. C. Commissioned second lieutenant, November 21, 1862, with rank from October 9, 1862, original.

FAGAN, JOHN.—Age, 28 years. Enlisted, August 21, 1862, at Tusten, to serve three years; mustered in as private, Co. K, October 9, 1862; mustered out with company, July 20, 1865, at Washington, D. C.

FERGERSON, ROBERT W.—Age, 21 years. Enlisted, August 13, 1862, at Cochecton, to serve three years; mustered in as private, Co. K, October 9, 1862; mustered out with company, July 20, 1865, at Washington, D. C.

FOSTER, JOHN A.—Age, 21 years. Enrolled, August 21, 1862, at Tusten, to serve three years; mustered in as sergeant, Co. K, October 9, 1862; promoted quartermaster-sergeant, no date; returned to ranks, Co. K, November 17, 1864; mustered out to date, July 20, 1865, while on furlough. Commissioned, not mustered, first lieutenant, February 2, 1865, with rank from January 1, 1865, vice Isaac Jelliff, promoted.

FUNDA, STEPHEN.—Age, 36 years. Enlisted, August 15, 1862, at Cochecton, to serve three years, as private, Co. K, and deserted, October 8, 1862, before muster-out of company, as Fundy.

GOFF, NATHAN.—Age, 45 years. Enlisted, August 14, 1862, at Cochecton, to serve three years; mustered in as private, Co. K, October 9, 1862; mustered out, July 1, 1865, at Fort Delaware, Del.

GORDON, ALBERT B.—Age, 19 years. Enrolled, August 21, 1862, at Tusten, to serve three years; mustered in as sergeant, Co. K, October 9, 1862; promoted first sergeant, May 1, 1864; mustered in as first lieutenant, Co. D, April 26, 1865; mustered out with company, July 20, 1865, at Washington, D. C. Commissioned first lieutenant, April 15, 1865, with rank from February 10, 1865, vice D. C. Apgar, promoted.

GREEN, EDWARD O.—Age, 20 years. Enlisted, August 21, 1862, at Tusten, to serve three years; mustered in as corporal, Co. K, October 9, 1862; promoted sergeant prior to December 18, 1863; transferred to Co. D, Fifth Regiment, Veteran Reserve Corps, April 1, 1865; discharged, July 19, 1865, at Burnside barracks, Indianapolis, Ind.

GUINNESS, CHARLES.—Age, 23 years. Enlisted, August 21, 1862, at Tusten, to serve three years; mustered in as private, Co. K, October 9, 1862; transferred to Veteran Reserve Corps, January 10, 1865.

HARRE, AUGUSTUS.—Age, 40 years. Enlisted, August 21, 1862, at Tusten, to serve three years; mustered in as private, Co. K, October 9, 1862; captured, July, 1863, near Aldee, Va.; died, August 18, 1864, at Andersonville, Ga.; also borne as Harra.

HENDRICKSON, ELIAS.—Age, 22 years. Enlisted, August 21, 1862, at Tusten, to serve three years; mustered in as private, Co. K, October 9, 1862; died of diarrhea, November 15, 1863, at Nashville, Tenn.

HENDRICKSON, JONATHAN H.—Age, 27 years. Enlisted, August 15, 1862, at Tusten, to serve three years; mustered in as private, Co. K, October 9, 1862; absent, on furlough, since July 3, 1865, and at muster-out of company.

HICKEY, JOHN.—Age, 33 years. Enlisted, August 21, 1862, at Cochecton, to serve three years; mustered in as private, Co. K, October 9, 1862; deserted, February 28, 1863, from guard house of camp.

HILL, ELIAS B.—Age, 44 years. Enlisted, August 21, 1862, at Tusten, to serve three years; mustered in as private, Co. K, October 9, 1862; wounded in action, July 20, 1864, at Peach Tree Creek, Ga.; transferred to One Hundred and Fifty-first Company, Second Battalion, Veteran Reserve Corps, October 7, 1864; mustered out, August 1, 1865, at Nashville, Tenn.

HILL, JAMES.—Age, 28 years. Enlisted, August 21, 1862, at Cochecton, to serve three years; mustered in as private, Co. K, October 9, 1862; mustered out with company, July 20, 1865, at Washington, D. C.

HILL, WILLIAM H.—Age, 18 years. Enlisted, August 21, 1862, at Tusten, to serve three years; mustered in as musician, Co. K, October 9, 1862; mustered out with company, July 20, 1865, at Washington, D. C.

HOFFMAN, AARON B.—Age, 22 years. Enlisted, August 21, 1862, at Tusten, to serve three years; mustered in as private, Co. K, October 9, 1862; died of diarrhea, January 2, 1864, at Murfreesboro, Tenn.

HOSIE, JOHN P.—Age, 27 years. Enlisted, August 14, 1862, at Cochecton, to serve three years; mustered in as private, Co. K, October 9, 1862; transferred to Co. G, same date; mustered out with company, July 20, 1865, near Alexandria, Va.

INGRICK, WALTER.—Age, 18 years. Enlisted, August 10, 1862, at Neversink, to serve three years; mustered in as private, Co. K, October 9, 1862; died of chronic diarrhea, January 5, 1864, at Lookout Valley, Tenn.; also borne as Ingric.

JELLIFF, ISAAC.—Age, 23 years. Enrolled, August 21, 1862, at Monticello, to serve three years; mustered in as first sergeant, Co. K, October 9, 1862; as second lieutenant, April 17, 1863; as first lieutenant, Co. B, March 26, 1864; mustered out with company, July 20, 1865. near Alexandria, Va.; prior service as first lieutenant, Co. K, Fifty-sixth Infantry. Commissioned second lieutenant, October 17, 1863, with rank from March 30, 1863, vice D. Divine, promoted; first lieutenant, April 18, 1864, with rank from March 26, 1864, vice E. C. Howard, appointed quartermaster.

KEESLER, AUGUSTUS H.—Age, 24 years. Enlisted, August 13, 1862, at Cochecton, to serve three years; mustered in as private, Co. K, October 9, 1862; mustered out, May 26, 1865, at hospital, Lookout Mountain, Tenn.

KEESLER, SOLOMON.—Age, 20 years. Enlisted, August 18, 1862, at Cochecton, to serve three years; mustered in as private, Co. K, October 9, 1862; mustered out with company, July 20, 1865 at Washington, D. C.

KEESLER, WALLACE.—Age, 21 years. Enlisted, August 18, 1862, at Cochecton, to serve three years; mustered in as private, Co. K, October 9, 1862; promoted corporal prior to October, 1864; mustered out with company, July 20, 1865, at Washington, D. C.

KESSLER, CONRAD.—Age, 37 years. Enlisted, August 30, 1862. at Callicoon, to serve three years; mustered in as private, Co. K, October 9, 1862; died, October 3, 1864, at hospital, Chattanooga, Tenn.

KNAPP, JOHN L.—Age, 21 years. Enlisted, August 21, 1862. at Tusten, to serve three years; mustered in as corporal, Co. K, October 9, 1862; returned to ranks prior to April 30, 1863; promoted corporal, no date; died of chronic diarrhea, December 25, 1863, at Field Hospital, Lookout Valley, Tenn.

LAYTON, CHARLES B.—Age, 24 years. Enlisted, August 22, 1862, at Cochecton, to serve three years; mustered in as private, Co. K, October 9, 1862; promoted corporal, no date; mustered out with company, July 20, 1865, at Washington, D. C.

LEE, AMOS.—Age, 31 years. Enlisted, August 29, 1862, at Cochecton, to serve three years; mustered in as private, Co. K, October 9, 1862; deserted, December 27, 1863, at Bellair, Md.

LENT, CHARLES.—Age, 21 years. Enlisted at Tenth Congressional District, to serve three years; mustered in as private, Co. K, May 7, 1864; mustered out with company, July 20, 1865, at Washington, D. C.

LENT, HENRY J.—Age, 21 years. Enlisted, August 8, 1862, at Cochecton, to serve three years; mustered in as corporal, Co. K,

October 9, 1862; died of typhoid fever, June 18, 1863, at hospital, Yorktown, Va.

LENT, JOSEPH A.—Age, 20 years. Enlisted, August 18, 1862, at Cochecton, to serve three years; mustered in as private, Co. K, October 9, 1862; wounded in action, May 25, 1864, at Dallas, Ga.; absent, in hospital, Jeffersonville, Ind., since and at muster-out of company.·

LENT, THOMAS O.—Age, 19 years. Enlisted, August 18, 1862, at Cochecton, to serve three years; mustered in as private, Co. K, October 9, 1862; mustered out with company, July 20, 1865, at Washington, D. C.

LILLEY, HARRISON.—Age, 18 years. Enlisted, August 25, 1862, at Cochecton, to serve three years; mustered in as private, Co. K, October 9, 1862; mustered out with company, July 20, 1865, at Washington, D. C.

MAROLD, PAUL.—Age, 28 years. Enlisted, September 3, 1862, at Cochecton, to serve three years; mustered in as private, Co. K, October 9, 1862; promoted corporal prior to October, 1864; sergeant, no date; mustered out with company, July 20, 1865, at Washington, D. C.

MAROLD, ROBERT.—Age, 25 years. Enlisted, August 21, 1862, at Cochecton, to serve three years; mustered in as private, Co. K, October 9, 1862; mustered out with company, July 20, 1865, at Washington, D. C.

MASON, JOHN H.—Age, 40 years. Enlisted, August 22, 1862, at Cochecton, to serve three years; mustered in as private, Co. K, October 9, 1862; transferred to Co. F, Eighteenth Regiment, Veteran Reserve Corps, March 31, 1864; mustered out, July 22, 1865, at Washington, D. C.

McGUEY, MATHEW.—Age, 21 years. Enlisted, August 19, 1862, at Cochecton, to serve three years; mustered in as private, ·Co. K, October 9, 1862; mustered out with company, July 20, 1865, at Washington, D. C.

MILLER, H. LEWIS.—Age, 38 years. Enlisted, August 19, 1862, at Callicoon, to serve three years; mustered in as private, Co. K,

October 9, 1862; mustered out with company, July 20, 1865, at Washington, D. C.

MORRIS, JOHN.—Age, 18 years. Enlisted, September 6, 1862, at Mamakating, to serve three years; mustered in as private, Co. K, October 9, 1862; mustered out with company, July 20, 1865, at Washington, D. C.

MUCK, PHILIP.—Age, 23 years. Enlisted, August 28, 1862, at Cochecton, to serve three years; mustered in as private, Co. K, October 9, 1862; missing in action, November 19, 1864, near Social Circle, Ga.; no further record.

MURRAY, THOMAS.—Age, 32 years. Enlisted, August 14, 1862, at Cochecton, to serve three years; mustered in as private, Co. K, October 9, 1862; deserted, June 28, 1865, near Alexandria, Va.

OSTERHOUT, CORNELIUS.—Age, 19 years. Enlisted, August 21, 1862, at Cochecton, to serve three years; mustered in as private, Co. K, October 9, 1862; mustered out with company, July 20, 1865, at Washington, D. C.

OSTERHOUT, WILLIAM H.—Age, 24 years. Enlisted, August 22, 1862, at Cochecton, to serve three years; mustered in as private, Co. K, October 9, 1862; deserted, April 21, 1865.

PENDERGASS, JOHN.—Age, 37 years. Enlisted, September 6, 1862, at Thompson, to serve three years; mustered in as private, Co. K, October 9, 1862; mustered out with company, July 20, 1865, at Washington, D. C., as Pendegrass.

PERRY, GEORGE.—Age, 21 years. Enlisted, August 21, 1862, at Cochecton, to serve three years; mustered in as private, Co. K, October 9, 1862; mustered out with company, July 20, 1865, at Washington, D. C.

POWELL, JOSEPH.—Age, 18 years. Enlisted, August 21, 1862, at Highland, to serve three years; mustered in as private, Co. K, October 9, 1862; wounded in action, Mar 19, 1865, near Bentonville, N. C.; discharged for disability, October 21, 1865, at De-Camp Hospital, David's Island, New York Harbor.

QUICK, JR., JOHN.—Age, 28 years. Enlisted, September 21, 1862, at Thompson, to serve three years; mustered in as private,

Co. K, October 9, 1862; deserted, September 29, 1863, near Callett's Station, Va.

QUICK, JOSHUA H.—Age, 18 years. Enlisted, August 21, 1862, at Highland, to serve three years; mustered in as private, Co. K, October 9, 1862; mustered out with detachment, June 24, 1865, at Mt. Pleasant Hospital, Philadelphia, Pa.

ROSS, JOHN G.—Age, 29 years. Enlisted, July 25, 1862, at Cochecton, to serve three years; mustered in as private, Co. K, October 9, 1862; died of chronic diarrhea, November 3, 1863, at Stevenson, Ala.

SACKETT, JAMES.—Age, 21 years. Enlisted, August 21, 1862, at Highland, to serve three years; mustered in as private, Co. K, October 9, 1862; discharged for disability, September 8, 1863, at Convalescent Camp, Alexandria, Va.

SAUNDERS, JOHN B.—Age, 44 years. Enlisted, August 21, 1862, at Mamakating, to serve three years; mustered in as private, Co. K, October 9, 1862; discharged for disability, January 4, 1863, at Carlisle, Pa.

SKINNER, WESTON D.—Age, 22 years. Enlisted, August 21, 1862, at Tusten, to serve three years; mustered in as private, Co. K, October 9, 1862; transferred to Third Company, Second Battalion, Veteran Reserve Corps, no date; mustered out with detachment, August 21, 1865, at Washington, D. C.

SMITH, WILLIAM H.—Age, 23 years. Enlisted, August 21, 1862, at Highland, to serve three years; mustered in as private, Co. K, October 9, 1862; died of dropsy, April 5, 1864, at Murfreesboro, Tenn.

SODEN, WILLIAM E.—Age, 22 years. Enlisted, August 22, 1862, at Tusten, to serve three years; mustered in as private, Co. K, October 9, 1862; discharged, May 26, 1865, at hospital, Madison, Ind.

STAHL, JOHN.—Age, 26 years. Enlisted, August 22, 1862, at Cochecton, to serve three years; mustered in as private, Co. K, October 9, 1862; absent, sick, since January 24, 1864, and at muster-out of company.

STANTON, LEWIS N.—Age, 21 years.   Enrolled, August 21, 1862, at Tusten, to serve three years; mustered in as first lieutenant, Co. K, October 9, 1862; as captain, Co. D, May 1, 1864; mustered out with company, July 20, 1865, at Washington, D. C. Commissioned first lieutenant, November 21, 1862, with rank from October 9, 1862, original; captain, April 18, 1864, with rank from November 25, 1863, vice J. Higgins, promoted.

SUTTON, ADOLPHUS.—Age, 18 years.   Enlisted, August 21, 1862, at Tusten, to serve three years; mustered in as private, Co. K, October 9, 1862; mustered out with company, July 20, 1865, at Washington, D. C.

SWAM, LEWIS.—Age, 19 years.   Enlisted, August 22, 1862, at Monticello, to serve three years; mustered in as private, Co. K, October 9, 1862; mustered out with company, July 20, 1865, at Washington, D. C., as Swalm.

TACY, GEORGE.—Age, 27 years.   Enlisted, August 25, 1862, at Bethel, to serve three years; mustered in as corporal, Co. K, October 9, 1862; died of diarrhea, November 24, 1863, at Nashville, Tenn.

TUTTLE, ISAAC F.—Age, 18 years.   Enlisted, August 21, 1862, at Highland, to serve three years; mustered in as private, Co. K, October 9, 1862; deserted, January 28, 1863, at Upton's Hill, Va.; no further record; also borne as Tuthill.

TYLER, LEMANDO.—Age, 18 years.   Enlisted, August 22, 1862, at Cochecton, to serve three years; mustered in as private, Co. K, October 9, 1862; deserted, January 28, 1863, at Upton's Hill, Va.

TYLER, WILLIAM.—Age, 22 years.   Enlisted, September 2, 1862, at Cochecton, to serve three years; mustered in as private, Co. K, October 9, 1862; mustered out with company, July 20, 1865, at Washington, D. C.

URBEN, HENRY.—Age, 29 years.   Enlisted, August 21, 1862, at Cochecton, to serve three years; mustered in as private, Co. K, October 9, 1862; discharged for disability, March 16, 1863, at Philadelphia, Pa.; also borne as Urban.

VANTRAN, JAMES.—Age, 23 years.   Enlisted, August 21, 1862, at Monticello, to serve three years; mustered in as corporal, Co. K,

October 9, 1862; returned to ranks prior to June, 1863; transferred to Co. G, Sixteenth Regiment, Veteran Reserve Corps, April 10, 1864; discharged for disability, May 25, 1865, at Camp Hinks, Harrisburg, Pa.; also borne as Vantren and Vantram.

VAN WAGNOR, HARMAN.—Age, 21 years. Enlisted, August 22, 1862, at Cochecton, to serve three years; mustered in as private, Co. K, October 9, 1862; mustered out with company, July 20, 1865, at Washington, D. C.

VAN WART, GEORGE.—Age, 30 years. Enlisted, August 21, 1862, at Tusten, to serve three years; mustered in as private, Co. K, October 9, 1862; deserted, April 9, 1865; also borne as George W. Van Wort.

WALLENSTEIN, LEWIS.—Age, 25 years. Enlisted, August 21, 1862, at Tusten, to serve three years; mustered in as private, Co. K, October 9, 1862; absent, at convalescent camp, Bridgeport, Ala., since October 26, 1863, and at muster-out of company; also borne at Wallenstine.

WHEELER, JOHN H.—Age, 42 years. Enlisted, August 21, 1862, at Cochecton, to serve three years; mustered in as private, Co. K, October 9, 1862; discharged for disability, August 26, 1863, at convalescent camp, Alexandria, Va.

WILLIAMS, BURRAS P.—Age, 18 years. Enlisted, August 21, 1862, at Highland, to serve three years; mustered in as private, Co. K, October 9, 1862; absent, at hospital, since November 11, 1864, and at muster-out of company, as Burroughs P.

WOOD, JEROME.—Age, 32 years. Enlisted, September 6, 1862, at Thompson, to serve three years; mustered in as private, Co. K, October 9, 1862; died of chronic diarrhea, November 12, 1863, at Nashville, Tenn.

WOODRUFF, WESLEY V.—Age, 18 years. Enlisted, August 19, 1862, at Cochecton, to serve three years; mustered in as private, Co. K, October 9, 1862; promoted corporal prior to October, 1864; sergeant, no date; mustered out with company, July 20, 1865, at Washington, D. C.

KILLED IN ACTION.

Dibble, David N., July 20, 1864, at Peach Tree Creek, Ga.
Much, Philip, missed, Nov. 19, 1864, at Social Circle, Ga.

WOUNDED IN ACTION.

Baird, Clinton L., no date or place.

DIED OF DISEASE AND WOUNDS.

Appley, Gilbert, Jan. 2, 1864, at Lookout Valley, Tenn.
Baird, Clinton L., April 16, 1865, at New Bern, N. C.
Bentley, William C., June 18, 1863, at Yorktown, Va.
Bouets, Benjamin, May 22, 1865, at David's Island, N. Y.
Chittenden, Albert W., May 11, 1863, at Chesapeake Hospital, Va.
Decker, George L., Nov. 28, 1863, at New Albany, Ind.
Elfrey, Peter, Dec. 20, 1863, at Chattanooga, Tenn.
Harre, Augustus, Aug. 18, 1864, at Andersonville, Ga.
Hendrickson, Elias, Nov. 15, 1863, at Nashville, Tenn.
Hoffman, Aaron B., Jan. 2, 1864, at Murfreesboro, Tenn.
Ingrick, Walter, Jan. 5, 1864, at Lookout Valley, Tenn.
Knapp, John L., Dec. 25, 1863, at Lookout Valley, Tenn.
Lent, Henry J., June 18, 1863, at Yorktown, Va.
Ross, John G., Nov. 3, 1863, at Stevenson, Ala.
Smith, William H., April 5, 1864, at Baltimore, Md.
Tacy, George, Nov. 24, 1863, at Nashville, Tenn.
Wood, Jerome, Nov. 12, 1863, at Nashville, Tenn.

DISCHARGED DURING SERVICE.

Bauernfeind, Christopher, Feb. 1, 1864, for disability.
Bessmer, Michael, June 5, 1865, for disability.
Cornish, Newton, Dec. 29, 1863, for disability.
Keesler, Augustus H., May 26, 1865, for disability.
Powell, Joseph, Oct. 21, 1865, for disability.
Sackett, James, Sept. 8, 1863, for disability.
Saunders, John B., Jan. 4, 1863, for disability.
Soden, E. William, May 26, 1865, for disability.

Urben, Henry, Mar. 16, 1863, for disability.
Vantran, James, May 25, 1865, for disability.

TRANSFERRED.

Barrett, John H., Sept. 1, 1863, to Veteran Reserve Corps.
Green, Edward O., April 1, 1865, to Veteran Reserve Corps.
Guinness, Charles, Jan. 10, 1865, to Veteran Reserve Corps.
Hill, Elias B., Oct. 7, 1864, to Veteran Reserve Corps.
Hosie, John P., Oct. 9, 1862, to Co. G, 143d.
Mason, John H., Mar. 31, 1864, to Veteran Reserve Corps.
Skinner, Weston D., no date, to Veteran Reserve Corps.

DESERTED.

Angel, Richard, Oct. 11, 1862, at New York city.
Elbert, Nicholas, no date, at Hagerstown, Md.
Funda, Stephen, Oct. 8, 1862, at ————?
Hickey, John, Feb. 28, 1863, from guard house at camp.
Lee, Amos, Dec. 27, 1863, at Bellair, Md.
Murray, Thomas, June 28, 1865, at Alexandria, Va.
Osterhout, William H., April 21, 1865, at ————?
Quick, John, Jr., Sept. 29, 1863, near Callet's Station, Va.
Tuttle, Isaac F., Jan. 28, 1863, at Upton's Hill, Va.
Tyler, Lemando, Jan. 28, 1863, at Upton's Hill, Va.
Van Wart, George, April 9, 1865, at ————? .

CAPTURED.

Harre, Augustus, July, 1863, near Aldee, Va.

UNASSIGNED.

AUSTIN, HENRY H.—Age, 36 years. Enlisted at Mamakating, to serve one year, and mustered in as private, unassigned, September 21, 1864; mustered out, October 28, 1865, at Elmira, N. Y.

CARY, JOHN.—Age, 19 years. Enlisted at Goshen, to serve one year, and mustered in as private, unassigned, February 9, 1865; mustered out with detachment, May 9, 1865, at Hart's Island, New York Harbor, as Carey.

DIVINE, JAMES H.—Age, 18 years. Enlisted at Liberty, to serve one year, and mustered in as private, unassigned, October 5, 1864; mustered out, October 18, 1865, at Albany, N. Y.

EVERITT, HARVEY A.—Age, 20 years. Enlisted at Neversink, to serve three years, and mustered in as private, unassigned, September 17, 1864; mustered out with detachment, May 9, 1865, at Hart's Island, New York Harbor, as Henry A.

FOLEY, MICHAEL.—Age, 24 years. Enlisted at Mamakating, to serve one year, and mustered in as private, unassigned, September 30, 1864; mustered out with detachment, May 9, 1865, at Hart's Island, New York Harbor.

HUNT, WILLIAM.—Age, 20 years. Enlisted at Goshen, to serve one year, and mustered in as private, unassigned, September 17, 1864; mustered out, July 2, 1865, at Louisville, Ky.

MILLER, GEORGE W.—Age, 18 years. Enlisted at Cornwall, to serve one year, and mustered in as private, unassigned, October 1, 1864; mustered out with detachment, May 9, 1865, at Hart's Island, New York Harbor.

MOORE, BYRON J.—Age, 20 years. Enlisted at Neversink, to serve one year, and mustered in as private, unassigned, September 9, 1864; mustered out with detachment, May 9, 1865, at Hart's Island, New York Harbor.

SHERWOOD, W. G.—Age, 21 years. Enlisted at Goshen, to serve one year, and mustered in as private, unassigned, September 27, 1864; mustered out, May 9, 1865, at Hart's Island, New York Harbor.

SHULTZ, SEBASTIAN.—Age, 29 years. Enlisted at Albany, to serve one year, and mustered in as private, unassigned, September 5, 1864; mustered out with detachment, May 9, 1865, at Hart's Island, New York Harbor.

STALTER, GEORGE L.—Age, 24 years. Enlisted at Cornwall, to serve one year, and mustered in as private, unassigned, September 28, 1864; mustered out with detachment, May 9, 1865, at Hart's Island, New York Harbor; also borne as Stolter.

SWINGLE, ASA S.—Age, 24 years. Enlisted at Goshen, to serve one year, and mustered in as private, unassigned, September 30, 1864; mustered out, May 9, 1865, at Hart's Island, New York Harbor.

WASHBURN, JAMES H.—Age, 18 years. Enlisted at Syracuse, to serve one year, and mustered in as private, unassigned, August 8, 1864; mustered out, October 7, 1865, at Albany, N. Y.

ADDENDA.

Quotations from an Address Delivered by George H. Carpenter, at a Re-union of the Members of the 143d Regiment, N. Y. V., at Liberty, N. Y., Oct. 12, 1909.

"Mr. President, Survivors of the 143d Regiment, Ladies and Gentlemen:—Here and now are gathered together the remnant of a regiment that forty-seven years ago marched out from Sullivan County ten hundred strong toward the seat of war, and the wonder is not that there are so few of you here, but that there are so many. It would be strange if in the old county of Sullivan, or in the older town of Liberty, a place could be found where the soldier would not be welcome. There is a charm about the Grand Army button and the old blue coat that opens all hearts and swings back all doors wherever old Glory floats in the breeze, and here at least every latch string hangs out for you. The town and the fulness thereof are yours.

"Forty-seven years is a far cry backward and furnishes time for 'colts to grow horses and beards to turn grey,' and both have done so since that glowering October morning when you marched down the broad pike from Monticello, wearing the army blue, and carrying the spick and span flags that you brought back faded, tattered and torn, but, as Webster said, 'without a stripe erased or a star obscured.'

"War had not then become a reality to you and there were many coltish fellows in the ranks that morning despite the fact that they were bound for a land where they were promised a 'welcome with bloody hands to hospital graves.'

"There have been three years of war and forty-four years of peace since that gloomy October morning in '62, and war, General Sherman said, is hell. He is a competent witness and his statement is accepted as establishing the fact, but I judge from the stories I have heard some of the old boys tell when in reminiscent moods, that the sulphurous parts of those three years were intermittent and not continuous. There were bright spots along the way then, and sometimes, I have been told, that roast pig, roast chicken and fresh eggs, commandeered, as the Dutch say, from their habitats, along the march, took the place on the menu of hardtack and beans.

"In the forty-four years of peace which have passed since 'the battle flags were furled,' while life hasn't been 'one grand sweet song' for you all, in the main it has been successful and honorable. Many of your number have held offices of trust and power and we have yet to learn that any of them defaulted or failed to make good. I think that I am justified in saying that all the world loves a soldier, and as I look around me here and see that bit of gun metal adorning your coats, I have a feeling of envy almost that I have no right to wear it. To me there is a magic about the Grand Army button that no other badge can possess. It speaks of patriotism, heroism and fraternity. A fraternity that a civilian may not know, which looks after the welfare of the soldier in life, buries him with the honors of war, and shields his widow and orphans after his death. To me that button seems vibrant with the melody of 'Raly round the flag,' 'Tramp, tramp, the boys are marching,' alive with the stirring refrain, 'We'll hang Jeff Davis on a sour apple tree,' and resonant with the rollicking melody of 'Marching through Georgia.' Like the shell picked up from the beach, which always retains somewhat of the sound of the sea, the Grand Army button carries with it the clamor of war as well as the music of peace, charity and love. Rich or poor, high or low, the wearer of the Grand Army button has a pearl above price, a token, which had I the right to wear it, I would not exchange for any diamond that ever adorned the tiara of a pope or glittered in the crown of a king. In the days to come the replica of that button cut on the simple slab that may mark the resting place of the poorest soldier of you all, shall make holy ground of the soil in which he sleeps and a sacred shrine of the humble stone above his head. It will be decorated with flags and strewn with flowers until the attrition of time shall wear away the stone and nature sink in years.

" 'Civilization does get forward on a powder cart,' and as much as war is to be deplored it is undeniable that the swords and spears of the ancients, the battle axes and bows of the middle ages and the firearms of modern times, while causing havoc and slaughter, have made for peace, prosperity and liberty.

"The 143rd was a typical Sullivan County Regiment. Made up as it was of the very flower of the youth of the county there was never any doubt but that on 'War's red touchstone it would ring true metal,' and it did. In one respect it treated friend and foe alike. It never turned its face from a friend or its back to a foe, and its record is bright and clean.

"I remember with what feeling of awe I saw the boys march away toward the southland in that battle autumn when, as Whittier sung,

> " 'The birds flew northward singing as they flew.
> The land we leave behind has swords for cornblades,
> Blood for dew.'

"I wouldn't have given much for the chances that any of you then had to see Old Sullivan again, but I didn't know, and as little did I dream that forty-seven years afterward I should be addressing the fragments of that stalwart host here within sight of the last resting places of so many of their number. Up yonder on the green hillside where the first rays of the sun glint upon the polished marble, and its last beams linger like a lover loth to leave his mistress, sleep some of the brightest and best of your number. Ratcliff, and Watkins and Decker are there and others whose names I do not recall. Over the big divide in the church yard at Parksville lies Reynolds, and near the edge of the smiling Callicoon at Youngsville, rests that wonderful genius and warm hearted comrade, W. T. Morgans. The little handful of survivors, not enough for a full company, here assembled, represent really the youth and the age of the regiment. A score of years hardly marks the difference between the extremes here represented, but all are cheerful and no doubt ready to say:

> " 'Hang the almanac's cheat and the muster roll's spite,
> Old Time is a liar, we're twenty to-night.'

"But despite this youthful feeling, gentlemen, the fact remains that the 'Road to Yesterday' has never been found; it isn't down on any map and is of 'the stuff that dreams are made of.' You are facing a declining sun, and marching steadily along the western reaches of life's highway toward the final camping ground, where the invisible bugler stands waiting to sound taps for you all as Eternity bids you 'Hail' and Time says 'Farewell.'

"There

> 'Where the rough road turns and the valley sweet,
> Smiles bright with its balm and bloom,

You'll forget the thorns that have pierced the feet,
And the nights with their grief and gloom;
And the sky will smile and the stars will beam,
And you'll lay you down in the light to dream.'

"Assured that the descendants of the blue and the gray, united
in a common love for the old flag and gathered under the crossed
swords and locked shields of the Northland and the South will sing
the songs of peace and learn war no more."

THE ASSOCIATION.

At a meeting of survivors of the 143d Regiment, N. Y. V. I.,
held at the Ratcliff Post rooms in Monticello, N. Y., October 10,
1888, an association was formed to be known as the "Survivors
of the 143d Regiment, N. Y. V. I."

The object of the association was to continue that spirit of loyalty and fidelity to country that brought us together in 1862; to perpetuate its principles; to collect facts and make a record of the same;
and to establish and maintain a complete roster of the Regiment.

The first two objects named have been accomplished by meeting every year since the organization of the Society on or near
October 10, the anniversary of the Regiment leaving Camp Holley for the front. The places of meeting have been at Monticello,
five times, four of which were on the old camp ground; Liberty,
six times; Hurleyville, five times; Livingston Manor, twice; Rockland, twice; and Centerville and Ellenville, each once.

There has been a marked interest in these meetings, not only
by the members of the Association, but also by the communities
where they have met.

The third object is being accomplished in the publication of this
history. It is to be regretted that this historical work had not been
completed earlier. No doubt it would have been, but for the un-
timely death of Colonel Watkins, who was deeply interested and is
known to have collected much material of which no trace can be
found.

The fourth object is being accomplished by the records of the
Secretary of the Association. They show, as far as possible, the
residence of members of the Regiment living, and the date of death
of those who have answered final "roll call."

Two hundred have been enrolled as members of the Association. One hundred and thirty deaths have been recorded, an average of seven per year.

Any information along these lines will be gratefully received by the Secretary of the Association, whether from survivors or friends of the Regiment.

The following persons were recruits on their way to the 143d in 1864, and belonged to the Provisional Company E, commanded by Lieutenant Dwight Divine. They died or were sent back sick before reaching the Regiment, and hence their names do not appear on the muster rolls of the Regiment:

Brown, P., a recruit, but cannot trace further. Probably sent back sick.

Cook, Elisha D., died of typhoid fever at Adairsville, Ga., Nov. 2, 1864.

Dice, Ezekiel J. Cannot trace.

Gillett, J. B. Cannot trace.

Mathews, R. Cannot trace.

Porter, Adna. Died at Chattanooga, Ga., in Autumn of 1864.

Sheeley, David S. Sent back sick to hospital at Nashville, Tenn. Discharged, June 10, 1865.

Vantran, John V. Died at Chattanooga, Ga., in Autumn of 1864.

POLLOCK, ROBERT.—A member of Company E. Record will be found among those of Company F. Was placed there by mistake. Can be found on page 157.

ROOVES, JOHN.—Record of whom is on page 142, came from Longstreet's Army. He deserted when the 143d was about to face Longstreet's Army, as he did not want to risk the chance of falling into the hands of the army from which he had deserted.

FITZGERALD, JAMES.—Age, 22 years. Enlisted August 20, 1862, at Bethel, to serve three years; mustered in as private, Co. B, October 8, 1862; died of dysentery, December 13, 1863, near Athens, Tenn.

HARGIN, JEFFERSON.—Age, 44 years. Enlisted, August 6, 1862, at Ithaca, to serve three years. Mustered in as wagoner, Co. D, October 8, 1862. Grade changed to private, no date. Died of fever at hospital, Fort Monroe, Va., July 27, 1863.

PERSONAL INDEX.

The letters inclosed in parenthesis ( ) indicates the original company, the (Un) the unassigned, and the numbers for the pages where record will be found.

Cogswell, Richard. (B).......90, 101
Cole, Asa. (F)............... 150, 161
Cole, Moses B. (E).......66, 137, 146
Cole, Philip D. (E)..........137, 146
Cole, Robert. (I)............... 193
Cole, Wm., Jr. (H)............. 179
Coleman, Henry R. (A).......... 72
Collins, John. (D)............. 122
Collins, Thomas D. (H),
       1, 58, 61, 179, 190
Comfort, Reeve. (B)..........90, 102
Conklin, Benjamin. (C)......105, 117
Conklin, David D. (H).......179, 191
Conklin, Eugene. (B)............ 90
Conklin, Frank. (D)............. 122
Conklin, George H. (G)......165, 174
Conklin, Harrison. (I).......194, 204
Conklin, James A. (F).......... 150
Conklin, Levi. (H)............. 179
Conklin, Mannings. (H)......... 179
Conklin, Theodore. (C)......105, 118
Conklin, Wm. (K)............... 209
Connell, Patrick. (K)........... 209
Conner, Thomas O. (A)......... 72
Connor, Jr., Patrick. (K)........ 210
Cook, Enoch R. (F)............. 150
Cook, Elisha D. (Un.)........... 222
Cook, Enos. (I).....194, 204
Cook, Mathias. (G).............. 166
Coons, Henry. (F)..........150, 161
Copley, John W. (I)..........194, 205
Corby, Oren T. (A)............. 72
Corgill, Thomas. (A)............ 72
Corkins, Asa A. (D)........122, 133
Cornelius, Horace. (D)......122, 134
Cornish, Newton. (K)......210, 220
Coykendall, Harrison. (I)....194, 205
Cox, Abraham. (A)............. 73
Cox, Joseph E. (C).........106, 118
Craft, Herman. (Staff)......27, 66, 68
Crane, Adam R. (G).........166, 175
Crary, Jerry. (H)............... 180
Crawford, Charles N. (E)....137, 146
Creamer, Jeremiah. (G)......... 166
Criddle, Wm. H. (D).........54, 122
Cromwell, Alexander. (B)....... 90
Cronce, Wm. H. (D)............ 123
Crosby, Scipo L. (B).........90, 100
Cross, Cornelius. (C)........... 106
Cross, George W. (C)....106, 117, 118
Cuddington, James. (E)......... 137
Curry, Richard C. (H).......... 180
Curtis, Edwin. (D)............. 123

Darbee, Cleveland. (C).......... 106
Darbee, John G. (C)............ 106
Darbee, John W. (C)............ 106
Darling, David. (A)...........73, 84
Daved, James B. (E).......138, 146
Davenport, Daniel D. (I)......... 194
Davenport, George W. (K)....... 210
Davis, James W. (D)............ 123
Davis, Joseph. (G).............. 166
Davis, Joseph D. (F)............ 150
Davis, Prosper P. (G).......166, 174
Davis, Wm. (E)................. 138
Dawson, David L. (H)........... 180
Deatrich, John. (K)............. 210
Deatrich, Lawrence. (K)........ 210
Decker, Charles H. T. (B).....90, 100
Decker, George H. (H)....8, 176, 180
Decker, George L. (K)......210, 220
Decker, Gideon W. (H).......... 180
Decker, John D. W. (H)....180, 191
Decker, Mathew. (H)........... 180
Decker, Peter. (E)..........138, 146
Decker, Rufus. (I)..........194, 204
Decker, Selar. (E)..........138, 146
Decker, Wm. (H)..........180, 190
Decker, Jr., Wm. N. (A)......... 73
Degroot, Charles. (E)........... 138
Dekay, James C. (C)............ 106
Delaney, Thomas. (G)........... 166
Demorest, Jonathan O. (B)...91, 101
De Munn, Francis M. (C)........ 106
Deniston, John G. (C)........... 106
Dennis, Wm. C. (C).........107, 118
De Pew, Elias G. (D)........... 123
Deschner, Theodore. (D)........ 123
Denel, James M. (I).........194, 204
Devaney, Gilbert (I).........194, 204
Devens, James P. (G).......166, 174
De Witt, David P. (Staff).9, 14, 65, 66
De Witt, John. (C).........107, 119
Dexter, Benjamin D. (K)........ 210
Dibble, David N. (K).......210, 220
Dice, Ezekiel J. (Un.)........... 222
Dice, Henry. (A)................ 73
Dickinson, John W. (D)......... 123
Dickinson, Marcellas. (G)....166, 174
Dickinson, Willet J. (D).....123, 133
Divine, Dwight. (C),
      1, 8, 54, 102, 107, 143
Divine, James H. (Un.)......... 222
Dobbs, Michael. (A)..........73, 84
Dodd, Reuben W. (D).......... 123
Dodge, Cyrenus. (K)........... 210

Lord, Joseph. (A)..............77, 85
Lord, Samuel. (A).............69, 77
Lorgan, James A. (B).........94, 102
Loring, Jonathan C. (B).......54, 94
Lounsbury, John M. (A).......77, 85
Low, James. (C).............66, 111
Low, Jonathan W. (C).......111, 118
Luckey, Theron B. (G).8, 163, 169, 174
Luckey, Wm. V. (G)........169, 175
Lybolt, Henry C. (B)............ 94
Lynson, John. (F)...........154, 162
Lyon, George. (B)............94, 100
Mackey, Linus S. (D)........127, 133
Mackney, Samuel J. (C)......111, 117
Maltby, Marcus. (F).....154, 151, 162
Manett, George V. (C).......... 111
Mapledoram, James C. (A)......78, 85
Marold, Paul. (K).............. 215
Marold, Robert. (K)............ 215
Martin, Gideon W. (C).......... 112
Marvin, Harrison. (I)...1, 8, 192, 198
Marvin, John B. (H)............ 185
Mason, James B. (A)............ 78
Mason, John H. (K)........215, 221
Masten, David W. (E)........66, 140
Mastin, Abram. (D).........127, 134
Mathews, David. (Staff).......66, 67
Mathews, James H. (D)......... 127
Mathews, Lorenzo. (C).......... 112
Mathews, R. (Un.)............. 222
Matson, John C. (I)........198, 205
Maxwell, Edward. (I)........198, 205
McCord, Andrew J. (A)........78, 85
McDermott, James. (I)......199, 205
McGovern, Patrick. (E)......... 140
McGuey, Mathew. (K)......... 215
McIntine, John L. (B).......... 94
McKellips, Enos C. (H)......66, 185
McLoughlin, Henry C. (E)....... 140
McLynn, James. (H)........... 185
McMillen, Wm. (A)............1, 78
McPhelomy, Robert. (H)........ 185
McPherson, Charles J. (A).....66, 78
McWorther, John T. (I)....199, 205
McWilliams, Charles S. (G)...66, 169
McWilliams, John. (A)......... 78
McWilliams, Wesley. (D)........ 127
Mead, Jacob. (D)...........127, 134
Mead, Wm. H. (A)............78, 85
Meddeuch, Abram. (C).......... 112
Medler, Wm. O. (C)........112, 118
Medler, Zachariah. (E).......... 140
Mellen, Barney. (D)............ 128

Merical, Wm. P. (C)............ 112
Mericle, Van Gasbeck. (D)...127, 133
Merns, Samuel. (D)............. 127
Middaugh, Dennis S. (A).......78, 85
Miller, David. (C)...........112, 118
Miller, George. (F)............. 155
Miller, George W. (Un.)......... 222
Miller, Henry. (F)............. 155
Miller, H. Lewis. (K).......... 215
Miller, John. (F)............... 155
Miller, Samuel J. (A)........... 78
Miller, Verdine H. (G)......... 169
Milligan, Wm. G. (G)........169, 174
Mills, George H. (F)............ 155
Mills, Seth B. (F)..........155, 162
Misner, George R. (F)......155, 161
Mitchel, Joseph. (D)............ 128
Mitchel, Wm. H. (F)............ 155
Mix, Henry. (D).............128, 133
Moffat, Wm. T. (I),
    8, 120, 163, 192, 199, 205
Moffitt, Ferris. (H)............ 185
Moore, Byron J. (Un.)........... 222
Morey, Wm. Alfred. (I).....199, 204
Morgan, Chester S. (D)......... 128
Morgan, Isaac. (C)..........112, 117
Morgan, Patrick. (H)........... 186
Morgan, Wm. T. (F)............ 155
Morris, George J. (A).......... 79
Morris, James D. (B)........... 95
Morris, John. (K)............. 216
Morrison, Edward. (D)......128, 133
Morse, John W. (H)............ 186
Mosher, Philip D. (I).......199, 204
Mowris, J. A. (Staff)........... 68
Muck, Philip. (K)..........216, 220
Muir, David. (E)............... 140
Muller, George. (F).........156, 161
Murphy, Edmund. (D)......128, 133
Murray, George. (F).....156, 161, 162
Murray, Thomas. (K)......216, 221
Murray, Wm. (F)...........156, 161
Murry, Adolphus E. (H)....186, 191
Murry, Andrew. (H)............ 186
Myers, Adelbert. (A).......... 79
Myers, George. (D)............. 128
Myers, Jr., John. (G)......169, 174
Myers, Jr., Moses D. (A)....... 79
Myers, Wm. (H)...........186, 191
Myers, Wm. D. (A)............. 79
Myers, Wm. H. (A)............. 79
Nash, David. (I)............... 199
Nation, Joseph W. (E)......141, 146

www.ingramcontent.com/pod-product-compliance
Lightning Source LLC
Chambersburg PA
CBHW060303100426
42742CB00011B/1851

9 780962 635748